Fairy Tales
of
Hans
Christian
Andersen

Fairy Tales
of
Hans
Christian
Andersen

Translated by Neil Philip
Illustrated by Isabelle Brent

PUBLISHED BY
THE READER'S DIGEST ASSOCIATION LIMITED
LONDON · NEW YORK · SYDNEY · MONTREAL

CONTENTS

INTRODUCTION

HE FAIRY TALES OF Hans Christian Andersen are among the imperishable treasures of world literature. 'The Princess and the Pea', 'The Ugly Duckling', 'The Little Mermaid', 'The Emperor's New Clothes', 'The Steadfast Tin Soldier', 'The Snow Queen'—the list of masterpieces goes on and on. Andersen was not only a writer for children. But while his novels, poems and travel books have faded, the fairy tales remain as fresh and arresting as the day they were written. It was Andersen's friend H.C. Ørsted, the discoverer of electro-magnetism, who first saw their extraordinary quality. In 1835, his thirtieth year, Andersen published a novel, *The Improviser*, and a first pamphlet of stories, *Fairy Tales Told for Children*. Ørsted told Andersen, '*The Improviser* will make you famous, but the fairy tales will make you immortal.'

Andersen came from a humble background, and the story of his struggle for education and literary success is a remarkable one. He called his autobiography *The Fairy Tale of My Life*. And this is how he understood his own life story, as a fairy tale in which he was the poor, despised hero whose special qualities would nevertheless enable him to achieve his destiny. As he told his mother, when aged 14 he set out to make his fortune in Copenhagen, 'First you go through terrible suffering, and then you become famous.'

Whatever else they are about, Andersen's stories are always first and foremost about Hans Christian Andersen. Even as a boy, he was teased by the other pupils at school because in his stories 'I was always the chief person'. The same is true in the fairy tales, no matter whether the protagonist is a snowman, a fir tree or even a shirt collar. He was the ugly duckling, ever the outsider; he was the shy student in 'Little Ida's Flowers', ill-at-ease with adults, but blooming when telling stories to children; he was the hypersensitive princess, able to detect a single pea of criticism beneath twenty mattresses and twenty featherbeds of praise.

A FAIRY-TALE LIFE

Hans Christian Andersen was born in Odense, Denmark, in 1805. His mother, Anne Marie Andersdatter, was in her late thirties. His father, Hans Andersen, was 22. They had been married for only two months, and Hans Christian was their only child.

The delicate and introspective young boy never played with the children in the street outside their one-room home, which doubled as his father's shoemaker's shop. Instead he made clothes for his dolls, and played with the toy theatre made by his father, who would also fire the boy's imagination with stories from the *Arabian Nights*. Although his parents were poor, Andersen was coddled, as his mother told him, 'like a nobleman's child'. He had some basic schooling, after which he was sent to work, like other children of his class, first in a cloth mill, then in a tobacco factory. These jobs lasted only days, before the sensitive boy was back home with his theatre, dreaming of becoming an actor, a singer or a dancer.

This impoverished but emotionally rich life ended in 1812 when Andersen's father was paid to serve in place of a local landowner in the Napoleonic wars. He returned a broken man and died in spring 1816—'the Ice Maiden has taken him', Anne Marie told Andersen. Mother and child were left destitute, so she took up work as a washerwoman, standing waist deep for hours in the icy river, warmed only by nips of schnapps. The memories of

Andersen painted in 1836, the year after his first collection of fairy tales was published.

7

this desperate time resurface in the tender yet brutally realistic story '"She Was No Good"'.

In 1818, Anne Marie married another shoemaker, who took no interest in her son. She wanted Andersen to take an apprenticeship with a tailor, but he was determined on an actor's life. So on September 4, 1819, he set off on the coach to Copenhagen. There, the utter self-belief of this naive pauper with artistic longings persuaded a succession of well-connected people—including Edvard Collin, a State Councillor, and Admiral Wulff, the Danish translator of Shakespeare—to take an interest in him, paying for singing lessons and enrolling him in the ballet school of the Royal Theatre. When his teachers judged that he 'lacked both the talent and the appearance necessary for the stage', that might have ended his ambitions. Instead, his patrons used a royal charitable fund to send Andersen, aged 17, to receive a gentleman's education at the grammar school in provincial Slagelse.

He found school a torment—the headmaster would, he felt, 'destroy my soul'—but while there, in a moment of intense unhappiness, he wrote a poem, 'The Dying Child', that was to make his name as a writer. The poem, written as the words of a dying child to its mother, seems unbearably sentimental today, but it was hailed as original and moving when published in the *Copenhagen Post* in September 1827. Two years later Andersen could hold in his hands his first book of verse, *Digte* (or *Poems*).

TWIST IN THE TALE

This story of a washerwoman's son who through sheer persistence, and some influential help from unlikely sources, overcame all obstacles to become a great poet *is* like a fairy tale. But there may be an even more incredible side to the story.

Andersen boasted to schoolmates that he was a switched child of noble birth. This was perhaps no more than idle fantasy, but there is a theory, woven from a web of hints and clues, that he was not the biological child of Anne Marie Andersdatter and Hans Andersen, but rather the illegitimate son of Crown Prince Christian Frederik, later King Christian VIII, and the teenage Countess Elise Ahlefeldt-Laurvig, his birthplace Broholm Castle, near Odense. At this same time, Anne Marie was a nursemaid at Broholm, while

Odense Castle, where the young Hans Christian Andersen played with Prince Fritz, future king of Denmark.

Hans Andersen worked for Countess Elise's family. Could the inconvenient baby have been adopted by them? Such adoptions were not uncommon—only the previous year, a castle servant had been entrusted with the Prince's illegitimate baby daughter, Fanny.

There is also the strange matter of Andersen's childhood friendship with Prince Christian Frederik's son, Prince Fritz, three years his junior. For a time in 1819, when Andersen had no friends among the poor boys of his neighbourhood, his mother often took him with her to Odense Castle to play with Fritz. Why Anne Marie was employed at the castle, and why Andersen was chosen, rather than a child of nobility, as a playmate for a prince are mysteries.

This royal bond is recalled in one of Andersen's finest fairy tales, 'The Bell', published in 1842. Set on Confirmation Sunday (the friendship with Prince Fritz coincided with Andersen's own confirmation), it tells of two boys who search for the source of a great bell that sounds through the forest. One is a poor boy, the other a king's son. Although they take different routes, one in sunshine and one in shadow, in the end they arrive at the same place, and embrace each other as brothers.

The connections with the Danish royal family were to continue throughout Andersen's life. In 1844, for instance, he was invited as the guest of King Christian VIII to join the royal family on holiday on the island of Føhr, where the only other non-family guest was Fanny, the king's illegitimate daughter. Prince Fritz continued to treat Andersen as an old friend. He liked to hear him tell his fairy tales, and once asked him, 'How can you think up all these things? How does it all come to you? Have you got it all inside your head?' When Fritz, then King Frederik VII, died, Andersen was the only non-family member allowed a private visit to view the king's body in its coffin.

THE ORIGINAL UGLY DUCKLING

Whoever his true parents were, Andersen grew up to be a troubled man. Except in the freedom of his imagination, he never truly felt like a magnificent swan. He was always the gawky, ill-at-ease ugly duckling, who felt picked on by all and sundry: 'The ducks bit him; the hens pecked him; the girl who came to feed the poultry kicked him out of the way.' All his life Andersen was extraordinarily sensitive to slights. Every cruel or careless remark bit into his soul, and he remembered them all.

Andersen's desperate need to flee from provincial Odense and test his wings in the wider world is echoed again and again in his fairy tales. The 'Five Peas from the Same Pod' are happy enough in their green world until one of them wonders if there is something outside. In 'The Shepherdess and the Chimney Sweep', the two central characters brave all kinds of dangers to climb the chimney to the wide world outside where they can be together. A kind of spiritual, emotional and physical wanderlust marked Andersen's life. He travelled relentlessly, to

Andersen drew this view of a Roman garden, framed by the window of his lodgings, in 1833. Such sketches, made on small scraps of paper, were kept as notes for his stories.

Germany, Italy, Greece, the Far East, often publishing accounts of his travels. But wherever he went he took his troubled soul with him. Always beside his bed lay a coil of rope, in case of fire, and a handwritten notice—'I only seem dead'—in case he lapsed into a coma in the night and was buried before he could wake up.

Despite this expansive existence, Andersen was destined to live his life alone. His was a passionate but thwarted nature. He fell in love easily, but never with someone who could love him back. There was something apart in him that would never have settled easily into a partnership, yet he desperately needed to be wanted and included. Therefore, while keeping his independence and freedom, he attached himself to several families, such as his early champions, the Collins and the Wulffs, as well as the Danish royal family.

Turning Tradition on its Head

While Andersen undoubtedly put much of himself into his tales, he was influenced also by a long custom of story-telling. Mankind seems always to have told and passed on fairy tales, but only in 1697, when the Frenchman Charles Perrault published a collection including 'Cinderella', 'The Sleeping Beauty', 'Little Red Riding Hood' and 'Puss-in-Boots', did this oral tradition enter fully into western literature. These stories have deep roots, reaching back to ancient Egypt, Greece and Rome, and even farther afield—the first recorded version of 'Cinderella' comes from 9th-century China.

Perrault wrote his tales as entertainments for the court of Louis XIV. It was not until 1808 that Jacob and Wilhelm Grimm founded the science of folklore by recording German folk and fairy tales in the words in which they were told. Andersen first heard such stories at the annual hop harvest and in the spinning room of the Odense pauper hospital-cum-asylum, where his grandmother was employed to take care of the garden. Here, he said, 'a world as rich as that of the Arabian Nights was revealed to me'. But he was not primarily a tradition bearer. Only eight, out of more than 150, of his tales are direct retellings of Danish folktales. Five—'The Princess and the Pea', 'The Tinderbox', 'The Wild Swans', 'The Swineherd' and 'Father's Always Right'—are included in this collection. Instead, he was an artist who used the narrative mode of the fairy tale as a means of accessing his inner world.

Even when he is retelling a folktale such as 'The Wild Swans', Andersen does it in his own style, reshaping the story and adding descriptive details and symbolic elements as he sees fit. A good example is the climax of 'The Wild Swans', when the innocence and goodness of the long-suffering Elise is proved by her brothers, who have been transformed from swans by her patient devotion. Elise is tied to a stake, about to be burned alive. As her eldest brother reveals the truth, a wonderful fragrance fills the air...

> 'For every piece of wood in the fire built around the stake had
> taken root, and sent forth branches, until they made a high
> hedge around Elise, full of red roses. At the very top there
> was a single pure white flower, bright as a shining star.'

This transcendent imagery of flowers as the symbol of perfection is central to Andersen's vision. Similar passages can be found throughout his work. But it would be hard to find parallels in true folktales, in which flowers, because they wither and die, are more often symbols of death and decay.

'THE WHOLE WORLD, AND A PAIR OF SKATES'

It was not until he began to write fairy tales that Andersen found a way of harnessing his child-like love of make-believe. Fairy tales offered him space for both the large picture and the tiny detail— 'the whole world, and a pair of skates', as the Snow Queen offers Kay in Andersen's masterpiece 'The Snow Queen'.

His first pamphlet of fairy tales, published in 1835, contained just four stories: 'The Tinderbox', 'Little Claus and Big Claus', 'The Princess and the Pea' and 'Little Ida's Flowers'. Already in these early stories, Andersen understood that it was not so much the story that mattered as the voice of the storyteller. He speaks directly to the reader: 'There was once a prince who wanted to marry a princess—only she must be a real princess. He went all over the world looking for one, but there was always something wrong. He found plenty of princesses, but were they real princesses? He couldn't quite tell.' His voice is so intimate and relaxed, he seems almost to step out of the book and into the room to tell his tale.

Once he had found the right voice for his tales, he could not stop writing them—'They forced themselves from me'—and continued to publish pamphlets of fairy tales for the rest of his life. His contemporaries were amazed at his ability to spin such stories out of thin air. The Danish sculptor Bertel Thorvaldsen once challenged him to write a

Andersen entertains a young audience (1863).

new story, adding, 'You're capable of writing about anything, even a darning needle.' Andersen's response was the story 'The Darning Needle', about 'a darning needle who was so fine she fancied she was a sewing needle'.

Andersen's voice was so new and so fresh that his tales quickly found fame and were translated into many languages. The first English versions appeared in 1846, and echoes of these stiff translations, so far removed from the relaxed informality of the true style, can still be found in many editions of the tales. But however inadequate the Victorian translations were, the power of Andersen's imagination still shone through, inspiring many writers, including George MacDonald, author of *At the Back of the North Wind* (1871) and *The Princess and the Goblin* (1872), and Oscar Wilde, whose greatest fairy tale, 'The Fisherman and His Soul', owes much to 'The Little Mermaid' and 'The Shadow'.

One of his earliest admirers was Charles Dickens. The two authors became friends, although Andersen, who was a demanding and self-centred guest with very limited English, outstayed his welcome when invited to Dickens's home in 1857. After he was gone, Dickens put up a notice in his bedroom reading, 'Hans Andersen slept in this room for five weeks—which seemed to the family AGES!'. Andersen may have driven the household to distraction, but Charles Dickens's son Henry remembered fondly a wordless way in which the writer entertained him...

'He had one beautiful accomplishment, which was the cutting out in paper, with an ordinary pair of scissors, of lovely little figures of sprites and elves, gnomes, fairies and animals of all kinds, which might well have stepped out of the pages of his books. These figures turned out to be quite delightful in their refinement and delicacy in design and touch.'

In a typically fanciful Andersen papercut, a windmill-shaped miller is depicted with two hearts and a ballerina dangling from one arm. To each side is a sandman—from Andersen's story 'The Sandman'—holding an umbrella.

Andersen, a talented artist, specialised in these intricate paper cut-outs, often on fairy tale themes. He describes them in his story 'Little Ida's Flowers', where he depicts himself as the student who tells Ida wonderful stories, 'and could cut amazing pictures out of a piece of paper—hearts with little dancers in them, flowers and great castles with doors that opened'.

A BITTERSWEET LEGACY

This book contains 40 of Andersen's best fairy tales; he wrote 156 in all. They do not altogether fit the popular idea of what a fairy tale should be. Read 'The Little Mermaid' or 'The Steadfast Tin Soldier' and you see Andersen as essentially a poet of human suffering. Not for nothing is the nightingale in 'The Nightingale' praised for singing 'so beautifully that it brought tears to the emperor's eyes'. Story after story ends sadly, in rejection, humiliation or disappointment. Yet they are saved from self-pity by the salt of Andersen's wit and the acuteness of his observation.

Even in the happy-ending stories such as 'The Snow Queen', the moments of joy have to be painfully earned. Yet we are more than willing to suffer alongside the characters, because we identify so completely with them. And in 'The Snow Queen' we are rewarded by a transcendent ending, in which all suffering is redeemed and transformed into happiness. The story is as glittering and dangerous as the Snow Queen herself, but the message is clear: love is stronger than death.

Andersen wrote 'The Snow Queen', almost his longest tale, in a frenzy—begun on December 5, 1844, and published two weeks' later on December 21. He told a friend, 'It came out dancing over the paper'. In this his greatest story he let his mind go back to the tiny room he shared with his parents in his earliest childhood, and the little window box on the roof where his mother grew her vegetables. 'In my story of "The Snow Queen",' he wrote, 'that garden still blooms.'

Andersen died in Copenhagen on August 4, 1875, worried to the end that he would be buried alive. His had been a strange, unsatisfied life, full of hurts and grievances and bitter regrets. Yet it had also been, as he chose to present it to the world, a kind of fairy tale, in which all the struggles and disappointments were transformed into a glorious success.

In his diary on Sunday, September 18, 1825, Andersen—still a struggling, overgrown schoolboy at the age of 20—wrote, 'I must carry out my work! I must paint for mankind the vision that stands before my soul in all its vividness and diversity; my soul knows that it can and will do this.' In the fairy tale, he found the form in which he could achieve his dream, and win himself, as his friend H.C. Ørsted had predicted, immortality.

Neil Philip

THE PRINCESS
AND THE PEA

HERE WAS ONCE a prince who wanted to marry a princess—only she must be a real princess. He went all over the world looking for one, but there was always something wrong. He found plenty of princesses, but were they real princesses? He couldn't quite tell; there was always something that didn't feel right. So he came back home, very put out, because he did so long for a real princess.

One evening there was a fearful storm. The rain came down in torrents, and the thunder and lightning were quite terrifying. In the middle of it all there was a knock at the palace gate, and the old king went to open it. Standing outside was a princess. Goodness! What a state she was in. She was drenched. The water was running through her hair and down her clothes, in at the tips of her shoes and out at the heels. Yet she said she was a real princess.

'We'll soon see about that!' thought the old queen. She didn't say a word, but went into the spare bedroom, stripped the bedclothes, and placed a pea on the base of the bed. Then she piled twenty mattresses on top of the pea, and twenty featherbeds on top of the mattresses. That was the princess's bed for the night.

In the morning they asked her how she'd slept.

'Oh, shockingly,' said the princess. 'I hardly got a wink of sleep all night. Heaven knows what was in the bed; I was lying on something hard, and it has bruised me black and blue all over. It's quite dreadful.'

So they could see that she was a real princess, as she had felt the pea through twenty mattresses and twenty featherbeds. Only a real princess could be as sensitive as that.

So the prince married her, now he knew for certain she was a real princess. And the pea was put in the museum, where you can see it for yourself, if it hasn't been stolen.

That's a real story!

THUMBELINA

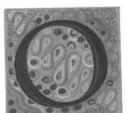NCE THERE WAS a woman who longed for a little child of her own, but she didn't know how to get one. So she went to an old witch and asked her, 'Can you tell me where I can find a little child? I would so love one.'

'That's easy,' said the witch. 'Take this barleycorn—but mind, it's not the sort that grows in the fields, or that you feed to the chickens. Put it in a flower pot, and you shall see what you shall see.'

'Oh, thank you!' said the woman, and she gave the witch a silver coin. Then she went home and planted the barleycorn, and right away it sprouted into a large, handsome flower that looked like a tulip. The petals were closed in a tight bud.

'What a lovely flower!' said the woman, and she kissed the red and yellow petals. As she kissed them, they snapped open. You could see that it was a real tulip, but right in the heart of the flower there sat a tiny little girl, so pretty and delicate that she was no bigger than the woman's thumb. So the woman called her Thumbelina.

A beautifully polished walnut shell served as Thumbelina's bed; she lay on violet petals, with a rose petal for her cover. That was where she slept at night; but in the daytime she played on the table, where the woman set out a soup bowl filled with water, with flowers wreathed around the edge. The stalks dangled in the water. A large tulip petal floated on the surface, and Thumbelina could sit on that and row from one side to the other, using two white horse hairs as oars. She looked so pretty! And she could sing, too, in the prettiest voice you ever heard.

One night, as she lay in her beautiful little bed, an ugly old toad hopped in through a broken window pane. It was a horrid, slimy thing, and it jumped right down onto the table where Thumbelina lay sleeping under her red rose petal.

'She would make just the wife for my son,' said the toad. So she grabbed the walnut shell in which Thumbelina was sleeping and hopped away with it, back through the window and into the garden.

At the bottom of the garden there was a wide stream, and it was on the muddy, marshy bank that the old toad lived with her son. He was a fright, just like his mother! *Koax, koax, brekke-ke-kex!* was all he could say, when he saw the pretty little girl in the walnut shell.

'Don't make such a noise, or she'll wake,' said the old toad. 'She might easily run away from us, for she's as light as swan's-down. Let's put her out in the stream, on one of those great water-lilies; she's such a slip of a thing, she'll think it's an island. She can't get away from there, and in the meantime you and I can prepare the best room under the mud, where you and she will make your home.'

There were many water-lilies in the stream, with broad leaves that floated on the surface. The biggest of them all was the farthest out, and the old mother toad swam over to it, and left Thumbelina there in her walnut shell.

Early next morning the poor little thing woke up, and when she saw where she was she began to weep bitterly, for the leaf was surrounded by water and there was no way to reach the bank.

The old toad had been busy in the mud, decorating a room with rushes and marsh marigolds, to make it all bright and snug for her new daughter-in-law. Then she swam out with her son to fetch Thumbelina's walnut shell bed, so that they could set it up ready in her room. The old toad curtseyed to Thumbelina from the water, and said, 'Well, this is my son! He's to be your husband,

and I'm sure you'll be very happy together, in your lovely home beneath the mud.'

Koax, koax, brekke-ke-kex! was all the son could say.

Then they took the neat little bed and swam away with it. Thumbelina, left alone on the green leaf, sat and wept. She did not want to live with the horrid old toad, or marry her ugly son.

The little fishes swimming in the water heard what the toad said, and they poked their heads up to catch sight of the little girl. As soon as they saw her, they were won over by her beauty. They couldn't bear to think that she must marry the ugly toad and live in the mud. It must not be! They gathered round the green stalk that held up the water-lily leaf, and nibbled at it till it gave way.

The leaf floated downstream, with Thumbelina aboard; it carried her far away, where the old toad could never follow.

Thumbelina sailed on past all sorts of places, and the wild birds in the trees sang out, 'What a pretty creature!' as she passed. On and on, farther and farther floated the leaf—and that was how Thumbelina set out on her travels.

A pretty white butterfly kept fluttering round and round her, till at last it settled on the leaf, for it was quite taken by the little girl. And she too was happy, now she had escaped from the toad. Everything was so beautiful. The sunshine on the water shone like burnished gold. She took off her sash and tied one end to the butterfly, and the other to the leaf. Then she sailed even faster.

Just then a big beetle came buzzing by. As soon as he saw Thumbelina, he snatched her round her slender waist with his claw, and flew up into a tree with her. But the green leaf still floated down the brook, and the butterfly had to go with it, because he was tied to the leaf and couldn't get loose.

Oh! How frightened Thumbelina was when the beetle carried her up into the tree! And she was sad, too, for her poor dear butterfly; for unless he could manage to free himself from the leaf,

he would surely starve. But that didn't bother the beetle. He settled beside her on the largest leaf in the tree, and fed her honeydew from the blossoms. He told her she was lovely, although she wasn't a bit like a beetle.

By and by all the beetles who lived in the tree came to inspect her. The young lady beetles shrugged their feelers, and said, 'She's only got two legs, the miserable creature! She hasn't any feelers! With that pinched little waist she might almost be a human. How ugly she is!' That's the kind of thing they said.

The beetle who had carried her off thought she was beautiful, but when all the others kept saying how ugly she was, he began to believe them. At last he would have nothing more to do with her; she could go where she pleased. They flew her down from the tree, and set her on a daisy. There she sat and wept, because she was so ugly that the beetles didn't want to know her; yet really she was as pretty as can be—as perfect as a rose petal.

All summer long poor Thumbelina lived alone in the greenwood. She plaited grass blades together to make a bed, and hung it under a large dock leaf to shelter from the rain. She ate the nectar from the flowers, and drank the dewdrops from the leaves; and so the summer and the autumn passed.

Then came winter—the long, cold winter. All the birds who had sung to her so sweetly flew away; the trees lost their leaves and the flowers withered. Even the big dock leaf under which she lived curled up into a faded yellow stalk. Poor Thumbelina was terribly cold, for her clothes were in rags, and she was so small and frail. It seemed she would freeze to death.

When it began to snow, every snowflake buffeted her like a shovelful thrown on us; for remember she was no bigger than your thumb. She wrapped herself up in a withered leaf, but there was no warmth in that. She trembled with cold.

On the edge of the wood lay a large cornfield. The corn had been harvested long before—only the hard bare stubble remained, sticking out of the frozen earth. But that was like a forest for Thumbelina to travel through—and oh! how she shook with cold.

At last she came to a field mouse's house. The field mouse had made herself a snug home in a hole beneath the stubble. There was a storeroom full of corn, and a warm kitchen, and a dining room. Poor Thumbelina stood like a beggar-girl at the door, and asked if she might have a piece of barleycorn, for she hadn't eaten a thing for two whole days.

'You poor mite!' said the field mouse, for she had a kind heart. 'Come into the warm and eat with me.'

She took a great liking to Thumbelina, so she said, 'Why don't you stay here with me? Just keep my room neat and tidy, and tell me stories, for I am very fond of stories.' And Thumbelina did as the good old field mouse asked, and made herself comfortable.

'We shall have a visitor soon,' said the field mouse. 'He lives nearby, and he pops in every week. His house is even bigger than mine, with huge rooms, and he wears a gorgeous black velvet coat. Now he would be a catch as a husband, although his eyesight's not good. You must save all your best stories for him.'

Thumbelina paid no attention to this, for she had no thought of marrying him, however many times the field mouse told her how rich and clever he was, and what a big house he had—twenty times larger than hers. He was a mole; and he came to call in his velvet suit. He knew about all sorts of things, but he couldn't abide the sunshine or the flowers—though he never saw them. Thumbelina had to sing for him. She sang 'Ring a ring o' roses' and 'I had a little nut tree', and the mole fell in love with her because she sang so sweetly. But he didn't say anything, because he was such a cautious sort.

He had dug a long passage from his house to theirs, and he told them that they could walk in it whenever they liked. They were not to be afraid of the dead bird that was lying there. It was a whole bird, with its beak and feathers intact, and he supposed it must

have died recently, at the start of winter, and been buried where he had made his underground passage.

The mole took a piece of rotten wood in his mouth—for in the darkness, that shines just like a torch—and led the way down the long dark passage. When they came to the place where the dead bird lay, he thrust his broad snout up through the earth, to let in some light. In the middle of the floor lay a swallow, his wings clenched to his sides, and his head and legs tucked beneath his feathers. The poor bird must have frozen to death.

Thumbelina felt so sorry, for she loved all the birds that had sung so delightfully for her all through the summer. But the mole just kicked it aside with his stumpy legs, saying, 'That one's chirped its last chirp! Who'd be born a bird? Thank goodness no child of mine will ever suffer that fate! A bird can't do anything but tweet, and when winter comes it starves to death.'

'That's the sensible view,' said the field mouse. 'What does a bird have to show for all its twittering when winter comes? It must starve and freeze. I can't see what people see in them.'

Thumbelina said nothing, but when the other two had turned their backs on the bird, she stooped down to smooth the feathers that covered his head, and kiss his closed eyes. 'Who knows?' she thought. 'This may be the very one that sang so beautifully to me last summer.'

The mole stopped up the hole he had made for the daylight, and saw the ladies home. But that night Thumbelina could not sleep. So she got up, and wove a covering out of hay, and took it and spread it over the dead bird; and she took some soft thistledown from the field mouse's room and tucked the bird in, to keep it warm under the cold earth.

'Goodbye, dear bird,' she said. 'Goodbye, and thank you for your lovely song in the summer, when all the trees were green, and the sun was so warm.' And then she laid her head on the bird's breast. That gave her a terrible fright, for it seemed something was beating inside. It was the bird's heart. He was not dead, he had fainted away, and now that he was warmer, he revived.

In autumn, the swallows all fly away to the warm countries; but if one lingers behind, it freezes and falls down as if it were dead. And there it lies, and the cold snow covers it.

Thumbelina was trembling with fright, for the bird was so much bigger than she, who was no bigger than a thumb. But she gathered her courage, and tucked the bird in even tighter, and fetched a mint leaf that she had been using as a blanket and laid that over his head.

The following night she stole down to the bird again, and this time he was more himself, though still very weak. He opened his eyes for a moment to look at Thumbelina, standing there with a piece of rotten wood in her hand, for she had no other light. 'Thank you, you dear child,' said the sick swallow. 'I'm warm again now, and soon I shall be strong enough to fly out in the bright sunshine.'

'Oh, no!' said Thumbelina. 'It's so cold out now! It's snowing and freezing. You stay here in the warm; I will take care of you.'

Then she brought the swallow some water in a leaf, and as the bird drank he told her how he had torn one of his wings on a thorn bush and so had not been able to keep up with the other swallows when they flew away to the warm countries. At last he had fallen to the ground; after that, everything was blank. He didn't know how he came to be where he was.

The swallow stayed in the passage all winter. Thumbelina looked after him, and became very fond of him. But she didn't say anything to the mole or the field mouse, for she knew that they did not care about the poor swallow.

As soon as spring came, and the sun began to warm the earth, the swallow said farewell to Thumbelina, who opened up the hole that the mole had made in the roof of the passage. The sun was so welcome as it flooded in; the swallow asked Thumbelina if she would like to come with him. She could sit on his back, and they would soar away into the greenwood. But Thumbelina knew that the old field mouse would be hurt if she left like that.

'No, I can't,' she said. 'I mustn't.'

'Then farewell, farewell, you dear kind girl,' said the swallow, and he flew away into the dazzling sun. Thumbelina's eyes filled with tears as she watched him go, for she had come to love the swallow.

Tweet, tweet! sang the bird, and flew off into the greenwood.

Thumbelina was so sad. She wasn't allowed to go out into the warm sunshine, and anyway in the field above the corn grew so tall that it seemed like a dense forest to the little girl, who was only the size of a thumb.

'You must get your wedding outfit ready this summer,' said the field mouse. 'You shall have clothes in linen and wool—the best of everything, for when you are married to the mole.'

So Thumbelina had to spin the wool, and the field mouse hired four spiders to weave for her, day and night. Every evening the mole came visiting, and the only thing he could talk about was how the summer was coming to an end, and once the sun had stopped scorching the earth so dry, he and Thumbelina would be married. This didn't make Thumbelina happy, for she did not care for the boring old mole.

Every morning, as the sun rose, Thumbelina would creep out of the door. When the wind bent the tops of the corn aside, she could see the blue sky, and she thought how beautiful and bright it was, and longed to see the swallow once more. But the bird never came; he must have been flying in the greenwood.

Then it was autumn, and Thumbelina's outfit was ready.

'Only four more weeks, and you shall be married!' said the field mouse. But Thumbelina broke down in tears, and said that she did not want to marry that dull mole.

'Hoity-toity!' said the field mouse. 'Don't take on such airs, or

I shall bite you with my white teeth. Why, the mole will make you a splendid husband. He's so handsome—why, the queen herself hasn't got a black velvet coat to match him. And he's rich—with the finest kitchen and cellar. You should be thankful.'

The wedding day arrived. The mole was to come early, to fetch Thumbelina. She was to live with him, deep down under the earth, and never come out into the bright sunshine, for he didn't like it. The poor child was heartbroken at having to say goodbye to the beautiful sun. At least while she was living with the field mouse she had been able to glimpse it from the doorway.

'Goodbye, bright sun!' she cried, lifting her arms up to it; and she took a few steps out into the open. The corn had been harvested, and once again only the stubble was left. 'Goodbye, goodbye!' she repeated, and she threw her arms round a little red poppy that was growing there. 'Give my love to the swallow, if ever you see him.'

Tweet, tweet! she heard overhead. It was the swallow! He was so pleased to see Thumbelina. But she was crying. She told him how she must marry the mole, and live underground where the sun never shone. She hated the thought.

'The cold winter will soon be here,' said the swallow. 'I shall fly away to the warm countries. Will you come with me? You can sit on my back, and tie yourself on with your sash. We'll fly far away from the stupid mole and his gloomy house—right across the mountains, to where the sun shines hot, and the flowers are in bloom because it's always summer. Come and fly with me, dear Thumbelina, who saved my life when I lay frozen in that dark passage under the earth.'

'Yes, I'll come with you!' said Thumbelina. And she climbed onto the bird's back, resting her feet on his wings, and tying herself to one of the strongest feathers with her sash. Then the swallow soared high into the air, and flew away over forest and lake, and across the high mountains where the snow always lies. Thumbelina

shivered in the keen frosty air; but she snuggled down into the bird's warm feathers, with just her head peeping out to gaze on the beauty below.

At last they came to the warm countries. The sun was shining much more brightly than at home, and the sky seemed twice as high. On the terraced slopes were growing green and purple grapes; there were lemons and oranges; the scent of myrtle and sweet herbs hung in the air. Laughing children ran along dusty paths, chasing bright butterflies. But the swallow kept on flying, and the countryside below seemed to grow ever more beautiful.

Beside a still blue lake, in the shade of tall trees, stood the ruins of an ancient palace, built of white marble long ago. Vines trailed round its pillars, and at the very top there were swallows' nests. One of these belonged to the swallow on whose back Thumbelina was riding.

'This is my home,' cried the swallow. 'But if you would rather live on the ground, you can choose the most beautiful flower of all, and make your house there.'

'That would be lovely!' said Thumbelina, and she clapped her tiny hands.

A great white column lay fallen on the ground. It had broken into three pieces, and between these there grew the most gorgeous white flowers. The swallow flew down with Thumbelina, to set her on one of the broad petals—and what a surprise she got! There, at the heart of the flower, sat a little man, so fair he was almost transparent, as if he were made of glass. He was wearing a tiny gold crown on his head, and fine, shining wings on his shoulders; he was no bigger than Thumbelina. He was the flower fairy. Each of the flowers had such a spirit living in it, and he was the king of them all.

'How handsome he is!' breathed Thumbelina to the swallow.

The fairy king was at first quite alarmed at the bird, which seemed a giant compared with him; but when he saw Thumbelina he was enchanted, for she was the loveliest girl he had ever seen. So he took the gold crown off his head and placed it on hers. He asked her what her name was, and if she would marry him, and be queen of all the flowers.

This was a husband Thumbelina could truly love—not like the old toad's ugly son, or the blind dull mole in his black velvet coat. So she said 'Yes' to the handsome king.

Then all the flower fairies came out of their flowers—each one so dainty and graceful, and each one with a gift for Thumbelina. Best of all was a pair of beautiful wings. They were fastened to her shoulders, and now she too could fly from flower to flower. Everyone rejoiced; and the swallow, sitting in his high nest, sang his sweetest song—though he was sad, too, for he loved Thumbelina, and didn't want to part from her.

'You shall not be called Thumbelina any more,' said the Fairy King. 'It's an ugly name, and you are so pretty. We shall call you Maia.'

'Farewell, farewell,' sang the swallow, and he flew away from the warm countries, far away back to Denmark. There he had a little nest by the window of a man who writes fairy tales. *Tweet, tweet!* sang the swallow. And the man listened, and he wrote down this story.

THE SWINEHERD

HERE WAS ONCE a prince who didn't have any money. But he had a kingdom, and though it was only small, it was enough for two. So he decided to get married.

Still it was daring of him to say to the emperor's daughter, bold as brass, 'Will you have me?' But he did, for his name was famous far and wide, and there were hundreds of princesses who would have answered, 'Yes, thank you.'

Listen, and you shall hear what *this* one said.

Growing on the prince's father's grave was a rose tree—a beautiful rose tree, which only flowered once every five years, and even then only produced one lovely bloom. This rose smelt so sweet that it made you forget all your troubles.

The prince also had a nightingale, that sounded when it sang as if all the loveliest melodies were stored up in its throat.

Those were presents fit for a princess; so the prince sent them to the emperor's daughter, in big silver caskets.

The emperor had them brought into the great hall, where the princess was playing 'grandmother's footsteps' with her ladies-in-waiting. They were getting bored with that, so when the princess saw the caskets she clapped her hands for joy.

'I do hope it's a clockwork kitten,' she said. But, instead, out came the rose tree.

'Isn't it prettily made!' exclaimed the ladies-in-waiting.

'It is more than pretty,' said the emperor. 'It's top-notch!'

But when the princess touched it, she said, 'Oh, Papa! It's not manufactured at all. It's natural!' She was so disappointed she could have cried.

'There, there,' said the emperor. 'Let's see what's in the other casket, before we get annoyed.'

Out came the nightingale, singing so beautifully it took their breath away.

'*Superbe!*' said one of the ladies-in-waiting, '*Charmant!*' said another—for they always spoke French when they wanted to sound intelligent.

'It sounds just like the musical box that belonged to the old empress,' said one old courtier. 'The same tone, the same delivery.'

'Yes!' said the emperor, and he shed a tear for old time's sake.

'I do hope it isn't a real bird,' said the princess.

'Yes, it is a real bird,' said the messengers who had brought it.

'Then let it fly away,' said the princess. And she refused point-blank to receive the prince.

But the prince was not to be deterred. He smeared his face with mud, pulled his cap over his eyes, and knocked at the palace door. 'Good morning, emperor,' he said. 'I'm looking for a job.'

'I can't give jobs to all and sundry,' said the emperor. 'But let me see—we do need someone to mind the pigs. There are such a lot of them.'

So the prince was made Imperial Swineherd. He was given a poky little room next to the pigsty, and he sat there all day, making something. By the evening, he had finished. It was a cooking pot, with bells hanging round it. When the pot was boiling, the bells tinkled against the sides and played a tune:

Oh! My heart is turned to dust!
All is lost! All is lost!

Even stranger was the fact that if you held your finger in the steam that rose from the pot, you could smell all the meals that were being cooked right across town. That was something quite different from the rose.

Before long the princess came walking by with her ladies-in-waiting. When she heard the tune, she stood still and listened. For she too could play that very song. It was the only one she knew, but she managed to pick out the notes with one finger.

'That's my tune!' she said. 'This new swineherd must be well-bred! Go and ask him how much he wants for the instrument.'

So one of the ladies slipped on some wooden clogs and went into the pigsty.

'How much do you want for your musical pot?' she asked.

'I want ten kisses from the princess,' he replied.

'Heavens above!' said the lady-in-waiting.

'I can't take any less,' said the swineherd.

'Well, what does he want?' asked the princess.

'I can't say it aloud,' said the lady-in-waiting. 'It's too awful.'

'Whisper it, then.' So the lady-in-waiting whispered it in the princess's ear.

'The cheeky so-and-so!' said the princess, and she stalked off. But as she left, all the bells began to ring out so prettily:

Oh! My heart is turned to dust!

All is lost! All is lost!

'I know,' said the princess. 'Ask him if he will accept ten kisses from my ladies-in-waiting.'

'No, thank you,' said the swineherd. 'I want ten kisses from the princess, or I will keep the pot.'

'How vexing!' said the princess. 'You ladies must stand behind me, so that no one can see.'

So the ladies-in-waiting shielded the princess from view, and she gave the grubby swineherd ten kisses in exchange for the musical cooking pot.

It was such fun! They kept the pot on the boil all day and all night. They knew what was cooking in every house in the town, whether it was the mayor's or the shoemaker's. It made the ladies-in-waiting skip about, and clap their hands with glee.

'We know who is making do with yesterday's soup!' they cried. 'We know who is treating himself to lamb cutlets!' They were fascinated.

'But don't say a word to anyone!' said the princess. 'I am the emperor's daughter, after all.'

The swineherd—that is to say, the prince, although nobody knew he hadn't worked with pigs his whole life long—was always making something new. The next thing he made was a rattle. When you swung it round, it played all the waltzes, jigs and polkas you could think of.

'Now that is *superbe*,' said the princess. 'I've never heard such lovely tunes. Go in and ask him the price of the instrument. But, mind, no more kisses!'

'He wants a hundred kisses from the princess,' said the lady-in-waiting, when she returned.

'He must be mad,' said the princess, and began to walk away. But when she had gone a little way, she stopped. 'It is a princess's duty to encourage the arts,' she said. 'Tell him he shall have ten kisses like yesterday, and the remainder from my ladies-in-waiting.'

'No! We couldn't!' said the ladies-in-waiting.

'Don't talk nonsense!' said the princess. 'If I can kiss him, so can you! Remember, I am the emperor's daughter!' And she sent the lady-in-waiting back into the pigsty.

'A hundred kisses from the princess,' said the swineherd. 'or I keep the rattle.'

'Shield me!' cried the princess, and all the ladies-in-waiting stood behind while she started kissing the swineherd.

'What on earth is going on by the pigsty?' asked the emperor, who happened to be looking out from his balcony. He rubbed his eyes, and put on his spectacles. 'It's the ladies-in-waiting playing some game; I'll go and see what they're up to.' So he hitched up his slippers at the heel, where he had trodden them down.

He couldn't wait to see what was going on!

As soon as he came into the courtyard, he began to creep along silently so that the ladies-in-waiting wouldn't hear him. But anyway they were so engrossed in counting the kisses, to make sure the swineherd played fair, that they never noticed the emperor.

The emperor rose up on tiptoe and peered over the heads of the ladies-in-waiting.

'What's this?' he cried, and he took off his slipper and thwacked them over the head, just as the swineherd was enjoying his eighty-sixth kiss.

The emperor was so angry. 'Get out!' he shouted, and both the princess and the swineherd were turned out of the kingdom.

The princess stood there crying in the pouring rain.

'Poor me!' wailed the princess. 'If only I had married the handsome young prince when I had the chance! Poor me!'

The swineherd went behind a tree, washed the mud from his face, threw away his filthy clothes, and stepped forward in his princely robes. He looked so royal, even the princess couldn't help making a curtsey.

'Don't expect me to be sorry for you,' he said. 'You would not marry an honest prince. You did not value the rose or the nightingale. But you were ready to kiss a swineherd for the sake of a jingling toy. You have got what you deserve.'

And with that he went back to his own kingdom, and shut the door of his palace in her face.

She was welcome to stand outside it and sing,
Oh! My heart is turned to dust!
All is lost! All is lost!

THE BUCKWHEAT

F YOU WALK through a field of buckwheat after a thunderstorm, you may notice that the buckwheat has turned quite black. Countryfolk will tell you, 'It's been scorched by the lightning.'

But how does it happen? I'll tell you what the sparrow told me—and the sparrow heard it from a gnarled old willow tree that stands close by a field of buckwheat. It's a mighty willow, but wrinkled and old, with a crack running right down the trunk, from which grass and brambles grow. It's bent with age, with branches that droop down almost to the ground, like long green hair.

In the fields round about, all kinds of corn were growing—rye, barley and oats, which look so lovely when they are ripe, like a line of little yellow canaries nodding on a bough. The cornfields were a lovely sight, and the richer the crop, the lower the corn stooped in meek humility.

But there was also a field of buckwheat, just in front of the old willow tree. The buckwheat didn't bow down, like the rest of the corn. It stood stiff and proud.

'I am just as rich as the rye,' it said, 'and much better-looking. My flowers are as beautiful as apple blossom. I'm a pleasure to look at. Do you know anything finer, old willow tree?'

The willow nodded his head as if to say, 'Yes, I do.' But the buckwheat was so puffed up with pride, it just said, 'Stupid old tree! He's so far gone, grass is growing out of his body!'

Now a terrible storm came on. All the flowers of the field folded their leaves or bent their delicate heads while the storm

39

passed over. But the proud buckwheat stood as tall and straight as ever.

'Bow your head, as we do,' said the flowers.

'I don't need to,' said the buckwheat.

'Bow your head, as we do,' said the corn. 'The angel of the storm is upon us. His wings reach from the clouds to the earth. He will strike you down before you can cry for mercy.'

'That may be so,' said the buckwheat, 'but I will not bow.'

'Shut up your flowers and fold your leaves,' said the old willow tree. 'Don't look at the lightning, when the cloud bursts. Even men dare not do that, for the lightning flash is the blinding light of heaven. If even man is dazzled by it, what would happen to us plants, who are so inferior?'

'Inferior?' said the buckwheat. 'Speak for yourself. As for me, I intend to stare right into God's heaven.' And in his arrogant pride, he did. When the lightning flared, it seemed the whole world was wrapped in flame.

When the storm had passed, the flowers and the corn lifted up their heads, refreshed by the rain and the pure air. But the buckwheat had been scorched as black as coal by the lightning. Now it hung shrivelled and dead, like a useless weed.

And the old willow tree's branches trembled in the wind, and great spots of water dripped from the leaves, as if the tree were crying. And the sparrows asked, 'Why are you crying? Look how beautiful the world is! The sun is shining, the clouds are sailing by. Just smell the perfume in the air! Why are you crying, old willow tree?'

'I am crying for the buckwheat,' said the willow, 'who would not bow down before the angel of the storm.'

And that's the story. I heard it from the sparrows. They told it to me one evening, when I begged them for a tale.

THE WILD SWANS

AR AWAY, where the swallows fly in winter, lived a king who had eleven sons, and one daughter, Elise. The eleven brothers went to school with stars on their breasts and swords at their sides. They wrote on golden slates with diamond pencils, and learned all their lessons off by heart; you could tell they were princes. Their sister Elise used to sit on a shining glass stool, reading a picture book that cost half a kingdom. The children had all they could want; but it didn't last.

Their father the king married a wicked queen, who disliked the poor children—they found that out on the very first day. There was a big party at the palace, and the children played their old game of pretending to be visitors. But the queen did not give them any cakes or baked apples, as usual. She just handed them a teacup full of sand, and told them to feed their imaginations on that.

A week later, she sent little Elise to the country to be brought up by peasants, and it was not long before she had filled the king's head with so many lies about the poor princes that he turned quite against them.

'Fly away, out into the world, and look after yourselves,' said the wicked queen. 'Fly away as great, voiceless birds.' But for all her ill-will, she couldn't do them as much harm as she wished; for they turned into eleven beautiful wild swans. With a strange cry, they flew out of the castle window, across the park and over the wood.

It was still early in the morning when they passed over the cottage where their sister Elise was sleeping. They hovered over the roof, flapping their great wings and stretching their long necks, but no one heard or saw them. They had to fly off again, up in the clouds, and out into the world. At last they came to a wide, dark forest that ran all the way down to the sea.

Poor Elise was left in the peasants' cottage, with only a green leaf to play with. She pricked a hole in it and peeped through it at the sun, which made her think of her brothers' bright eyes; and whenever the sun fell warm upon her face, she thought of her brothers' kisses.

One day passed like another. When the wind blew through the rose hedge in front of the cottage, it whispered to the roses, 'Is there anyone more beautiful than you?' And the roses would nod their heads, and answer, 'Elise.' And when the peasant wife sat in the doorway of a Sunday, reading her hymn book, the wind used to turn the pages and ask the book, 'Is there anyone more faithful and pure than you?' And the book would rustle its answer, 'Elise.' And it was all true, what the roses and the hymn book said.

When Elise was fifteen, she had to go home. When the queen saw how beautiful Elise had grown, she hated her. She would have liked to turn her into a wild swan like her brothers, but she did not dare, because the king wanted to see his daughter.

So the next morning the queen went into her bathroom, which was made of marble, but softly carpeted, with cushions everywhere. She fetched three toads, kissed them, and said to the first one, 'Sit on Elise's head when she gets into the bath, so that she will turn dull and stupid like you.' To the second one she said, 'Sit on Elise's forehead, so that she will turn ugly and loathsome like you, and her father won't know her.' And to the third she whispered, 'Sit on Elise's heart, and fill her with wicked thoughts to torment her.' Then she put the toads in the clear water, which at once turned brackish and green.

She called Elise, undressed her, and made her get into the bath. The first toad sat on her head, the second on her forehead, and the third on her heart. But Elise did not seem to notice them.

When Elise got out of the bath, three red poppies were left floating on the water. If the toads had not been poisonous, and kissed by a witch, they would have been turned into roses as they rested on Elise's head and heart; she was too good to be hurt by any witchcraft.

When the wicked queen realised this, she rubbed walnut-juice all over the girl's body, and smeared a vile, smelly ointment all over her face, and tangled her beautiful hair. When the king saw her, he was horrified, and said it couldn't possibly be his daughter. No one wanted to know her, except for the old watchdog and the swallows, and their opinions didn't count.

Poor Elise wept and thought of her eleven brothers, who had all disappeared. With a troubled heart, she crept out of the castle and walked all day over fields and moorland till she reached the forest. She didn't know where she was going, but she was so sad, and she missed her brothers so much. They must have been cast out just like her, and she made up her mind to find them.

She had not been long in the forest when night fell. She was lost in the dark, so she lay down on the soft moss, said her evening prayer, and rested against a tree trunk. It was very still in the forest, and the night air was soft. All around gleamed the green fire of hundreds of glow-worms. When Elise idly touched a branch above her, the shining insects fell about her like shooting stars.

All night long she dreamed about her brothers. They were all children again, playing together and writing on their gold slates with their diamond pencils, or looking at the pictures in the beautiful book that had cost half a kingdom—but this time they weren't just copying letters onto the slates, as they used to. They were writing down all the brave deeds they had done, and the bold adventures they had had. And in the picture book, everything had come alive—the birds sang, the people stepped out of the pages and talked to Elise and her brothers. But when she turned a leaf, they jumped back in again, so the pictures didn't get muddled.

When Elise awoke, the sun was already high. She couldn't see it properly through the trees, but the sunbeams danced through the dense branches in a shimmering haze. There was a fresh, green smell, and the birds almost came and perched on her shoulders. She could hear the sound of water splashing; there were several springs flowing into a pool. Elise made her way down to the water, by a path that had been worn through the undergrowth by deer going for a drink. The water was so clear that if the wind hadn't disturbed the trees and bushes she might have thought they were painted on the water—every leaf was so sharply reflected, whether it was in the sunshine or the shade.

When Elise saw her face reflected in the water she got a shock—it didn't look like her at all. But she dipped her hand in the water, and rubbed her eyes and forehead till she could see her own face again. Then she took off her clothes and stepped into the fresh water to bathe. In the whole world there was no one as lovely as Elise.

When she had dressed and plaited her hair, she went to the bubbling spring and drank from her cupped hands. Then she carried on into the forest, though she still did not know where she was going. She thought of her brothers, and of God who would surely not forsake her. It was He who made the wild apples grow, so that the poor would not go hungry. Here was just such a tree, heavy with fruit.

Elise ate a midday meal beneath its shade, and afterwards propped up the groaning branches. Then she walked on, into the darkest part of the wood. It was so still she could hear her own footsteps, and even the rustling of the withered leaves as she trod them underfoot. No bird was to be seen, and not a single ray of sun could pierce through the thick foliage. The tall tree trunks were so close together it looked as though she were completely enclosed by interlaced branches. Oh, this forest was a lonely place!

And the night was so dark! Not a single glow-worm showed its light. Sad and forlorn, she lay down to sleep. And it seemed to her that the branches above her parted, and that God watched over her gently, with angels crowding to peep over His shoulders. In the morning when she woke she did not know if this was a dream.

She walked on a short while, and met an old woman with a basket full of berries; the old woman gave her some. Elise asked her if she had seen eleven princes riding through the forest.

'No,' said the old woman, 'but yesterday I saw eleven swans with gold crowns on their heads, swimming down by the river near here.' And she led Elise to a hill, at the foot of which a river was winding. The trees on each bank leaned over the water to touch each other; with the effort, the roots had wrenched themselves from the earth to trail out over the water.

Elise said goodbye to the old woman and followed the river till she came to the place where it met the sea.

The great, endless ocean lay before her. But there was not a ship or a boat to be seen—how could she go on?

She gazed at the countless pebbles on the beach, worn smooth by the waves: glass, iron, stone, all had been shaped and subdued by the water, though this was softer even than Elise's delicate hand. 'The waves just keep rolling,' she said, 'making the rough stones smooth. I will be just as tireless. Thank you for your lesson, you bright waves. Some day, my heart tells me, you shall carry me to my dear brothers.'

Scattered on the seaweed at the tide-line, Elise found eleven white swan's feathers, which she carefully gathered up. Drops of water clung to them—whether they were dew, or tears, Elise couldn't tell. She was quite alone on the shore, but she didn't mind, for the sea was always changing. The sea changes more in an hour than a lake does in a year. If a black cloud passed overhead, the sea seemed to say, 'I can frown, too'; and then the wind would get up, and ruffle the waves white; when the sky flushed pink, and the wind dropped, the sea could look just like a

rose petal. It was now green, now white. It was never fully at rest; for always along the shore there was a gentle heave and swell, like the breathing of a sleeping child.

At sunset, Elise saw eleven wild swans with golden crowns on their heads flying in from the sea; they streamed one after another through the air like a long winding ribbon. Elise hid behind a bush, while the swans settled near her, flapping their great white wings.

As the sun sank below the horizon, the swans' feathers suddenly fell away, and there stood eleven handsome princes, Elise's brothers. She uttered a sharp cry: for though they were much changed, she knew them at once—she was sure they were her brothers. She ran to their arms, calling their names. They were overcome with joy to recognise their sister, who had grown so tall and beautiful. Between laughter and tears, the story was soon told of how wickedly their stepmother had treated them.

'So long as the sun is in the sky,' said the eldest of the brothers, 'we fly as wild swans. But when the sun has set, we regain our human form. So we must take care at sunset to reach dry land: for if we were out riding the air when we became human, we should fall to our death. We don't live here. Across the sea there is a land just as beautiful as this, but it's a long way there. We must cross the wide ocean, where there is no island for us to rest overnight— just one lonely little rock sticks up above the waves, just big enough for us to stand side by side. There we spend the night, in human form, and when the sea is rough, the spray soaks us; but we are thankful for that little rock. Without it, we could never return to visit our own country.

'We can only come once a year, for we need two of the longest days for our flight. We can only stay eleven days, but during that time we can fly over this forest, from which we can see the castle where we were born, and where our father lives, and also the tower of the church in which Mother is buried. Here, we feel at home with the trees and bushes; here, the wild horses gallop across the plain, as they did in our childhood; here, the charcoal-burner sings the old songs we heard in our childhood; we are drawn here, and here we have found you, our dear sister. We may stay here two days more, then we must fly back across the sea, to a fine land, though not our own. How can we take you with us? We have neither ship nor boat.'

'And how shall I free you?' asked Elise. And they talked it over through the night; they only had a few hours' sleep.

Elise was woken by the whirring of swans' wings overhead. Her brothers were again transformed; they were flying above her in wide circles. At last they flew far, far away—but one of them, the youngest, stayed behind. The swan laid his head in her lap, and she stroked his white wings; they stayed like that all day. As the day wore on the others returned, and when the sun set they were all standing on the firm land in their human form.

'Tomorrow we shall fly away, and cannot return for a whole year—but we don't want to leave you. Dare you come with us? Between us we must surely have enough strength in our wings to carry you across the sea.'

'Yes, take me with you,' said Elise.

They spent the whole of that night weaving a net from supple willow bark and tough rushes, till it was really strong. Elise lay down on it and, when the sun rose and the brothers were again transformed into wild swans, they seized the net in their beaks and flew high into the clouds with their dear sister, who was still asleep. The sun's rays shone full on her face, so one of the swans flew above her, to shade her with his outstretched wings.

They were far from land when Elise awoke. She thought she was still dreaming, so strange did it seem to her to be carried through the air, high above the sea. By her side she found some ripe berries and tasty roots, which the youngest of the brothers had gathered for her. She thanked him with a smile, for she knew that he was the one flying overhead, and shading her with his wings.

They flew so high that the first ship they saw beneath them looked like a white seagull skimming over the water. Behind them, on a huge white cloud as big as a mountain, Elise could see giant shadows of herself and the eleven swans. Never before had she seen such a splendid picture—but as the sun rose higher, and they left the cloud behind, the shadow picture disappeared.

All day long they whizzed through the air like arrows—yet not so fast as usual, because they had their sister to carry. A storm was brewing, and evening was approaching. Elise watched anxiously as the sun went down; still there was no sign of the lonely rock. She felt the swans beating their great wings ever more furiously. Oh! It was all her fault if they could not fly fast enough. When the sun set, they would become human beings again, and then they would fall into the sea and be drowned. She prayed to God from the bottom of her heart, but still she could not see the rock. The black clouds gathered; the gusting winds heralded a storm. The waves seemed turned to lead, and in the clouds lightning flashed.

The sun was now on the rim of the ocean. Elise's heart thumped. Then, all of a sudden, the swans darted downwards—so quickly that she thought she was falling—but the next moment they were hovering. The sun was half below the horizon. At that moment she saw the little rock below; it looked like a seal's head raised above the water. The sun was sinking fast; now it was as small as a star. As her foot touched the solid rock, the sun winked out, like the last spark on a piece of burning paper, and there were her brothers, standing arm in arm around her. There was only just room for her and them—no more. The sea dashed itself against the rock, drenching them in a shower of foam; the sky was ablaze with the glare of lightning, and thunder crashed. Elise and her brothers kept hold of each other's hands and sang a hymn, which comforted them and gave them courage.

By daybreak, the air was pure and still, and as soon as the sun rose, the swans flew off with Elise from the rock. There was still a strong sea running, and as they looked down from the clouds the white-flecked waves seemed like millions of swans swimming on the dark green sea.

When the sun was high in the sky, Elise saw in front of her, floating in the air, a land of mountains and glaciers. In the very middle was a palace. Below it, palm trees waved, and gorgeous flowers bloomed as big as millwheels. She asked if this was their destination, but the swans shook their heads. What she saw was the ever-changing cloud palace of the fairy Morgana, which no mortal could enter. Even as she looked, the mountains, and the palm trees, and the palace vanished, and in their place rose twenty high-towered churches. She thought she could hear an organ playing, or was it the sea? As she got near to the churches, they changed into a fleet of ships sailing below. She looked down—and all she could spy was a sea mist drifting across the ocean.

At last she caught sight of the beautiful blue mountains of the land for which they were heading. Cedar woods, towns and castles rose into view. And at sunset, Elise was sitting on a mountainside, in front of a large cave that was so overhung with delicate green creepers that they looked like embroidered curtains.

'I wonder what you will dream of tonight,' said the youngest brother, as he showed her where to sleep.

'If only I could dream how to set you free!' she answered.

She could think of nothing else. She prayed so hard; yes, even in her dreams she was praying. And it seemed to her that she flew high up through the air, to Morgana's cloud palace. The fairy welcomed her. She was dazzlingly beautiful, yet somehow she reminded Elise of the old woman who had given her berries in the forest, and told her of the swans with golden crowns.

'You have the power to set your brothers free,' she said. 'But have you the courage and the determination? It is true that the sea is softer than your fair hands, and yet can mould hard stones to its will. But the sea cannot feel the pain your fingers will feel; and the sea has no heart to feel the fear and grief that you will suffer.

'Do you see this stinging nettle in my hand? There are many such growing by the cave in which you sleep; only those, and the ones that grow in the churchyard, are any use—remember that. You must gather them, though they will burn blisters on your skin. Then you must tread on them with your bare feet to break them into flax. This you must weave into eleven shirts with long sleeves. Throw them over the eleven wild swans, and the spell is broken. But remember—from the moment you begin your work until it is finished, even if it takes years, you must not speak. The first word that falls from your lips will strike like a dagger at your brothers' hearts. Remember!'

And then the fairy touched Elise's hands with the nettle. It burned like fire, and she awoke.

It was broad daylight. Close by lay a nettle just like the one she had seen in her dream. She knelt down in silent thanks to God, and went out of the cave to begin her work. She plucked the stinging nettles with her delicate hands, though they seared her skin, burning great blisters on her hands and arms. She did not mind the pain, if it would set her brothers free. She trampled the nettles with her bare feet, and wove them into green flax.

At sunset her brothers returned. They were worried when they found Elise so silent; they thought it must be some new spell of the wicked stepmother's. But when they saw her blistered hands, they realised what she was doing for their sake. The youngest brother wept, and where his tears fell on her burned hands the pain was soothed.

That whole night Elise worked without rest. How could she rest until her brothers were free? All next day she worked alone, while the swans flew far away; never had time passed so quickly. As soon as the first shirt was finished, she began on the second.

Suddenly a hunting horn rang out among the hills. Elise was frightened. The noise came nearer; now she could hear the baying of the hounds. In terror she fled into the cave. She tied the nettle-yarn into a bundle, and sat on it.

At that moment a huge hound sprang out of the bushes; then another, then another. They kept barking and running to and fro. Soon the hunters were outside the cave; the handsomest of them all was the king of the land. He stepped up to Elise; never had he seen such a beautiful girl.

'How did you come here, fair maid?' he asked. Elise shook her head; she didn't dare to speak, for a single word would cost her brothers their lives. She hid her hands under her apron, so that the king should not see her suffering.

'Come with me,' he said. 'You cannot stay here. If you are as good as you are beautiful, I will dress you in velvet and silk. I will put a gold crown on your head, and you will live in my palace.' He lifted her onto his horse. She wept and wrung her hands, but he said, 'I only want to make you happy. You will thank me one day.' And away he rode across the mountainside, holding her in front of him, and the rest of the hunt following on.

As the sun set, the domes and spires of the splendid royal city lay before them. The king took Elise to the palace. Fountains were playing in the high marble hall, and the walls and ceiling were covered with beautiful paintings. But Elise had no eyes for such things—her eyes were blinded by tears. She let the waiting women dress her in royal clothes, and weave pearls into her hair, and draw long soft gloves over her blistered hands.

As she stood there in such finery, her beauty was so overpowering that the courtiers all bowed low before her, and the king chose her for his bride, even though the archbishop shook his head, and muttered that this pretty wood sprite must be a witch, to enchant everybody so and enthrall the king.

But the king wouldn't listen. He called for music, and a feast,

and dancing girls. Elise was led through sweet-scented gardens into a magnificent apartment, but still she grieved. Nothing brought a smile to her lips, or a light to her eyes.

Then the king showed her the little room where she was to sleep. It was hung with a costly green tapestry, and looked much like the cave where she had been found. On the floor lay the bundle of flax that she had spun from the nettles, and on the wall hung the shirt that she had already finished. One of the hunters had brought it all along.

'Here you can dream you are back in your old home,' said the king. 'Here is the work you were doing. Sometimes, amid all this grandeur, it may amuse you to think of the old days.'

When Elise saw these things that were so dear to her heart, she smiled, and the blood returned to her cheeks at the thought that she might still save her brothers. She kissed the king's hand; he hugged her to his heart, and ordered the church bells to chime out the news of their wedding. The lovely silent maiden from the woods was to be queen of all the land.

The archbishop whispered his malice into the king's ear—but not into his heart. The wedding went ahead, and the archbishop himself had to crown her. Out of spite he forced the narrow circlet down so hard that it hurt. But sorrow already squeezed such a tight ring round her heart—sorrow for her brothers—that she never noticed the pain.

She remained silent, for a single word would cost her brothers' lives; but the light from her eyes told the king that she returned his love. She grew fonder of him every day. If only she dared tell him of her sorrow! But she must remain silent, until her work was done. Therefore she used to steal away every night, to the little room that was fitted out like the cave, and weave the shirts. But just as she was beginning the seventh, she ran out of flax.

She knew that the right kind of nettles grew in the churchyard, and that she must gather them herself. But how was she to bear it?

'What is the pain in my fingers compared with the agony in my heart?' she thought. 'I must try. God will not forsake me.'

Then, as fearful as if she were creeping out to perform some evil deed, she crept down into the moonlit garden, through long avenues and empty streets until she reached the churchyard. There she saw, sitting on one of the big tombs, a group of fearsome witches. They were stripping off their rags as if to bathe, and digging with their bony fingers into the newly dug graves; they were scrabbling out the corpses and feasting on their flesh. Elise had to pass right by them, and they fixed her with their eyes; but she said a silent prayer, gathered the stinging nettles, and carried them back to the palace.

Only one person had seen her—the archbishop. He was on the watch, while others slept. Now he was certain: the queen wasn't what she appeared. She was a witch, who had enchanted the king.

In the confessional, he told the king what he had seen, and what he feared. When the false words fell from his lips, the carved saints shook their heads, trying to say, 'It's not true. Elise is innocent!' But the archbishop said that they were shaking their heads in horror.

Two great tears rolled down the king's cheeks. He went home with a troubled heart. At night he pretended to sleep, but sleep never came; he noticed Elise slip from her bed every night, and he followed her in secret, and saw her go into the little room.

Day by day his looks darkened. Elise noticed, but she couldn't think why. It fretted her; and besides, her heart was heavy with sorrow for her brothers. Her salt tears ran down onto her velvet dress of royal purple; they lay there like sparkling diamonds, so that everyone who saw her said, 'How wonderful! I wish I were queen!'

Now she had nearly completed her task. There was only one shirt to make, but she didn't have a single nettle left. So one last time she must venture to the churchyard and gather the final few handfuls. She shivered at the thought of that lonely walk and those awful witches, but her will was set as strong as her trust in God.

Off she went; the king and the archbishop followed her. They saw her disappear through the churchyard gates. As they entered, they saw the hag-like witches sitting on the tomb, just as Elise had seen them. The king turned away, for he thought she must be one of them—his own Elise, whose head had rested upon his breast that very evening. 'Let the people judge her!' he said, and the people condemned her to be burned at the stake.

She was dragged to a dark damp cell, where the wind whistled through a barred window. Instead of velvet and silk, they gave her the nettles she had gathered; these must be her pillow. The shirts she had woven must be her blankets. But they couldn't have given her anything more precious to her, and she continued to work, praying hard all the time. Outside, children in the street sang jeering songs about her; not a soul had a word of comfort or kindness for her.

Then, as evening fell, she heard the beating of swans' wings at the grating. It was the youngest of her brothers, who had found her at last. She sobbed aloud for joy, although she knew that the coming night might be her last. For her work was nearly done, and her brothers were near.

The archbishop came to keep her company in the final hours; he had promised the king to do that. But she shook her head, and made signs for him to go. That night she must finish her task or all her suffering—the agony, the tears, the sleepless nights—would have been in vain. The archbishop went away, with cruel words. But Elise knew she was innocent and went on with her work.

Little mice scurried about the floor, dragging the nettles to her to help her; a thrush sat on the windowsill all night, and sang as merrily as he could, to keep up her spirits.

It was still twilight; the sun would not rise for an hour. There stood the eleven brothers at the palace gate, demanding to see the king. But they were told that could not be. It was night; the king was still asleep; they dared not wake him. The brothers begged, and threatened. The guard was called. At last, the king himself turned up to find out what was going on. But at that moment the sun rose, and the brothers could not be seen—just eleven white swans flying away over the palace.

The people poured out of the city gates, eager to see the witch burned. One poor nag pulled the cart in which Elise sat. She was dressed in a coarse dress made of sacking; her beautiful long hair hung limply over her shoulders; her cheeks were pale as death; her lips were moving gently as she wove the green flax. Even on the road to death she would not give up her work. The ten shirts lay at her feet, and she worked at the eleventh, while the rabble mocked and jeered.

'Look at the witch, mumbling away! That's no hymn book in her hands, but some witch's work. Take it from her, and tear it up!'

And they all crowded round her to tear up what she had made. But eleven white swans came flying down, and settled on the cart, flapping their great wings. The crowd were terrified.

'It's a sign from heaven!' some whispered, though they didn't dare say it aloud. 'She must be innocent.'

The executioner took her by the hand—but she quickly threw the eleven shirts over the swans, and they turned into eleven handsome princes. Only the youngest had a swan's wing instead of one arm, for his shirt was missing a sleeve—it had not been finished.

'Now I may speak!' she cried. 'I am innocent.'

And the people, who had seen what had happened, bowed down to her as to a saint. But Elise, worn out by worry, fear and grief, sank back lifeless into her brothers' arms.

'Yes, she is innocent,' said her eldest brother. And he told them all that had happened. As he spoke, a wonderful fragrance filled the air. For every piece of wood in the fire built around the stake had taken root and sent forth branches, until they made a high hedge around Elise, full of red roses. At the very top there was a single pure white flower, bright as a shining star. The king plucked it, and laid it on Elise's breast; and she awoke, with peace and joy in her heart.

Church bells rang out, and the air was filled with flying birds.

What a joyous parade it was back to the palace! No king could command anything so fine.

THE DARNING NEEDLE

HERE WAS ONCE a darning needle who was so fine she fancied she was a sewing needle.

'Watch what you're doing!' she snapped to the fingers of the cook, who picked her up. 'Don't drop me! If I were to fall on the floor, you might never find me again, I'm so fine.'

'Enough of your airs and graces,' said the fingers, clasping her round the waist.

'See, I come with a train!' said the darning needle, trailing a long thread behind her. The fingers guided her to the cook's slipper, for the leather upper had come away and needed to be sewn back on.

'What rough work this is,' said the darning needle. 'I shall never get through. I shall break! I shall break!' And break she did. 'I told you so,' said the darning needle. 'I'm too fine.'

'Now she is good for nothing,' thought the fingers. But still, they didn't want to throw her away. The cook dropped some sealing wax on her, and pinned the darning needle in her shawl.

'Look! Now I am a brooch,' said the darning needle. 'I knew I would make my way up in the world. Some people are just destined for success.' And she laughed—inwardly, of course, for you can't tell from the outside if a darning needle is laughing or not. There she sat, taking her ease, as proud as if she were driving in a carriage and acknowledging the crowds.

'May I take the liberty of asking if you are made of gold?' she

asked a pin that was next to her. 'I like the look of you, although your head is so small. You should try to make it grow, for we can't all have sealing wax dropped on us.' And the darning needle drew herself up so proudly that she fell out of the shawl into the sink, just as the cook was letting out the plug.

'Now I'm off on my travels!' said the darning needle. 'I hope I don't get lost!' But she did.

'I am too fine for this world,' she said, when she came to rest in the gutter. 'But my conscience is clear, and that's a comfort.' And the darning needle kept her spirits up by holding herself as straight as ever.

All sorts of things floated past her—sticks, straws, scraps of old newspaper. 'Look at them sailing along!' said the darning needle. 'They have no idea what treasure lies below. Here I am, and here I shall stay. Look at that stick, he doesn't have a thought in his head except being a stick. And look at that straw, twisting and turning this way and that. Watch where you're going, or you'll crash into the kerb! And there goes a page of newspaper—its news is all forgotten, yet it still flaps about. I lie here patient and quiet. I know what I am, and I shan't change.'

One day something landed up next to her that was so shiny the darning needle thought it must be a diamond; it was really only a bit of broken glass, but as it was so bright the darning needle spoke to it, introducing herself as a brooch. 'Aren't you a diamond?' 'Something like that' was the reply. And as they each believed the other to be a valuable jewel, they had a good gossip about the airs and graces of others.

'Yes, I have lived in a box belonging to a young lady,' said the darning needle. 'And this young lady was a cook. She had five fingers on each hand, and anything so conceited as those fingers I have never known. They had nothing to do all day but take me out of the box, hold me while I did all the work, then put me back in again.'

'And were they shiny?' asked the bit of broken glass.

'Shiny?' said the darning needle. 'Not a bit of it. But they were full of themselves, all the same. They were five brothers, all fingers by birth. The first was called Tom Thumb—he was short and fat, and he stood on the outside of the others; he only had one joint, so he could only make a simple bow, but even so he told me once that if he were cut off a man's hand, that man could never be a soldier. The second was called Lickpot—he couldn't resist a sauce, whether it was sweet or sour; he used to point at the sun and moon, and hold on to the pen when the fingers wrote. Lanky Lawrence looked down on the others. Goldband wore a gold ring. And little Peter Playboy never did anything at all, and was proud of it! They were stuck-up, the lot of them—so I jumped into the sink.'

'And now we sit here and shine,' said the bit of broken glass. Just then, a torrent of water streamed through the gutter and swept the piece of glass away.

'He has moved on,' said the darning needle. 'But I am still here. I am too fine for my own good—but that's something to be proud of—people respect you for it.' So she lay there stiffly and thought her own thoughts.

'I'm so fine, I could almost believe I was born from a sunbeam. I'm sure the sun often searches for me under the water. I'm so fine, even my own mother can't find me! If I still had my old eye, which broke, I believe I could cry—though I wouldn't, of course, it's not refined.'

One day some boys were grubbing about in the gutter, looking for old nails, coins and the like. They got very dirty doing it, but that was what they liked.

'Ouch!' cried one—he had pricked himself on the darning needle. 'Rotten thing.'

'I'm not a thing, I'm a young lady,' said the darning needle, but no one heard her. The sealing wax had come off, and she had turned black. But black is slimming, so she thought herself finer than ever.

'Here comes an eggshell, floating on the water,' said one of the boys. And they stuck the darning needle in the shell, like a mast in a ship.

'I look very fine in black against a white background,' said the darning needle. 'If only everyone could see me now! But I hope I won't be seasick, for then I should break.' But she needn't have worried, for she wasn't seasick, so she didn't break.

'I have a constitution of steel,' she said. 'That's the best defence against seasickness, and a reminder that one is finer than others. I feel so much better now. The finer one is, the more one can put up with.'

Crunch! went the eggshell. A cart had run over it.

'Oh! I'm in a tight spot!' said the darning needle. 'I shall be sick after all! I shall break! I shall break!'

But she didn't break, even though she was run over by a cart. She was lying full length in the road—and there let her lie.

THE NIGHTINGALE

OU KNOW THAT in China the emperor is Chinese, and all the people around him are Chinese too. This story happened there a long time ago, which is all the more reason I should tell it to you now, before it is forgotten.

The emperor's palace was the finest in the world, made entirely of the most delicate porcelain, so precious and so fragile that you had to be very careful about touching anything. The garden was full of rare flowers, and the loveliest had little silver bells tied to them that tinkled to attract the attention of passers-by.

Yes, everything in the emperor's garden was very well thought out, and it stretched so far that even the gardener had no idea where it ended. If you kept on walking you came at last to a beautiful wood, with tall trees and still lakes. The wood went right down to the sea, which was blue and deep; big ships could sail right in under the high branches of the trees.

Among those branches lived a nightingale, who sang so sweetly that even the poor fisherman, with all his cares, would stop to listen while casting his nets each night. 'It does my heart good to hear it,' he would say; but then he had to get on with his work, and forget the bird. Yet the following night he would stop again to listen to her song: 'It does my heart good.'

Folk came from all over to admire the emperor's city, his palace and his garden; but when they heard the nightingale, they all said, 'That's the best of all.' And when they returned home, they never forgot the bird when telling their tales, so that when learned men wrote books about the city, the palace and the garden, the

nightingale always got the highest praise; poets wrote lovely poems about the nightingale in the wood by the sea.

These books went all over the world, and one of them at last reached the emperor. There he sat in his golden chair, reading away; every now and then he nodded his head, to show how pleased he was with the splendid descriptions of his city, palace and garden. 'But best of all is the nightingale,' said the book.

'What's this?' said the emperor. 'The nightingale? Why, I've never heard of it. Can there really be such a bird in my empire— in my own garden—and no one told me? Fancy having to find it out from a book.'

So he called for his lord-in-waiting. This gentleman was so grand that whenever anyone of lower rank dared to speak to him, he only answered '*Pah!*', which doesn't mean anything much.

'It says here that we have a most remarkable bird, called a nightingale,' said the emperor. 'Her song is supposed to be the finest thing in all my empire. Why have I never been told about her?'

'I have never heard of her,' said the lord-in-waiting. 'She's never been presented at court.'

'It is my wish that she should be brought here tonight to sing for me,' said the emperor. 'The whole world knows about this treasure of mine, except for me!'

'I have never heard of her,' repeated the lord-in-waiting. 'But she shall be found.'

But where? The lord-in-waiting ran upstairs and downstairs, along the corridors and back again, but none of the people he questioned had ever heard of the nightingale. So the lord-in-waiting hurried back to the emperor and said that it must be a story invented by the writer of the book. 'Your Majesty must not believe everything you read. These writers make it all up—the artful rogues.'

'This book,' said the emperor, 'was sent to me personally by the high and mighty Emperor of Japan, so it cannot be untrue. I *will* hear the nightingale, and I will hear her tonight! If she fails to appear, immediately after supper every courtier shall be punched in the stomach.'

'*Tsing-pe!*' said the lord-in-waiting, and he ran upstairs and downstairs, along the corridors and back again, this time with half the court at his tail, for they didn't fancy the idea of being punched in the stomach directly after supper. Everywhere, they asked about this nightingale, who was known to all the world except the court.

At last they came across a poor little kitchen-maid, who said: 'Oh yes, the nightingale! I know her well. How she sings! Every evening I take some scraps from the table to my poor sick mother, who lives by the shore. On my way back, I rest in the wood, and the nightingale sings to me. It brings tears to my eyes, as if mother were kissing me.'

'Little kitchen-maid,' said the lord-in-waiting, 'if you can take us to this nightingale, you shall have a proper job in the kitchen, and be allowed to watch the emperor at his dinner. For the emperor has commanded her presence at court.'

So they all went to the wood where the nightingale sang. On the way, they heard a cow moo. 'Ah, there she is!' cried the courtiers. 'What a powerful voice for such a small bird! Yes, we've heard her before.'

'That is a cow mooing,' said the little kitchen-maid. 'There's still a long way to go.'

Then some frogs began to croak in the pond.

'Divine!' said the emperor's chaplain. 'Just like church bells!'

'No, those are frogs,' said the little kitchen-maid, 'but I expect we will hear her soon.'

And then the nightingale began to sing.

'There she is,' cried the little girl. 'Listen! Listen! She's up there.' And she pointed to a drab little bird up in the branches.

'Is it possible?' said the lord-in-waiting. 'Who would have thought it? How plain she is. But perhaps she is abashed by such distinguished visitors.'

'Little nightingale,' called the kitchen-maid, 'our gracious emperor would like you to sing for him.'

'With all my heart,' said the nightingale, and at once she began to trill and sing.

'It's like glass bells chiming,' said the lord-in-waiting. 'See how her throat moves! It is extraordinary we've never heard of her before; she'll be a great hit at court.'

'Shall I sing once more for the emperor?' said the nightingale, who thought that the emperor must be one of the visitors.

'Most excellent nightingale,' replied the lord-in-waiting, 'it is my privilege to summon you to a concert at the court tonight, where you will enchant His Imperial Majesty with your delightful song.'

'It sounds best among the green trees,' said the nightingale, but she went with them willingly when she heard that that was what the emperor wanted.

The whole palace had been scrubbed and polished, till the porcelain walls shone in the light of thousands of gold lamps. The loveliest flowers were arranged in the corridors, with bells tied to them, that tinkled in the air stirred by servants scurrying to and fro—you could hardly hear yourself think.

In the middle of the great hall where the emperor sat, a golden perch was put up for the nightingale. The whole court was there, and the little kitchen-maid had special permission to stand behind the door, now that she had the official title Imperial Kitchen-Maid. Everyone was dressed up in all their finery, and all eyes were on the plain little bird.

The emperor nodded; that was the signal to begin.

The nightingale sang so beautifully that it brought tears to the emperor's eyes; they actually rolled down his cheeks. At that, the nightingale's song grew even lovelier—it touched the hearts of all who heard. The emperor was so delighted that he said the nightingale should have his gold slipper to wear around her neck; but she said no, thank you, she already had her reward. 'I have seen tears in the emperor's eyes, and that is all the reward I ask. There is a strange power in the tears of an emperor.' And then the nightingale sang again.

'She's quite bewitching!' sighed the ladies of the court; and they each took a gulp of water and tried to gurgle it in their throats, to see if they could be nightingales too. Even the lackeys and chambermaids were pleased, and that's saying a lot because they're the hardest audience of all. No doubt about it, the nightingale was a great hit.

So the nightingale was to stay at court, and have her own cage, with permission to fly out twice each day, and once each night. But whenever she flew, she had twelve attendants holding tight to a silk ribbon tied round her leg, so there wasn't much fun in it.

Still, she was the talk of the town. When two people met, one would say 'night', and the other would answer 'ingale', and that was all that needed to be said. Eleven new babies were called Nightingale, though none of them could sing a note.

One day, a large parcel arrived for the emperor. On it was written NIGHTINGALE.

'This must be a new book about our famous bird,' said the emperor. But it wasn't a book. It was a mechanical toy in a box— an artificial nightingale. It looked just like the real one except it was covered all over with diamonds, rubies and sapphires. All you had to do was wind it up and it would sing one of the songs that the real bird sang; and all the while its tail bobbed up and down, glittering with silver and gold. Round its neck hung the message: 'The Emperor of Japan's nightingale is a poor thing beside the nightingale of the Emperor of China.'

'How wonderful!' they all exclaimed. The man who had brought the gift was given the title Imperial Nightingale Bringer.

'Let's hear them together,' someone said. 'What a duet that will be!'

So the two birds sang together, but it wasn't a success. For the real nightingale sang in her natural way, while the artificial bird sang by clockwork. 'And none the worse for that,' said the Imperial Music Master. 'She keeps perfect time; she knows the rules.'

After that, the artificial bird sang by itself. It was just as popular as the real one, and so much better looking.

Over and over it sang its song—thirty-three times and never got tired. Everyone wanted it to sing again, but the emperor said it was time for the real nightingale to have a turn.

But where was she? She had flown away to the greenwood from an open window, and no one had noticed.

'Dear, dear, dear,' tutted the emperor. 'Is this the thanks I get?' And all the courtiers agreed that the nightingale was the most ungrateful creature, and called her names.

'At any rate,' they said, 'we have the better bird here.' So the clockwork bird had to sing once more. This was the thirty-fourth time they had heard the very same tune; but it was a very complicated one, so they didn't notice.

The Imperial Music Master praised the bird very highly; it was better than the real bird in every way—not just because of the jewels on the outside, but for the clockwork on the inside. 'You see, ladies and gentleman, and above all Your Imperial Majesty, with the real nightingale you could never tell what was coming, but with the artificial bird it's all pre-arranged. You know what you will hear. Open it up, and you can see the science of it: how the wheels turn to grind out the notes.'

Everyone agreed. The Imperial Music Master got permission to show off the new bird to the public on the following Sunday. 'They must hear it sing,' said the emperor. And hear it they did. It made them quite tipsy; they all said, 'Oh!' and wagged their fingers in the air, and nodded their heads. Only the poor fisherman who used to listen to the real nightingale said, 'It's like, yet … not like. There's something missing, though I can't put my finger on it.'

The real nightingale was banished from the empire.

The artificial bird lived on a silken cushion by the emperor's bed; all the presents it received, gold and precious stones, lay beside it; it was made Chief Imperial Bedside Minstrel, First Class on the Left—even emperors keep their hearts on the left.

The Imperial Music Master wrote a book in twenty-five volumes all about the artificial bird, using the longest and most difficult words he could find; everyone pretended to have read it and understood it, for no one wants to be thought stupid.

This went on for a year, until the emperor, his court and all his subjects knew by heart every trill of the toy bird's song; but that only made them like it all the more, as they could sing along. The boys in the street sang, *Zi-zi-zi! Kluk-kluk-kluk!* and the emperor sang it, too. It was great fun.

But one evening, when the artificial bird was in full song, and the emperor was lying in bed and listening, something went, *Snap!* inside the bird. *Whirr-rr-rr-r-.* The wheels whizzed round, and the music stopped.

The emperor sprang out of bed, calling for the doctor—but what could he do? Then they fetched the watchmaker, and with a lot of muttering and poking he managed to get the bird going after a fashion; but he said it mustn't be used too often, as the clockwork was almost worn out, and it couldn't be repaired.

It was all very sad. Once a year the artificial bird was allowed to sing, and even that was a struggle. Still, the Imperial Music Master made a speech full of long words, saying the bird was as good as ever, so of course it must have been.

Five years passed, and a great sorrow fell on the empire. The people really were fond of the emperor, and now it was reported that he was ill and close to death. A new emperor had already been chosen, and when people in the street asked the lord-in-waiting for news, he just said, '*Pah!*' and shook his head.

Cold and pale lay the emperor in his magnificent bed. The whole court regarded him as dead already, and had rushed off to greet the new emperor; the lackeys were standing around gossiping, and the chambermaids were all drinking tea. Heavy cloth had been laid down on all the floors to deaden the noise; the whole palace was still, so still.

But the emperor wasn't dead yet. He lay, pale and unmoving, in his great bed with its heavy velvet curtains and its golden tassels; through an open window, the moonlight shone down on the Emperor and the clockwork bird.

The poor emperor could scarcely breathe; he felt as if something were sitting on his chest; he opened his eyes and saw that it was Death, wearing the emperor's gold crown and holding in one hand the imperial sword and in the other the imperial banner. All around the bed, in the folds of the velvet curtains, were strange faces—some kind and friendly, some hideous and hateful. They were the emperor's good and evil deeds, clustered around him, as Death sat on his heart.

'Do you remember this?' they whispered, one after another. 'Do you remember that?' They went on and on, until the sweat broke out on the emperor's forehead.

'I never knew,' cried the emperor. 'I didn't realise.' Then he called out, 'Music! Music! Sound the great drum, so I can't hear what they're saying!' But still they went on, and Death nodded his head at every word.

'Music! Music!' pleaded the emperor. 'Beautiful little golden bird, I beg you, sing! I've given you gold and precious stones; I've hung my golden slipper round your neck. Sing, please, sing!'

But the bird was silent. There was no one there to wind it up, and it couldn't sing without that. Death just stared at the emperor with his great hollow eyes, and everything was still, so still.

All at once, by the window, the sweetest song rang out. It was the living nightingale, sitting on a branch outside. She had heard of the emperor's illness, and come to bring him what comfort she could. And as she sang, the ghostly faces grew fainter and fainter; the blood began to pulse more strongly through the emperor's feeble limbs; even Death listened in, and said, 'Go on, little nightingale, go on!'

'Yes, if you'll give me that fine sword … yes, if you'll give me that splendid banner … yes, if you'll give me the emperor's gold crown.'

And Death gave up each treasure for a song. The nightingale went on singing. She sang of the quiet churchyard where the white roses bloom, and the elderflowers smell so sweet, and the green grass is watered with tears. She filled Death with longing for his garden, and in a cold white mist he floated out of the window.

'Thank you, thank you!' said the emperor. 'You heavenly little bird. I remember you. I banished you from my lands, yet you have sung away those terrible phantoms from my bed, and lifted Death from my heart. How can I ever repay you?'

'You have already given me my reward. When I first sang to you, I saw tears in your eyes; that, I shall never forget. Those are the only jewels I value. But sleep now and wake refreshed, and strong. I will sing you a lullaby.'

And the nightingale sang, and the emperor fell into a sweet sleep—such a calm, peaceful sleep.

When the sun woke him, shining through the window, he was himself again. None of his servants had bothered to come; they all thought he must be dead. But the nightingale was still there, still singing.

'You must stay with me for ever,' said the emperor, 'but only sing when you want to. As for the artificial bird, I shall break it into a thousand pieces.'

'Don't do that,' said the nightingale. 'It did its best. Keep it. As for me, I can't live in a palace. Let me come when I like, and sit in

the evening on this branch by your window, and sing to you—happy songs, and sad songs, too. I will bring you news of joy and sorrow—everything that happens, good and bad, in your lands—news that has always been kept from you. For this little bird flies far and wide; I visit the fisherman's hut and the peasant's cottage, far from you and your court. I love you for your heart, not for your crown—yet the crown has its own magic. I shall come and sing to you. But you must promise me one thing.'

'Anything!' said the emperor. He was standing, dressed in his imperial robes, and holding the imperial sword against his heart.

'All I ask is this. Tell no one that you have a little bird that brings you all the news; then all will be well.' And the nightingale flew away.

The servants came in to have a look at their dead master. They stopped in their tracks!

'Good morning,' said the emperor.

THE TEAPOT

HERE WAS ONCE a proud teapot—proud of her porcelain, proud of her long spout, proud of her wide handle. She had something to boast about at the front and the back. She never talked about her lid, because the lid had been broken and glued back together. We don't like to talk about our shortcomings—other people will do that for us. The rest of the tea set—the cups, the cream jug, the sugar basin—preferred to gossip about the broken lid rather than praise the fine handle and the excellent spout. The teapot was well aware of that.

'I know them!' she said to herself. 'But I also know my own faults, and admit them. That's because I'm so humble, so modest. We all have our failings, but we all have our special qualities, too. The cups have their handles, the sugar basin has its lid—but I have both, as well as something neither of them has. I have my spout, and that makes me queen of the tea table. The sugar basin and the cream jug are the handmaidens—I am the mistress. I pour out a blessing for thirsty humanity. Inside me, the fragrant leaves of Chinese tea are infused in boiling water, which doesn't taste of anything by itself.'

That's how the teapot talked, in the glad confident days of her youth. Then one day, when she was standing on the tea table, she was lifted up by the most delicate hand—but the most delicate hand was careless, and the teapot fell to the floor. The spout broke off, the handles broke off, and as for the lid—we shan't talk about the lid, we've said enough already.

The teapot lay in a faint on the floor, with boiling water

gushing out of her. And that wasn't the worst thing. They laughed at her! At the teapot, not at the careless hand that dropped her!

'That's something I shall never forget,' said the teapot, when later she told herself the story of her life. 'They said I was a useless old crock, and shoved me in a corner. The very next day, I was given away to a woman who came to beg for kitchen scraps. I was a pauper, and nothing I could say or do would change it. Yet that was the start of a better life for me. For though you begin as one thing, in time you become something completely different.

'I was filled with earth, which for a teapot is like being buried. But into the earth a bulb was placed. Who planted it there, I don't know. But it was a gift, to make up for the Chinese tea leaves, and the boiling water, and the loss of my handle and my spout.

'The bulb lay in the earth, the bulb lay in me, and it became my heart, my living heart. I was alive, as I had never been before. I pulsed with power and energy. The bulb sprouted, so full of thoughts and feelings it almost burst. And then it broke out into flower. I saw it, I carried it, and I forgot myself in its beauty. It's a wonderful thing to forget yourself in another.

'It never thanked me, it never gave me a thought. Everyone admired it. That made me so happy, and it must have made the bulb even happier. Then one day I heard someone say that the flower was so lovely it deserved a better pot. So they broke me in two, which hurt terribly.

'The bulb was moved to a proper flowerpot, and I was thrown out into the yard. And here I lie, an old piece of broken pot. But I have my memories—they can't take those away from me.'

THE UGLY
DUCKLING

 T WAS THE HEIGHT of summer in the countryside. The corn was yellow; the oats were ripe; the hay was stacked in the green meadows, where the stork wandered on his long red legs, muttering to himself in Egyptian, a language he learned from his mother. The open fields were skirted by thick woods, and hidden in the woods were deep cool lakes. Yes, it was lovely out in the country.

The bright sun fell on an old manor house, and glinted on the moat that surrounded it. On the wall by the water's edge grew huge dock leaves—the biggest were so tall that a child could make a secret hideaway beneath them. The place was as densely tangled as the heart of the woods, and it was here that a duck was sitting on her nest, waiting for her ducklings to hatch. That's a long job, and she was getting tired of it. No one ever came to visit her; the other ducks swimming around in the moat never thought to drop in under the dock leaves for a quack.

But at last the eggs began to crack, one after another. *Peep! Peep!* All the chicks were poking their little heads out the shells.

Quack, quack! said Mother Duck, and the little ones waddled to their feet as best they could, staring all the time at the green world under the dock leaves; she let them look as long as they liked, as green is good for the eyes.

'How big the world is!' said the ducklings; and to be sure, there is more room under a leaf than inside an egg.

'Do you suppose that this is the whole world?' said Mother Duck. 'Why, the world stretches far away—right across the garden and into the parson's field, though I've never ventured so far myself. Now, are you all hatched?' And she got up from the nest. 'No, not all. The largest egg is still here. How much longer will it be? I'm so tired of this.' And she sat down again.

An old duck happened by, and asked how she was getting on.

'There's just one egg that's taking forever to hatch. But look at the others: they're the prettiest ducklings you ever did see. They take after their father—that layabout, why does he never come and see me?'

'Let me look at that egg,' said the old duck. 'I bet it's a turkey's egg. I was fooled that way once, and the chicks gave me no end of trouble. They were afraid of the water, if you can believe it, and I just couldn't coax them in. I quacked and clucked but it was no use. Let me see it—yes, that's a turkey's egg. Leave it, and teach the others how to swim.'

'I'll sit on it a while longer,' replied Mother Duck. 'I've been at it so long, I may as well finish the job.'

'Please yourself,' said the old duck, and she waddled away.

At long last the big egg cracked open. *Peep! Peep!* said the little one, as he tumbled out. How ugly and gawky he was! Mother Duck looked at him. 'What a huge duckling that is! Can it be a turkey after all? Well, there's only one way to find out. Into the water he shall go, if I have to push him in myself.'

The weather next day was glorious, so Mother Duck took all her family down to the moat in the sunshine. Splash! she jumped into the water. *Quack, quack!* she called, and one by one the ducklings plopped in. The water closed over their heads, but they all bobbed up again, and began to swim happily on the surface, their little feet paddling away beneath them. They were all there, even the ugly one.

'Well, it's not a turkey,' said Mother Duck. 'Look at those legs go! He knows how to keep upright—he is my own chick! And really quite pretty, if you look closely. *Quack, quack!* Follow me, and I will show you the world—that is, the farmyard. Stay close to me, and keep your eyes skinned for the cat.'

So they went into the farmyard. Two duck families were making a terrible commotion, squabbling over the head of an eel—and then the cat got it after all.

'That's the way of the world,' said Mother Duck, with a downturned beak, for she could have just fancied a bit of eel's head. 'Now then, use your legs; slip over and pay your respects to that old duck over there. She is our most distinguished resident; she has Spanish blood. And look, she has a piece of red cloth tied round her leg. That marks her out as special—no one would dream of behaving rudely to her. Look lively, and don't turn your toes in; a well-bred duckling splays its feet out, like its father and mother. That's it. Now, make a bow, and say *Quack!*'

The little birds did as they were told. Meanwhile, all the other ducks in the yard were eyeing them up, and one of them said out loud, 'Look at that rabble! As if there weren't enough of us already. And look how ugly that one is! We can't put up with him!' And the duck flew at the ugly duckling and pecked him in the neck.

'Leave him alone,' said Mother Duck. 'He's not doing any harm.'

'He is gawky and different, so he must be put in his place.'

'Now, now,' said the old duck with the red rag on her leg. 'The other ducklings are all very pretty, it's just this one that doesn't seem to have hatched right.'

'If you please, my lady,' said Mother Duck, 'he may not be handsome, but he's good-natured, and swims just as well as the others—maybe better. I'm sure his looks will improve, and he won't stay so outsized; it's just that he was so long in the egg, that's all that's wrong.' And she plumed his neck for him and smoothed out the feathers. 'Besides, he's a drake, so looks aren't everything. He's fit and strong, so he'll be able to look after himself.'

'Anyway, the others are charming,' said the old duck. 'Make yourselves at home, and if you happen on an eel's head, my dears, that would be very welcome.'

So they made themselves at home.

But the poor little duckling who was last out of the egg and looked so ugly got jostled and pecked, and teased by ducks and hens alike. 'You big booby!' they all mocked. And the turkey, who was born with spurs and carried himself like an emperor, puffed up his feathers like a ship in full sail and ran straight at him, all red in the face and gobbling. The poor little duckling was quite beside himself, what with being so ugly, and being the butt of every joke.

That was just the first day; after that, it got worse and worse. Everyone picked on the ugly duckling. The ducks bit him; the hens pecked him; the girl who came to feed the poultry kicked him out of the way. His own brothers and sisters looked down on him, and jeered 'Yah! Boo! Hope the cat gets you!' One day, even his mother sighed, 'If only I didn't have to see you.'

So he ran away. He fluttered over the hedge, and frightened some little birds that flew into the air. 'That's because I'm so ugly,' he thought, and shut his eyes. But he kept on going, until he came to a wide marsh, where wild ducks lived. He lay there all night, worn out and miserable.

In the morning the wild ducks flew up to have a look at their new companion. 'What in the world are you?' they asked, and the duckling squirmed this way and that, trying to be polite.

'You really are an ugly-mug,' said the wild ducks. 'But that doesn't bother us, as long as you don't want to marry into our family.' Poor thing! He wasn't dreaming of getting married; all he wanted was to be allowed to sleep among the reeds, and drink a little marsh water.

There he lay for two days, and on the third two wild geese came along—or, rather, two young wild ganders, full of high spirits and self-importance. 'Listen, kid,' they said, 'you may be a freak, but you make us laugh. Come with us and we'll show you a good time. There's another marsh nearby full of tender young geese, the sweetest creatures who ever said *Hiss!* A clown like you will really tickle their fancy.'

Bang! Bang! a gun fired twice. Both the young ganders fell dead in the reeds, and the water was stained red with their blood. *Bang!* went another gun. Flocks of wild geese rose into the air. *Bang! Bang!* A big shoot was on. Hunters lay all around the marsh; some were even sitting in the trees at the edge. Clouds of blue gunsmoke curled over the water and drifted among the trees. The gun dogs splashed through the mud, flattening the reeds. The poor little duckling was so frightened. He tried to bury his head beneath his wing, but just then a fierce dog bounded up to him, its tongue slobbering from its mouth and its eyes flashing fire. It opened its gaping jaws and lunged at the duckling, but then it was gone with a splash, without touching him.

The duckling sighed in relief. 'I'm so ugly, even the dogs don't want to sully their mouths with me.' Then he lay quite still, listening as shot after shot rained down on the marsh.

It was late in the day before it grew quiet, and even then the poor duckling didn't dare to move for several hours. Then he hurried away from the marsh as fast as he could; he ran over fields and meadows, struggling against the strong wind that had got up.

Near nightfall he reached a wretched little cottage, so tumbledown that it couldn't decide which way to fall, which was the only reason it remained standing. The wind howled, and the poor duckling had to sit on his tail so as not to be blown over. It grew worse and worse. Then the duckling noticed that the cottage door had lost one of its hinges, and was hanging awry. There was just enough of a crack for him to creep inside; so he did.

An old woman lived there, with her cat and her hen. The old woman called the cat Sonny; he could arch his back and purr, and even send out sparks if you stroked him the wrong way. The hen

had bandy little legs, and so was called Chickabiddy-Shortshanks; she was a very good layer, and the old woman loved her dearly.

Next morning, they all noticed their strange new guest. The cat purred, the hen clucked and the old woman said, 'Whatever's that?' Her sight was failing, and she thought the ugly duckling was a plump full-grown duck that had lost its way. 'What a find!' she said. 'Now we shall have duck's eggs; unless it's a drake. Time will tell.'

And so the duckling was taken into the household, on three weeks' trial; but he didn't lay any eggs.

Now the cat was master of the house, and the hen was mistress. They always talked about 'We and the world', because they thought they made up half the world, and the better half at that. The duckling tried to put another opinion, but the hen wouldn't allow it.

'Can you lay eggs?' she asked.

'No.'

'Well, then, hold your tongue.'

And the cat asked, 'Can you arch your back? Can you purr? Can you give out sparks?'

'No.'

'Then keep your opinions to yourself, when your betters are talking.'

So the duckling sat alone in the corner, feeling very low. He tried to think about the fresh air and the sunshine, but that just made him long to go for a swim. At last, he couldn't help telling the hen about it.

'That's just a sick fancy,' said the hen. 'It's because you're idle. You should lay an egg, or purr, then you'd forget all this nonsense.'

'But it's so delicious to swim on the water,' said the duckling. 'It's wonderful to dabble about and dive to the bottom.'

'If that's what you call delicious,' said the hen, 'then you must be mad. Go and ask the cat—he's the one with the brains—if he wants to go swimming in all that wet water. Ask the old woman, our mistress, the wisest woman in the world! Do you imagine *she* wants to dabble and dive?'

'You just don't understand,' said the duckling.

'Well, if we don't understand, who would? If you think yourself wiser than the cat or the old woman, or even myself, you're sorely mistaken. So don't be silly and count your blessings. Haven't you come to a nice warm room with good companions who can teach you a thing or two? But you're too stupid for words and I can't be bothered with you. Believe me, I wish you well, but I must speak as I find—it takes a real friend to point out home truths. So why not make a bit of effort in return: try to lay an egg, or purr, or give out sparks.'

'I think I had better go back out into the wide world,' said the duckling.

'Well, go then,' said the hen.

So the duckling went. He swam on the water; he dived down—but he made no friends, and thought that was because he was ugly.

Autumn came. The leaves in the wood turned yellow and brown; the wind caught them and whirled them into a dance; the sky grew steely; the clouds hung heavy with hail and snow; the raven perched on the fence squawked *Caw! Caw!* in the cold air. It was enough to give anyone the shivers, and the poor duckling had a hard time of it.

One evening, just as the setting sun flamed across the sky, a flock of large, lovely birds rose from the rushes. The duckling had never seen such beautiful birds; they were brilliant white with long, graceful necks. They were swans. They called out—a harsh, compelling *Honk!*—spread their magnificent wings and wheeled away, flying to the warm lands, where the water didn't freeze over.

They soared high, so high, and the ugly duckling was seized with a wild excitement. He turned round and round in the water like a millwheel, craning his neck to keep them in sight, and let out a cry so shrill and strange that he scared himself. Oh! he would never forget those noble birds. When they were lost to view, he plunged to the bottom of the water; when he rose again he was almost beside himself. He did not know what the birds were called, he did not know where they were going, and yet he felt drawn to them in a way he had never felt before. He didn't envy them—such beauty was utterly beyond him. Not even the ducks would put up with him—poor, ugly creature.

The winter was cold, bitter cold. The duckling had to swim round and round in the water to stop it from freezing over. Every night, the little circle of free water grew smaller; the duckling had to work his legs frantically to keep the ice at bay; at last, he was worn out, and the ice froze him fast.

Early next morning a peasant saw him and broke the ice up with his wooden clog, and took the duckling home to his wife.

The duckling soon revived, and then the children wanted to play with him. But the duckling was afraid, and fluttered panic-stricken into the milk-pail. The milk splashed everywhere; the wife screamed and clapped her hands; the duckling flew into the butter-tub, then into the flour-bin, and out again. What a sight he was! The wife shouted and tried to hit him with the fire-tongs; the children cackled and shrieked as they chased him about the room. It was just as well that the door was open; the duckling sprang through and hid in the bushes on the new-fallen snow; he lay there in a daze.

It would be too sad to tell you all the hardships the duckling had to endure through that hard winter. He was huddling in the shelter of the reeds on the moor when one day the sun began to shine warmly again, and the larks sang: spring had arrived.

The duckling stretched out his wings. They were stronger than before and carried him swiftly along. Almost before he knew it he was in a big garden with blossoming apple-trees and sweet-smelling lilac overhanging a stream. It was so lovely, so fresh and spring-like.

From the thicket ahead came three beautiful swans, ruffling their feathers and sailing calmly on the water. The duckling recognised the stately creatures and was overcome with a sudden sadness.

'I will fly to them, those noble birds,' he said. 'They may peck me to death for daring to approach them, ugly as I am; but I don't care. Better to be killed by them than to be bitten by the ducks, pecked by the hens, kicked by the girl who feeds the poultry and left to freeze in the winter.'

He flew down and landed on the water, and swam toward the glorious swans. As they caught sight of him, they darted toward him, ruffling their feathers. 'Kill me, if you will,' said the poor creature, and he lowered his head to meet his death. But what did he see reflected in the water? He saw his own likeness—no longer a gawky, ugly duckling, but a swan!

It's no wonder you don't feel at home in the farmyard, if you've been hatched from a swan's egg.

This was the end of all his suffering—this blissful happiness. The three great swans swam round him, stroking him with their beaks.

Some little children came running into the garden. They threw corn and bread into the water, and the littlest one called out, 'Look, there's a new swan!' The others shouted with delight, 'Yes, a new one!' They clapped their hands and cavorted with pleasure, and ran to tell their father and mother. They threw bread and cake into the water and everyone said, 'The new one is the most beautiful of all—so young and handsome!' And the older swans bowed before him.

He felt quite overcome, and shyly tucked his head underneath his wing, he was so flustered. He was almost too happy, but not proud, for a good heart is never vain.

He thought of how he had been persecuted and despised, and now everyone said he was the most beautiful of these beautiful birds. The lilacs bowed their branches to him on the water, and the sun sent down its welcoming warmth. His heart was filled with joy. He ruffled his feathers and stretched his slender neck, and said, 'I never dreamed of such happiness, when I was the ugly duckling!'

THE SNOW QUEEN

A STORY IN SEVEN PARTS

PART ONE

THE MIRROR AND
THE SPLINTERS

LISTEN! THIS IS THE BEGINNING. And when we get to the end we shall know more than we do now.

Once there was a wicked demon—one of the worst: it was the Devil. He was very pleased with himself because he had made a mirror that had a strange power. Anything good and beautiful reflected in it shrunk away, while everything bad and ugly swelled up. The loveliest countryside looked like boiled spinach; the prettiest people looked horrible, and seemed to be standing on their heads or to have no stomachs at all. As for faces, the mirror twisted them so that you couldn't even recognise yourself. One single freckle would turn into a great blotch over your nose and your mouth. That's the Devil's idea of a joke!

If a good thought went through anyone's mind while he was looking in the mirror, it pulled a face at him. The Devil had a good laugh at that, too. All the pupils at his school for demons said it was a miracle. This is the real world, they said; this mirror shows what people are really like. And they ran around with it until there wasn't anyone or any place that hadn't been twisted by it.

Then the demons wanted to fly up to heaven, to make fun of the

93

angels and even of God himself. The higher they flew, the more the mirror grinned like a gargoyle. They could scarcely hold it still. The mirror shook and grinned, and grinned and shook, till they dropped it, and it fell straight down here to earth and broke into a million billion splinters.

That was only the start of the trouble. Some of the splinters were scarcely the size of a grain of sand, and they blew everywhere, getting into people's eyes and making them see everything ugly and twisted. Some splinters even got into people's hearts, and that was awful, because their hearts became like blocks of ice.

Some of the pieces of glass were big enough to use as window-panes, but it didn't do to look at your friends through that sort of window. Others were made into spectacles, and the people who wore them never could see things straight. The Devil laughed so much he nearly split his sides. And he's laughing still, because there are plenty of those splinters flying about right now, as you will hear.

PART TWO
A LITTLE BOY AND A LITTLE GIRL

 N THE CITY there are so many houses not everyone can have a garden. Most people make do with a few flowers in a flowerpot. But once there were two children who did have a garden a bit bigger than a flowerpot. They weren't brother and sister, but they loved each other just as if they were. Their families lived next door to each other, right up in the attics. Where the roofs joined, they each had a little

window, face to face, and you only had to clamber over the gutter to get from one window to the other.

Their fathers each put a wooden box across this gutter, to grow herbs for the kitchen. There were little rose trees, too, one in each box, that grew like anything. What with sweet peas trailing over the sides of the boxes and the rose trees twining their branches over the windows, the little garden was just perfect. Of course, as it was so high up, the children weren't allowed to climb on the boxes, but they often went out to sit under the roses and play together.

In winter these games had to stop. The windows were all iced up. But if you warmed a coin on the stove and put it to the frozen pane, it made a round peephole, and behind each peephole was a friendly eye of a little boy or a little girl. He was Kay and she was Gerda. In summer they could meet with one jump, but in winter they had to climb down a lot of stairs and then climb up a lot of stairs, and all the time the snowflakes were falling outside.

'Those are the white bees swarming,' said the little girl's old grandmother.

'Have they got a queen?' asked the boy, because he knew that real bees have one.

'Yes, they have,' said Grandmother. 'She flies at the heart of the swarm. She's the biggest of them all. *She* never lies on the ground; she soars up again into the dark cloud. Many's the winter night she flies through the streets of this very town and spies through the windows, making them freeze over with patterns like flowers.'

'I've seen that,' cried both the children, and so they knew it was true.

'Could the Snow Queen come in here?' asked the little girl.

'Just let her try!' said the boy. 'I'd put her on the hot stove and melt her.'

But Grandmother stroked his hair and went on to other stories.

In the evening, when little Kay was back at home and nearly ready for bed, he climbed onto the stool by the window and peeped out through the little hole. A few snowflakes were sifting down, and one of these, the biggest of them all, rested on the edge of the window box outside. This snowflake grew and grew until it became a lady dressed in the finest white gossamer, made of millions of starry flakes. She was so delicate and beautiful—but she was ice, dazzling, glittering ice. Yet she was alive. Her eyes burned like stars, and there was neither peace nor rest in them. She nodded at the window and beckoned with her hand. The little boy was scared and jumped down from his stool. Outside he fancied he saw a huge bird swoop past the window.

Next day there was a clear frost. Then there was a thaw, and then it was spring. The sun shone and the trees budded green. The swallows built their nests, and the windows were opened wide so that the children could sit once more in their little garden high above the houses.

How wonderful the roses were that summer! They were more beautiful than ever. Gerda had learned a hymn that made her think of the roses, and she sang it to Kay, and he sang along:

> *When Jesus Christ*
> *Was yet a child*
> *He had a garden*
> *Fair and wild.*

And that's how it felt to them in those glorious summer days, as they sat holding hands among the roses, in God's own golden sunshine.

One day Kay and Gerda were looking at a picture book full of animals and birds, when suddenly—just as the clock struck five in the old church tower—Kay cried, 'Oh! What's that pain in my heart? And, oh! What's that in my eye?'

The little girl put her arm around his neck, and he blinked his eye, but there was nothing to be seen.

'It must have gone,' he said, but it had not gone. It was one of those splinters of glass from the mirror—you remember, the Devil's mirror, the one that made anything good look ugly and small and anything bad look fine and grand. Poor Kay! He had a splinter in his heart, too, which would slowly turn it into a block of ice. It didn't hurt anymore, but it was there all right.

'What are you bawling about?' he asked. 'You look so ugly! There's nothing wrong with me.' Then, '*Ugh!* That rose is all wormy! And that one's all bent! What horrible roses!' He kicked the window box and tore off the rose blooms.

'Kay, what are you doing?' cried the little girl. When he saw how frightened she was, he pulled off another rose and ran away from his friend Gerda, back through the window.

After that, when Gerda brought out the picture book, he scoffed and said it was for babies. And when Grandmother told them stories now, he interrupted all the time and kept saying, 'But … '. Sometimes he would get behind her and put on her spare glasses and make fun of her. He really was like her, so people had to laugh.

Soon he could mimic everyone in the street, especially their quirks and faults. People said, 'He's so sharp he'll cut himself!' It was the splinter in his eye and the splinter in his heart that had changed him and made him tease even little Gerda, who loved him more than all the world.

He never wanted to play now, he just made experiments. For instance, one winter's day when it was snowing, he brought out a big magnifying glass and then held out the tail of his blue jacket to catch some flakes. 'Look through the glass, Gerda,' he said. And she saw that the flakes looked much bigger, and each one was like a lovely flower or a six-pointed star. It was beautiful.

'Isn't that clever?' said Kay. 'So much nicer than real flowers. They're just perfect—until they melt.'

Later Kay came around with his big gloves on and his sledge on his back. He shouted right in Gerda's ear, 'They're letting me go and sledge in the square with the other boys,' and off he went.

Out in the square the boldest boys were tying their sledges to the farmers' carts to hitch a ride. It was great fun. As they were playing, a great big sleigh drew up. It was painted white all over, and in it was a figure muffled up in white fur, with a white fur cap. This sleigh drove twice around the square, and Kay, quick as anything, tied his sledge behind it. The big sleigh went fast and then faster still and turned off into the main street. The driver turned and gave Kay a nod, as if they were old friends. And every time Kay thought of untying his sledge, the stranger nodded again, so Kay stayed where he was. They drove right out of the city gates.

Then it began to snow so heavily that the little boy could barely see his hand in front of his face, but still the great sleigh rushed on and on. And even when he did manage to untie the rope, it was no use. His little sledge clung fast to the big sleigh, as they sped on with the wind at their tail. He called out at the top of his voice, but no one could hear him. The snow kept falling, and the sleigh drove on. Now and then it seemed to give a little jump as if it were leaping over hedges and ditches. Kay was filled with terror, and he tried to say the Lord's Prayer—but all he could remember was the twelve-times table.

The snowflakes were getting bigger and bigger, until they looked like great white birds. Then suddenly they swerved aside, the big sleigh stopped and its driver stood up, in a fur cloak and a cap made of thick, thick snow. It was a lady—tall and slender and dazzlingly white. It was the Snow Queen.

'We have come far,' she said. 'But why do you tremble? Come, creep under my fur.' And she put Kay beside her in her sleigh and wrapped the fur around him. Kay felt as if he were sinking into a deep drift of snow.

'Are you still frozen?' she asked, and she kissed him on the forehead. Oh! Her kiss was colder than cold. It went straight to his

heart, which was nearly a lump of ice anyway. He thought he would die—but only for a moment. Then everything was all right, and he didn't feel cold anymore.

'My sledge! Don't forget my sledge!' That was his first thought. So it was tied to one of the white birds, which flew behind them with the little sledge at its back. Then the Snow Queen kissed Kay once more, and he forgot little Gerda, and her grandmother, and everyone at home.

'No more kisses now,' she said, 'or I'll kiss you to death.'

Kay gazed at her. She was so beautiful, more beautiful than he could grasp. Now she didn't seem to be made of ice, as she had been when she beckoned him at the window. He thought she was perfect, and he was not afraid. He told her he could do mental arithmetic—with fractions, too!—and that he knew exactly how many square miles there were in the country and how many people lived in it. But she just smiled, till it seemed to him that he really didn't know anything at all. Then he looked up into the huge, huge sky, and they rose up into it, up above the storm clouds, while the winds whistled snatches of sad old songs into their ears. They flew over forests, they flew over lakes, they flew over sea and land, while below them howled the icy blast and above them wheeled the black, screaming crows. Wolves cried, the snow glittered. Rising above everything, the great clear moon shone in Kay's eyes the length of the long, long winter night. And come day, he slept at the feet of the Snow Queen.

PART THREE
THE OLD WOMAN'S FLOWER GARDEN

UT WHAT DID little Gerda think when Kay didn't come back? Where could he be? Nobody knew, nobody could tell her. All the boys could say was that they had seen him tie his little sledge to a big one, which drove off down the street and through the city gate. Nobody knew what had become of him. Oh, the grief! Little Gerda wept bitter tears. People said Kay must be dead—drowned in the river that flowed past the city. It was a long, dark winter.

But at last the spring came, and the warm sunshine.

'Kay is dead and gone,' said little Gerda.

'I don't believe it!' said the sunshine.

'He is dead and gone,' she said to the swallows.

'We don't believe it!' they said. And after that, Gerda didn't believe it either.

'I will put on my new red shoes,' she said one morning, 'the ones Kay has never seen, and I'll go down to the river and ask for him.'

It was still early. Gerda kissed her grandmother as she lay asleep and set off through the town gate to the river.

'Have you really taken my friend?' she asked. 'I'll give you my red shoes if you'll bring him back again.'

It did seem as if the rippling water nodded to her, so she took off her precious red shoes and threw them into the river. But they fell close to the bank, and the little waves brought them straight back to her. It was as if the river didn't want her dearest possession, because it didn't have Kay. Or perhaps she hadn't thrown them far enough. So she clambered into a boat that was drawn up in the reeds, went right to the far end, and threw the shoes into the water once more. But the boat wasn't tied up, and her motion made it push off from the bank. Before she could move, it was yards out and drifting faster all the time.

Little Gerda was frightened and began to cry. But only the sparrows heard her, and they couldn't fetch her back to dry land. Instead they flew along the bank, singing as if to comfort her, 'Here we are! Here we are!' Down the stream went the boat, faster and faster, while Gerda sat quite still in her stockinged feet. Her little red shoes bobbed along behind, but they couldn't catch up.

The riverbanks were beautiful. There were lovely flowers, ancient trees, and meadows dotted with sheep and cows, but there wasn't a single human being. 'Perhaps the river is taking me to Kay,' thought Gerda, and that cheered her up. She stood up to get a better look at the beautiful green banks.

At last she came to a cherry orchard, where there was a little thatched house with funny blue and red windows and two wooden soldiers standing guard outside, presenting arms to anyone who passed. Gerda thought they were alive and called out to them, but of course they didn't answer. Then the river took her even closer, and she called again, louder, and out of the house came an old, old woman leaning on a shepherd's crook. She was wearing a big sunhat, painted all over with beautiful flowers.

'You poor little thing,' said the old woman. 'Whatever takes you on this big rushing river, floating out into the wide, wide world?' And with her crook she pulled the boat to the bank, and she lifted little Gerda out. Gerda was so pleased to be back on dry land, though she was just the least bit scared of the strange old woman.

'Now tell me all about yourself,' the old woman said, 'who you are, and how you got here.'

So Gerda told her everything, and the old woman kept shaking her head and going, *Hmmm, hmmm!* till Gerda was finished. When

Gerda asked her if she had seen Kay, the old woman said he hadn't come that way, but not to worry, for he was sure to do so. 'Don't fret! Come and taste my cherries, and look at my lovely flowers. They're prettier than any picture book and can tell a better story, too.' She took Gerda by the hand, and they went into the little house, and the old woman locked the door.

The windows were all high up, and the glass in them was red, blue and yellow, so the daylight shone through them strangely. But there were the most delicious cherries on the table, and Gerda was allowed to eat as many as she liked. While she ate them, the old woman combed Gerda's hair with a golden comb till her curls shone like gold around her rosy little face.

'I've longed for a dear little girl just like you,' the old woman said. 'You'll see how happy we shall be.' And the more she combed Gerda's hair, the more the little girl forgot about Kay. For though she wasn't a witch, the old woman could work magic. She just made spells for her own pleasure, and she wanted to keep Gerda for herself. So now she went into the garden and made all the roses hide under the dark earth so that you couldn't see where they had been. She was afraid the roses would remind Gerda of Kay, and then she might run away.

Now she showed Gerda the flower garden. It was such a perfect garden, you can't imagine. The blooms! The scents! Every plant you can think of, from every season of the year, all in flower at the same time. They were better than any picture book. Gerda played in the garden until the sun sank behind the cherry trees. Then she was given a lovely bed with red silk pillows stuffed with violets. She slept as happy as a queen on her wedding night.

On the next day and for many days she played among the flowers in the bright sunshine. Soon she knew every flower, and although there were so many, she couldn't help feeling that one was missing—which one, she couldn't say. Then one day she was sitting looking at the old woman's sun hat with the flowers painted on it,

and she saw that the prettiest of all was a rose. The old woman had forgotten that one when she magicked the others underground. That's what happens if you don't keep your wits about you.

'Oh!' said Gerda. 'Why are there no roses here?' And she ran from flowerbed to flowerbed, searching, searching, but she couldn't find a single one. Then she sat down and cried, and her warm tears fell just where a rose had buried itself, making the rose spring up as full of flowers as before. Gerda put her arms around it and kissed the roses, and thought of the roses in the roof garden at home, and then she remembered Kay.

'What am I doing here?' she cried. 'I ought to be looking for Kay!' She asked the roses, 'Do you know where he is? Do you think he's dead and gone?'

'He is not dead,' they replied. 'We have been in the earth among the dead, and he was not there.'

'Thank you,' said little Gerda, and she went around to all the other flowers and looked into their cups and asked, 'Do you know where Kay is?' But the flowers were just dozing in the sunshine, dreaming their own fairy tales. Gerda heard her fill of these, but none of them mentioned Kay.

What did the tiger lily say?

'Listen! The drums go *Boom! Boom!* Always the same notes: *Boom! Boom!* Listen to the wailing of the women! Listen to the chanting of the priests! The Hindu woman stands by the funeral pyre in her long red robe. The flames leap up around her and around her dead husband. But the woman is thinking of the living one in the circle, he whose eyes burn fiercer than fire, whose eyes consume her heart as the flames consume her body. Can the heart's flame ever be quenched?'

'I don't understand that at all,' said Gerda.

'But that's my story,' said the tiger lily.

What did the bindweed say?

'High above the narrow path hangs the old castle. The ivy is thick on the old stone walls, leaf after leaf twining up to the balcony where a beautiful girl is standing. She leans out and gazes down the path. No rose is fresher on the branch than she, no apple blossom more delicate as the wind spins it from the tree. Her silk gown rustles as she moves … "When will he come?"'

'Is it Kay?' asked Gerda.

'I'm only telling my story,' said the bindweed.

What did the tiny snowdrop say?

'The swing hangs on ropes between the trees. Two pretty girls, in frocks as white as snow, are swinging. Green silk ribbons are fluttering from their hats. Their brother is bigger than they. He stands on the swing with his arm round the rope to keep steady. In one hand he has a saucer, in the other a clay pipe. He is blowing bubbles. The soap bubbles drift, back and forth. The swing swings, back and forth, back and forth. The last bubble sways from the bowl of the pipe. A bubbly little black dog is on his hind legs trying to get on the swing. But it flies past, and he falls down with an angry yelp. The children laugh, the bubble bursts. A swinging plank, a flash of foam. That's my song.'

'Well, that's all very pretty, but you make it sound so sad, and you don't say anything about Kay.'

What did the hyacinths say?

'There were three lovely sisters, as fine as fine. The first was dressed in red, the second in blue, the third in pure white. The moon shone on them as they danced hand in hand by the still lake. They were not fairies, but of human kind. The breeze blew sweet, and the girls vanished into the forest. The breeze blew strong, and three coffins, with the lovely maids lying in them, floated out from the dark wood, over the lake. The fireflies hovered around them, like tiny lamps. Are the dancing sisters dead, or do they sleep? The scent of the flowers tells me they are dead. The bells toll for them.'

'You make me feel so sad,' said Gerda, 'and your own scent is so cloying, I can't help thinking of the dead girls. Can Kay be dead too? The roses have been down underground, and they say he isn't.'

Dong! Dong! Dong! tolled the hyacinth bells. 'We're not ringing for little Kay, we don't know him. We're just singing our song. It's the only one we know.'

The buttercup shone bright among its green leaves. 'Bright little sun,' pleaded Gerda, 'tell me where I can find my friend.'

The buttercup beamed. But what song did it sing? Nothing about Kay.

'In the small backyard the sun was shining. It was the first day of spring, and the sunbeams slid down the whitewashed wall. The first yellow flowers were showing, gleaming gold in the warm sunshine. The old grandmother was sitting outside, and her granddaughter, a poor, pretty servant girl, who was home on a visit, kissed her. There was pure heart's gold in the blessing of that kiss. And that's my story,' said the buttercup.

'My poor old grandmother,' said Gerda. 'She must be missing me, and Kay too! But I'll be home soon, bringing Kay with me. It's no use asking these flowers. They only know their own songs and can't tell me anything.'

She hitched up her skirt so that she could run faster, but the narcissus caught at her leg, so she stopped to ask, 'Do you know anything?' What did it say?

'I can see myself! I can see myself! Ah! How sweet my scent is! Up in the attic, I see a little dancer. First she stands on one foot, then the other, and then she aims her high kicks at the whole world. But of course it's all make-believe. She is pouring water from a teapot onto a bit of stuff she's holding. It's her bodice. Well, cleanliness is next to godliness. Her white dress is hanging from a peg. She's washed that in the teapot, too, and hung it up to dry. Now she's putting it on, with a yellow scarf. That makes the dress even whiter. Up goes her leg! How she struts on just one stalk. I can see myself! I can see myself!'

'I can't stand around listening to this,' said Gerda. 'It's no use to me.' She ran to the end of the garden. The gate was locked, but she shook it till the rusty bolt gave way and the door flew open. Little Gerda ran out barefoot into the wide world. She looked back three times, but nobody followed.

When she couldn't run anymore, she sat down on a big stone. She looked around. Summer was gone, it was late autumn. You couldn't tell in the garden because the sun always shone there and the flowers of all the seasons were always in bloom.

'I have tarried too long,' said little Gerda. 'Autumn has come. I must go on.' And she limped off.

How tired and sore her feet were. Everything was so bleak and cold. The long willow leaves were all yellow and damp with dew. One by one they fell. Only the sloe still kept its fruit, and that was so bitter it made you wince. Oh, how mournful and grey it was in the wide world!

PART FOUR
A PRINCE AND A PRINCESS

 ERDA HAD TO REST AGAIN. Hopping about in the snow just by her was a great big crow, who looked at her for a long time before he nodded his head and said, 'Caw! Caw! Hallaw! Hallaw!' That was the best he could manage at human speech. He liked the look of the little girl and asked her where she was heading, all alone in the wide world. 'Alone'—Gerda knew all too well what that word meant.

She told the crow all about herself and asked if he had seen Kay.

The crow nodded gravely and said, 'Cawed be! Cawed be!'

'Oh! Do you really think so?' cried the little girl, and she hugged the bird so tightly she nearly throttled him.

'Wawtch out! Wawtch out!' said the crow. 'It might have been he. But if it was, he's forsaken you for a princess.'

'Is he living with a princess?' asked Gerda.

'Yes. Listen!' said the crow. 'But your talk makes my poor throat hurt. If only you spoke Crow!'

'I've never learned it,' said Gerda. 'But my grandmother could speak it, and Gobbledegook, too.'

'Never mind,' said the crow. 'I'll do my best.' And this is what he tried to say.

'In this kingdom there lives a princess who is so clever that she has read all the newspapers in the world. And what's more, she's forgotten them again, which just shows you how clever she is. Now, she was sitting on her throne the other day, at a bit of a loose end, when she started humming a song that went like this:

> *I'm getting tired of the single life,*
> *It's about time I was a wife.*
> *They can run but they can't hide,*
> *I'll find the man to make me a bride.*

'And she said, "*Hmmm*. There's something to be said for that." So she decided she would get married, but only to a man who could speak when he was spoken to, not one who just stood around looking important—that would be even more boring. So she drummed up all her ladies-in-waiting, and when they heard what she planned, they were as pleased as pleased. "What a good idea! We thought of it ourselves only the other day!" This is not a word of a lie,' said the crow. 'I got this from my sweetheart, who is tame and has the run of the palace.' Of course the sweetheart was a crow too; birds of a feather flock together, as they say.

'The next day's newspapers were printed up with a border of

hearts and the princess's initials. And inside they said that any good-looking young man was free to come up to the palace and meet the princess. And the one who could chat away as if he were at home would win her. Take it from me, it's true! Well, come one, come all, there were crowds of them. But none of them was up to scratch. Out in the street they all had the gift of the gab, but once inside the palace gates, under the eye of the guards in their silver uniforms and the footmen in gold, they lost their tongues. And when they stood in the glittering throne room and the princess spoke to them, they couldn't do anything but parrot the last thing she said, and she didn't need to hear that again. It was as if they'd taken something to make them sleepy, and they didn't wake up till they got outside again. They could talk nineteen to the dozen then! There was a line all the way from the town gates to the palace. They were hungry and thirsty, and they didn't get so much as a glass of water from the palace. The sensible ones had brought sandwiches with them, but they wouldn't share them with the others. They thought, "The princess won't waste her time on starvelings."'

'But Kay, little Kay!' said Gerda. 'When did he come? Was he in the crowd?'

'Give me a chance! Give me a chance! I'm just getting to him. On the third day a perky little chap marches up to the palace without a horse or a carriage. His eyes were bright like yours, and he had lovely flowing hair, but his clothes were in a wretched state—quite threadbare.'

'That was Kay!' cried Gerda. 'I've found him at last!' And she clapped her hands.

'He had a little knapsack on his back,' said the crow.

'That must have been his sledge,' said Gerda. 'He had that with him.'

'Maybe,' said the crow. 'I didn't look too closely. But my sweetheart told me that when he walked through the palace gates and saw the sentries in silver and the footmen in gold, he wasn't the least put out. He just nods at them and says, "It must be very boring standing around on the stairs all day. I'd sooner go inside!" And even though the rooms were glittering with lights, and important-looking folk were tiptoeing about with golden dishes, he wasn't outfaced. His boots squeaked like anything, but he wasn't worried.'

'That's my Kay,' said Gerda. 'He had new boots, I heard them squeak in Grandmother's kitchen.'

'Yes, they squeaked all right,' said the crow, 'but he went cheerfully up to the princess, who was sitting on a pearl as big as a spinning wheel. All the ladies-in-waiting with their maids and their maids' maids, and all the courtiers with their footmen and their footmen's footmen, were ranged about, and the nearer they were to the door the prouder they looked. The palace bootboy was standing in the door, and he was so proud you daren't look at him!'

'Oh, how awful!' said Gerda. 'And Kay still won the princess?'

'If I wasn't a crow I'd have had a go myself, even though I am engaged. My sweetheart said he spoke as well as I do when I'm speaking Crow. He was witty and charming, he said he hadn't come to woo the princess but just to hear her talk—she was so wise! So no wonder she liked him!'

'It must have been Kay!' said Gerda. 'He's so clever, he can do mental arithmetic, with fractions! Oh, take me to him.'

'That's more easily said than done,' said the crow. 'But I'll talk to my sweetheart, and she'll know what to do. All I know is, a girl like you wouldn't get near the palace in the normal run of things.'

'I would,' said Gerda. 'As soon as Kay heard it was me, he'd come straight out to fetch me.'

'Well, just wait for me by that stile,' said the crow, wagging his head, and off he flew.

It was late afternoon when the crow came back again. '*Caw! Caw!*' he said. 'My sweetheart sends her best wishes, and this crust of bread from the kitchen—they won't miss it, and you must be hungry. It's out of the question for you to go to the palace barefoot as you are, the guards in silver and the footmen in gold won't stand for it. But don't fret, you'll still get in. My sweetheart knows a little back staircase that leads up to the bedchamber, and she knows where the key is kept.'

So they went into the garden and along the wide avenue where the leaves were falling, one by one, and as the palace lights went out, one by one, the crow brought little Gerda to a back door that was open just a crack.

Oh, how Gerda's heart was beating with fear and longing! She felt she was doing wrong, yet all she wanted was to see if Kay was there. Surely it must be he. In her mind's eye she could see his bright eyes and his long hair. She could just picture him back home, smiling among the roses. He would be glad to see her, and to hear how far she had come for his sake and how much they all missed him at home. She was so happy, and so afraid.

Now they were on the stairs. A little lamp was burning on a stand, and the tame crow was waiting for them. Gerda curtseyed, as her grandmother had taught her.

'My fiancé has told me a lot of nice things about you, my dear,' said the tame crow. 'The fairy tale of your life, if I may call it so, touches the heart. If you take the lamp, I will lead the way. If we go straight on, we'll not meet anyone.'

'But someone is following us,' said Gerda. Something rushed past her: shadows on the wall, horses with flowing manes and slender legs, huntsmen, lords and ladies on horseback.

'Those are but dreams,' said the tame crow. 'They fetch the grand folks' thoughts to the midnight hunt. And that's just as well, for you'll be able to look more closely while they sleep. All I can say is, when you come into fame and fortune, don't forget us.'

'That goes without saying,' said the crow from the forest.

Now they came into the first room. The walls were hung with

rose-red satin, embroidered with flowers. Here the dreams were rushing past so swiftly that Gerda could not make them out. Each new room was more sumptuous than the last, it made her quite dizzy. And now they were in the royal bedchamber. The ceiling was like a huge palm tree with leaves of crystal, and in the middle of the room there were two beds shaped like lilies, hanging from a golden stalk. One of them was white, and that was where the princess was lying. The other was red, and that was where Gerda looked for Kay. She bent back a red petal and saw a brown neck. It was Kay! She cried his name aloud, holding the lamp over his face. His dreams whirled back to him. He awoke, he turned his head, and—no! It wasn't Kay.

It was only the neck that looked like Kay's, though the prince, too, was young and handsome. The princess woke up in her lily bed and asked what was happening. Little Gerda burst into tears and told her whole story, with everything that the crows had done for her.

'You poor little thing,' said the prince and princess. They praised the crows and weren't angry at all, this once. The crows would even get a reward.

'Would you like to fly away free,' asked the princess, 'or would you like to be appointed Crows to the Court, with a right to all the kitchen scraps?'

Both the crows bowed and said they would like the official appointment, as they had to think of their old age and, 'You want something put by for a rainy day.'

Then the prince got out of his bed and put Gerda to sleep in it. He couldn't do more than that. She folded her hands and thought, 'How kind everyone is—animals and people.' She closed her eyes and went to sleep. The dreams all came back again, and they looked just like angels, pulling a little sledge with Kay on it, nodding at her—but it was just a dream, gone as soon as she woke.

The next day the prince and princess dressed her from top to toe in silk and velvet. They invited her to stay at the palace and join in the fun. But all she wanted was a little horse and carriage and a pair of boots so she could drive out once more into the wide world to look for Kay.

They gave her the boots and a muff as well. And when she was all dressed up in her beautiful new clothes, a carriage of pure gold drew up at the door, with the coats of arms of the prince and princess glittering on it like stars. The coachmen, the footmen and the outriders—yes, she even had outriders—had gold crowns on their heads. The prince and princess themselves helped her into the carriage and wished her good luck, and the forest crow, who was married now, saw her on her way for the first few miles. He sat beside her in the carriage. The tame crow stayed behind in the gateway, flapping her wings. All those kitchen scraps had given her a headache. Inside, the carriage was lined with sugar candy, and underneath the seat were ginger nuts.

'Goodbye! Goodbye!' cried the prince and princess. Little Gerda wept, and so did the crow. They went on like that for three miles, and then the crow said 'Goodbye!' too, and that was the hardest parting of them all. He flew up into a tree and flapped his gleaming wings as long as he could see the carriage, which shone back at him like bright, bright sunshine.

PART FIVE
THE LITTLE ROBBER GIRL

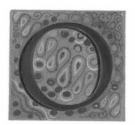N THEY DROVE THROUGH THE FOREST. The carriage shone so fiercely it dazzled the robber band. 'It's gold! It's gold!' they cried. They rushed out, seized the horses, killed the coachman and the footmen and the outriders, and dragged little Gerda from the coach.

'She's plump; she's a dainty morsel; she's been fattened on nuts!' said the old robber woman, who had a bristly beard and shaggy eyebrows. 'She's a tasty lambkin. She makes my mouth water.' And she drew her bright knife, which glittered menacingly.

'Ouch!' screeched the old hag all of a sudden. She had been bitten in the ear by her own fierce daughter, who was clinging to her back. 'You vile brat!' said her mother, quite forgetting to kill Gerda.

'She can play with me,' said the little robber girl. 'She shall give me her muff and her pretty dress and sleep in my bed.' And she bit her mother again, so that the robber woman leaped right round in the air and the other robbers laughed at her, shouting, 'Look at the tigress dancing with her cub!'

'I want to go in the carriage,' said the little robber girl. She always got her own way, she was so spoiled and stubborn. So she and Gerda sat inside while they rattled over bushes and briars through the forest. The little robber girl was the same height as Gerda but broader, stronger and darker-skinned. Her eyes were quite black, with an odd, sad look. She put her arm round Gerda's waist and said. 'They won't kill you, as long as I'm not cross with you. Are you a princess?'

'No,' said Gerda. 'I'm not a princess.' And she told her everything that had happened, and how much she loved Kay.

The robber girl listened solemnly and said. 'I won't let them kill you, even if I do get angry. I'll do it myself!' Then she dried Gerda's eyes and wrapped her hands in the warm muff.

The carriage pulled up in the courtyard of the robbers' castle. There were cracks right up the walls; crows and ravens were flying in and out of holes; great bulldogs, which looked as if they could gulp down a man, were leaping about, though they weren't allowed to bark. A huge fire was burning on the stone floor of the old hall, which was hung with cobwebs and soot; soup was simmering in a massive cauldron, and hares and rabbits were roasting on the spit.

'Tonight you'll sleep with me and my pets,' said the robber girl. They had something to eat and drink and then made their way to a corner where there was straw and some blankets. About a hundred pigeons, asleep on their high perches, ruffled themselves when the girls arrived. 'They're all mine,' said the little robber girl, and she grabbed the nearest one by its legs and shook it till its wings flapped. 'Give it a kiss!' she cried, shoving it in Gerda's face.

Then she pointed to some wooden slats nailed over a hole above their heads. 'Those two wood pigeons in there are forest riffraff. They'd fly off if you didn't keep them locked up.' Then she pulled a reindeer forward by its antlers; it was tethered and had a bright copper ring round its neck. 'This is my old love, Bae! I've got to keep him tied up, too, or he'd be up and off. Every night I have to tickle his neck with my dagger, just to put some fear in him!' And the little girl drew a long knife from a crack in the wall and slid it across the reindeer's neck. The poor beast kicked out, and the robber girl chuckled and pulled Gerda down into her bed.

'Do you keep your knife with you while you sleep?' asked Gerda, looking at it nervously.

'I always sleep with a knife by me,' said the little robber girl.

'You never know what will happen. But now tell me again about little Kay, and why you've come out into the wide world.' So Gerda told her tale once more, from the very beginning, while the wood pigeons murmured in their cage and the other pigeons slept. The little robber girl put her arm round Gerda's neck, with her knife in the other hand. She fell asleep—you could hear that—but Gerda couldn't close her eyes for a moment, not knowing if she was to live or die. The robbers sat round the fire, drinking and singing, while the old robber woman turned somersaults. Little Gerda was filled with dread.

Then the wood pigeons said, '*Coo! Coo!* We've seen little Kay. A white bird was carrying his sledge, and he was sitting in the Snow Queen's carriage, which flew low over the forest as we lay in our nest. She breathed on the young ones and all of them died except us two. *Coo! Coo!*'

'What's that?' asked Gerda. 'Where was the Snow Queen going? Can you tell me?'

'She was probably going to Lapland, to the everlasting ice and snow. Ask the reindeer who's tied up over there.'

'Yes,' said the reindeer, 'there's ice and snow in Lapland. It's wonderful! You can run free across the great shining valleys. That's where the Snow Queen has her summer tent. But her palace is up by the North Pole.'

'Oh, Kay! Poor Kay!' said Gerda with a sigh.

'Lie still!' said the robber girl. 'If you don't want a knife in your belly!'

When morning came, Gerda told her everything the wood pigeons had said, and the little robber girl looked at her solemnly and said, 'Never mind. Never mind.' Then she asked the reindeer, 'Do you know where Lapland is?'

'Who better than I?' he answered, his eyes alight. 'I was born there and I was bred there, running free across the fields of snow.'

'Listen,' said the robber girl to Gerda. 'All the men have gone out, but my Ma's still here, and she'll stick around. Later in the morning she'll have a swig from that big bottle, and after that she'll have a snooze. Then I'll see what I can do for you.' She jumped out of bed, threw her arms round her mother's neck, pulled her beard, and said, 'Morning, you old nannygoat!' And her mother gave her a punch on the nose that turned it red and blue—just as a token of affection.

When the old woman had swigged her drink and dropped off into her snooze, the robber girl went to the reindeer and said, 'I'd like to tickle your throat some more with my knife because it makes me laugh, but never mind. I'm going to let you off your rope and set you free so that you can go to Lapland. But you must put your best foot foremost and carry this little girl to the Snow Queen's palace for me. That's where her playmate is, but you'll have heard that, because she wasn't quiet about it and you were listening!'

The reindeer jumped for joy. The robber girl lifted Gerda onto his back and carefully tied her on, with a little cushion for comfort. 'You'll be all right,' she said. 'You can have your fur boots, because it's getting cold, but I'm keeping your muff, because it's so pretty. You won't freeze. You can have my Ma's big gloves. They'll reach right up to your elbows. Put your paws in! Now they look just like my ugly old Ma's!'

Gerda wept with happiness.

'I can't abide that grizzling,' said the little robber girl. 'You ought to be pleased. Anyway, here are two loaves and a ham, so you won't starve.' She tied these on the reindeer. Then she opened the door, called in the dogs, cut the rope and said to the reindeer, 'Off you go! Take care of the little girl!'

Gerda stretched out her hands in the huge gloves and said goodbye to the robber girl, and then the reindeer leapt away over bush and briar, through the great forest, over marsh and moor, as fast as he could go. Wolves howled, ravens shrieked, the wind

whistled past, *shioo, shioo*. The sky flashed red as if the world were sneezing.

'Those are my dear old Northern Lights,' said the reindeer. 'Putting on their show!' And he ran on faster than ever, through the night, through the day. The loaves were eaten. The ham was eaten. They were in Lapland.

PART SIX
THE LAPP WOMAN AND THE FINN WOMAN

HEY STOPPED AT a ramshackle little hut. The roof came right down to the ground, and the door was so low that the family had to crawl on all fours to get in or out. There was no one at home except an old Lapp woman, who was cooking fish over an oil lamp. The reindeer told her Gerda's story, though first he told his own, which he thought was much more important. Gerda was too bone-cold to speak.

'Oh, you poor things!' said the Lapp woman. 'You've still a long way to go! It's over a hundred miles to Finmark, and that's where you'll find the Snow Queen. She's staying in the country there, setting off her fireworks every night. I'll scribble a note on a piece of dried cod—I haven't any paper—and you can take that to the Finn woman up there. She can give you better directions than I.'

When Gerda was warm again and had had something to eat and drink, the Lapp woman scribbled her note on a piece of dried cod, telling Gerda to take good care of it, then tied her securely on the reindeer's back, and off he went. *Shioo! Shioo!* went the wind, and

123

up in the sky the Northern Lights burned blue and beautiful through the night.

And so they came to Finmark and knocked at the chimney of the Finn woman's house, as she didn't have a door.

Inside it was sweltering. The Finn woman herself barely had a stitch on. She was very dumpy and rather dirty. The first thing she did was loosen little Gerda's clothes and take off her gloves and boots; otherwise it would have been far too hot for her. She put a hunk of ice on the reindeer's head, and then read what was written on the cod. She read it three times, and when she had it by heart she dropped the cod into the cooking pot, because it was a tasty bit and she didn't like waste.

Now the reindeer told first his story, and then little Gerda's, and the Finn woman blinked her wise eyes but said nothing.

'You know so much,' said the reindeer. 'You can bind the winds of the world with a thread of cotton. When the sailor unties the first knot, he gets a strong wind. If he unties the second, the wind begins to gust. If he ventures the third and fourth, he calls up a gale that will destroy a forest. Will you give the little girl a drink so that she'll have the strength of twelve to overcome the Snow Queen?'

'The strength of twelve!' said the Finn woman. 'Much good that would do!' She went over to a shelf, took down a rolled-up parchment and unrolled it. Strange characters were written on it; the Finn woman read till the sweat poured from her brow.

The reindeer begged so hard for little Gerda, and Gerda looked at her with such tearful, beseeching eyes, that the Finn woman began to blink her own eyes. She took the reindeer into a corner and put more ice on his head, and whispered, 'Little Kay is with the Snow Queen, right enough, and he's glad of it. He thinks he's in the best place in the world, because he's got a splinter of glass in his heart and a speck of glass in his eye. Unless you get them out, he'll never be human again, but will remain under the Snow Queen's sway.'

'Can't you give Gerda something that will give her power?'

'I can't give her any more power than she has within her. Don't you feel how strong that is? Humans and beasts are at her service as she makes her way through the wide world on her two bare feet. But she must not learn of her power from us. It comes from the innocence of her dear child's heart. If she can't find her own way into the Snow Queen's palace and free little Kay by herself, there's nothing we can do to help. The Snow Queen's garden begins two miles on. Take her there, and put her down by the big bush with the bright red berries that stand out against the snow. Don't waste any time on idle chatter, but come back here as quick as you can.' And with that the Finn woman lifted little Gerda onto the reindeer's back, and off he ran.

'Oh! I haven't got my boots! I haven't got my gloves!' shouted little Gerda as the cold started to bite, but the reindeer didn't dare stop. He ran till he came to the big bush with the red berries, and there he sat Gerda down and gave her a kiss, with big shining tears trickling down his face. Then he ran back swiftly, leaving poor Gerda standing without boots, without gloves, in the icy middle of freezing Finmark.

She ran forward as best she could, and a whole regiment of snowflakes appeared beside her. They weren't falling from the sky, which was clear and lit up by the Northern Lights. They were running along the ground, and the closer they came the bigger they grew. Gerda was reminded how strange and cleverly made the flakes had seemed when she saw them through the magnifying glass. Now they were even bigger and much more frightening. They were alive! They were the Snow Queen's border guards. They took weird shapes: some were like great ugly hedgehogs; some were like knots of writhing snakes; others were like stumpy little bears with icicle fur. They were all living white snowflakes.

Then Gerda began to say the Lord's Prayer. The cold was so bitter she could see her own breath coming from her mouth like smoke. The clouds of smoke grew thicker and thicker, and turned into little shining angels, who got bigger and bigger when they touched the ground. They had helmets and shields and spears. By the time Gerda had finished her prayer, she was surrounded by a whole army of them. They thrust their spears into the terrible snow creatures and shattered them into a thousand pieces, so that Gerda could go forward without fear. The angels rubbed her hands and feet, and at once she felt less cold. She hurried on towards the Snow Queen's palace.

But now let's see what Kay has been up to. He hasn't been thinking about Gerda, that's for sure. He never dreamed she was standing there outside the palace.

PART SEVEN

WHAT HAPPENED IN THE SNOW QUEEN'S PALACE AND WHAT HAPPENED AFTER THAT

 HE PALACE WALLS were of driven snow, and the doors and windows were of biting wind. There were over a hundred rooms, all made by the drifting snow. The biggest was miles long. The whole vast, empty, glittering palace was lit by the Northern Lights. It was icy. No revels were held there, not so much as a frolic for the foxes or a dance for the polar bears, though the storm could have made the music while

the beasts walked on their hind legs and performed their party pieces. Bare and cold was the palace of the Snow Queen.

In the very middle was a frozen lake. It had split into a thousand pieces, each piece exactly like every other. It was a miracle of science. And in the middle of that lake the Snow Queen sat, when she was at home. She called it the Mirror of Reason and said it was the only one of its kind, and the best.

Little Kay was blue with cold. In fact he was almost black. But he didn't notice, as the Snow Queen had kissed his shivers away and his heart was just a lump of ice. He was dragging sharp, flat blocks of ice here and there, as if he were trying to make them into patterns. And so he was. They were the intricate patterns of the Puzzle of Reason and Ice. To him these patterns seemed utterly important and remarkable; that's because of the speck of glass in his eye. He was trying to join complete patterns to make a word, but somehow it wouldn't come out right. The word was ETERNITY. The Snow Queen had told him, 'If you can work out that pattern for me, you will be your own master. I shall give you the whole world, and a new pair of skates.' But he couldn't.

'I must be off to the warm countries,' said the Snow Queen. 'I'm going to have a peep into the black cauldrons, Etna and Vesuvius. I shall frost them over a bit. It's what they need, and good for the lemons and grapes.' And away she flew, leaving Kay all alone in the vast ice halls, staring at the blocks of ice and thinking so hard you could hear him crack inside. There he sat, so stiff and still he might have frozen to death.

It was then that little Gerda stepped through the gate of wind into the palace. She said the Lord's Prayer, and the fierce winds lay down to sleep. She entered the vast, icy hall and saw Kay. She knew him at once and flung her arms tight round him, crying, 'Kay! Dear Kay! I've found you at last!' But he sat quite still, stiff and cold.

Little Gerda wept: hot tears that fell upon his breast and sank right inside him. They melted the lump of ice and consumed the splinter of glass that was in his heart. Kay looked at Gerda, and then she sang the hymn they used to sing:

When Jesus Christ
Was yet a child
He had a garden
Fair and wild.

Then Kay burst into tears, and he cried away the splinter of glass that was in his eye. Then he recognised Gerda and shouted, 'Gerda! Dear Gerda! Where have you been for so long? And where have I been?' He looked about him. 'Oh, it's so cold here! It's so vast and empty!' And he hugged Gerda to him, and they both laughed and cried for joy. The very blocks of ice danced with them, and when they were tired, the blocks laid themselves down in the pattern the Snow Queen had told Kay to work out, so that he should be his own master and have the whole world, and a new pair of skates.

Then Gerda kissed his cheeks and brought the bloom back to them; she kissed his eyes, and they shone like her own; she kissed his hands and feet, and he was safe and sound. The Snow Queen could come back whenever she liked; Kay's freedom was written plain on the shining ice.

Hand in hand they made their way out of the great palace, talking about Grandmother and the roses on the roof. Wherever they walked, the winds dropped away and the sun shone. When they reached the bush with the red berries, the reindeer was waiting for them. With him was a young reindeer doe, who kissed the children and let them drink the warm milk from her full udders. Then the reindeer carried Kay and Gerda first to the Finn woman, to get warm in her hot room and learn how to get home, and then to the Lapp woman, who had new clothes and a sleigh ready for them.

The reindeer kept them company to the borders of their

homeland, where the first green shoots were beginning to show. There Kay and Gerda said farewell to the reindeer and the Lapp woman. 'Goodbye! Goodbye!' they all cried.

The small birds were twittering, and the woods were green with buds. And out of the woods there came a handsome horse. Gerda knew it—it was the horse that had pulled her gold carriage. And on it was a girl with a bright red cap on her head and pistols at her side. It was the little robber girl, who was fed up with home and heading north, or for any other part that took her fancy. She and Gerda were very happy to see each other.

'You're a fine fellow to go off on a spree,' she said to Kay. 'I wonder if it was worth anyone's while running to the ends of the earth for you.'

But Gerda stroked her cheek and asked about the prince and princess.

'They've gone off to foreign parts,' said the robber girl.

'And what about the crow?' asked Gerda.

'Oh, the crow's dead,' was the answer. 'His tame sweetheart is a widow now and wears a twist of black wool round her leg. She's such a misery-guts; but it's all an act. But now you tell me your story, and how you found him.'

So Gerda and Kay told her the whole story.

'Ah, well,' said the robber girl. 'Snip-snap-snout, your tale's told out.' Then she took them both by the hand and promised that if she was ever passing through their town she would look them up. And then she rode off into the wide world.

Kay and Gerda walked on hand in hand. As they went, the flowers of spring blossomed about them. Church bells rang out, and they saw the high towers of the city where they lived. They went to Grandmother's door, up the staircase and into the room. Everything was just as it had been. The clock still said *Tick, tock* as it always had. But as they entered the room, they felt that they were not the same. They had grown up.

The roses were flowering on the roof gutter, and near them were the children's stools. Gerda and Kay sat down and held each other's hands. The Snow Queen's frozen, hollow majesty was forgotten like a bad dream. Grandmother sat with them in God's good sunshine, reading from the Bible: 'Except ye become as little children, ye shall not enter the Kingdom of Heaven.'

Kay and Gerda looked into each other's eyes, and now they understood the words of the hymn:

> *When Jesus Christ*
> *Was yet a child*
> *He had a garden*
> *Fair and wild.*

They were still children at heart. And where they sat it was summer: warm, blessed summer.

THE SHEPHERDESS
AND THE
CHIMNEY SWEEP

AVE YOU EVER SEEN a really old carved-wood cupboard, quite black with age? There was once one just like that in a sitting room; it had been in the family for generations. It was carved from top to bottom with roses and tulips, and little stags' heads with branching antlers peeping out from the twining leaves. And on the central panel was carved a funny man. He had a long beard and little horns on his forehead, and the legs of a billygoat, and he had a grin on his face—you couldn't call it a smile. The children of the house called him 'Brigadier-General Private Sergeant-Major Goatlegs', because it was hard to say, and there aren't many—living or carved—who can boast a title like that.

Anyhow, there he was. From the cabinet, he kept a close eye on the table under the mirror, because that was where the china shepherdess stood. She had golden shoes and a golden hat, and a dress that was fetchingly pinned with a red rose. Oh, she was pretty as a picture!

Standing right next to her was a little chimney sweep; he too was made of china. Although he was as black as coal, you could tell he was only pretending to be a sweep. He was too neat and tidy, and his face was as pink and white as a girl's, without so much as a smut of soot on it. At the china works they might just as easily have made him into a prince as a chimney sweep.

Since the sweep and the shepherdess had always stood side by side on the table—he holding his ladder, and she her shepherd's crook—they naturally fell in love. They were a good match: two young people, both made of the same kind of porcelain, and each as fragile as the other.

Nearby there was another china figure, three times their size. It was an old Chinese mandarin, who could nod his head, and who always claimed to be the shepherdess's grandfather. That made him her guardian, according to him, so when Brigadier-General Private Sergeant-Major Goatlegs asked for her hand in marriage, the old mandarin nodded his consent.

'There's the husband for you,' he said. 'I am almost certain he is made of mahogany; and he will make you Lady Brigadier-General Private Sergeant-Major Goatlegs. He has a cupboard full of silver, and who knows what else.'

'I don't want to go into that dark cupboard,' said the shepherdess. 'I've heard that he has eleven china wives locked away in there already.'

'Then you can be the twelfth,' said the mandarin. 'For tonight, as soon as the cupboard starts creaking, you shall be married, as sure as I'm a Chinaman.' And with that he nodded off to sleep.

The little shepherdess was in tears. She looked imploringly at her true love, the china chimney sweep, and said, 'Please, take me out into the wide world. We can't stay here now.'

'I'll do anything you want,' the sweep replied. 'Let's go at once. I feel sure I can earn enough to keep us, by working as a chimney sweep.'

'If only we could get off the table,' sighed the shepherdess. 'I shall never be happy until we are out in the wide world.'

He did his best to comfort her, and showed her where to place her foot on a piece of tracery to begin the climb down. He took his ladder, too, to help her in the difficult places; and at last they reached the floor. But when they looked up at the dark old cupboard—what an uproar! The carved deer were straining their necks out, waving their antlers and shaking their heads. And Brigadier-General Private Sergeant-Major Goatlegs was hopping up and down and shouting to the old mandarin, 'They're running away! They're running away!'

That gave them a fright, and they jumped out of harm's way into an open drawer. Inside they found three or four packs of cards—none of them quite complete—and a ramshackle toy theatre. The puppets were performing a play, and all the queens—diamonds, hearts, clubs and spades—were sitting in the front row fanning themselves with flowers. Behind them stood the knaves, with their two heads, one at the top and one at the bottom; all playing cards are like that. They were watching a play about star-crossed lovers, and it made the shepherdess cry, because it was just like her own story.

'I can't bear it,' she sobbed. 'I must get out of this drawer.' But by the time they got back to the floor again, the old mandarin had woken up. He was rocking himself to and fro in a frenzy of nodding; that was the only way he could move.

'The old mandarin is after us!' shrieked the little shepherdess. She was so frightened that she sank down onto her porcelain knees.

'I've got an idea,' said the chimney sweep. 'Let's creep into the big potpourri jar in the corner; we can hide on a bed of roses and lavender, and if he comes after us we can throw salt in his eyes.'

'That wouldn't be any good,' she said. 'Besides, I happen to know that the old mandarin and the potpourri jar were once engaged; and there is always some fellow-feeling left when people have been as close as that. There's nothing for it but to go out into the wide world.'

'Are you really brave enough to come with me into the wide world?' asked the chimney sweep. 'Do you realise how vast it is, and that we can never come back again?'

'Yes, I do,' she said.

The sweep looked her straight in the eyes. 'The only path I know is up the chimney. Are you really brave enough to crawl right inside the stove, up the flue and into the chimney? Once there, I can find the way. We must climb up and up, so high that no one can reach us; right at the top there's a hole that leads out into the wide world.'

And he led her up to the door of the stove.

'How dark it looks!' she said. But she went with him all the same, past the firebricks and up the flue, into the pitch dark.

'Now we are in the chimney,' he said. 'Look up there! There's a lovely star twinkling above our heads.'

Yes, there was a real star shining right down on them, as if to light their way. So they clambered and crawled towards it, up, up, up through the horrible dark. The sweep kept giving the shepherdess his hand, and showing her where to put her little china feet, until at last they reached the very top. They sat on the edge of the chimney pot, tired out, and no wonder.

Above them was the sky with all its stars; below was the town with all its roofs. The wide, wide world was all about them. The poor shepherdess had never dreamed it could be so vast; she laid her little head on the chimney sweep's shoulder, and wept so bitterly that her tears washed the gold from her sash.

'It's all too much,' she said. 'I can't bear it; the world is far too big. I wish I were back on the table below the mirror. I shall never be happy until we are back there again. I have followed you into the wide world; now, if you love me, take me home.'

The chimney sweep pleaded with her. He reminded her about the old mandarin, and Brigadier-General Private Sergeant-Major Goatlegs, but that just made her cry even harder. She kissed him

and clung to him, and finally he had to give in, though he knew it was a bad idea.

It was a hard and dangerous climb, down the chimney, through the flue, past the firebricks and into the stove. There they paused, listening to hear what was happening. All was quiet, so they peeped out.

Oh! There in the middle of the floor lay the old Chinese mandarin. He had rocked himself right off the table and was lying where he fell, smashed into three pieces—his back, his front and his head, which had rolled off into a corner. Brigadier-General Private Sergeant-Major Goatlegs was just standing where he always did, deep in thought.

'How terrible,' cried the little shepherdess. 'Old Grandpa is broken to bits, and it's all our fault. I shall never forgive myself!' And she wrung her tiny hands.

'He can still be mended,' said the chimney sweep. 'That's not hard. Don't get in such a state. When they have glued him together, and put a rivet in his neck, he'll be as good as new, and able to give us a piece of his mind.'

'Do you really think so?' she said. And then they climbed back up to the table top.

'We have been a long way,' said the chimney sweep, 'yet here we are back where we started. We might have saved ourselves the trouble.'

'If only old Grandpa were mended,' said the shepherdess. 'Do you think it will be expensive?'

The family did have the mandarin mended. His back was glued on; a rivet was put in his neck; he looked as good as new. But he couldn't nod his head any more.

'You have got high and mighty since you were broken,' said Brigadier-General Private Sergeant-Major Goatlegs, 'though I can't see what there is to be proud of in being glued. Tell me, am I to have her or not?'

THE SHEPHERDESS AND THE CHIMNEY SWEEP

The chimney sweep and the shepherdess looked anxiously at the old mandarin; they were terrified that he might nod. But he had a rivet in his neck, and would never nod again, though he didn't want to admit that to a stranger. So the porcelain couple stayed together, and loved each other until they broke.

THE LAST DREAM
OF THE OLD
OAK TREE

T THE EDGE OF THE WOOD, on a cliff above the seashore, stood an old oak tree. It was three hundred and sixty-five years old. But years to a tree are like days to us. We are awake in the day and asleep at night, and that's when we dream, but a tree is different. A tree is awake for three seasons of the year, and sleeps only in winter. Winter is the night after the long day that is called spring, summer and autumn.

Many a warm summer's day the mayflies danced lightheartedly around the tree, and if ever one of them took a moment's rest on a leaf, the tree would say, 'Poor little thing! Just one day is your whole life! How short a time you have. It's so sad.'

'Sad?' the mayfly would answer. 'What do you mean by that? Everything is perfect. It's so warm and lovely, and I'm quite happy.'

'But only for one day, and then it's all over.'

'All over!' said the mayfly. 'What do you mean? Won't you be here?'

'Oh yes, I shall live for thousands of your days, and my day is a whole year long—longer than you could understand.'

'No, I don't understand. You may live thousands of my days, but I have thousands of moments to be happy in. Do you think all the beauty in the world will die when you do?'

'No,' said the tree, 'I expect it will go on, longer than I can understand.'

'Well, then, you and I have the same time as each other; we just reckon it differently.'

And the mayfly danced and flirted in the air, delighting in its lovely wings. The air carried the scent of clover in the fields and roses in the hedgerows, of elder trees, and honeysuckle, cowslips and wild mint. Their perfume was so strong that the mayfly was quite drunk with it. It was a long, beautiful day, full of happiness, full of joy. When the sun finally set, the little fly felt tired from so much fun. Its wings couldn't carry it any longer. Ever so gently, it drifted down onto the soft grass. Its head began to nod, and it fell into a happy sleep. That was death.

'Poor little mayfly,' said the oak tree. 'What a brief life that was!'

Every summer it was the same story. The same dance, the same conversation, the same outcome. Whole generations of mayflies lived and died, and each was as happy and carefree as the first. The oak tree stayed awake through the spring morning, summer afternoon and autumn evening. Then winter drew near. Soon it would be time to sleep. Already the storms were singing, 'Good night! Sleep tight! Shed your leaves! Pluck one, pluck two! Off with those leaves, let us ruffle your branches, we'll make you creak with pleasure. Sleep well, sleep tight, this is your three hundred and sixty-fifth night. You're still a youngster really. Sleep. Snow is falling, it will keep your toes warm. Sweet dreams!'

Now the oak tree's branches were bare, and it was ready for bed. It would sleep the whole winter long, and dream many dreams, full of adventure just like human dreams.

Once it had been tiny, with an acorn cup for its cradle. By human reckoning it was well into its fourth century. It was the biggest and finest tree in all the forest. It grew so high above the others that sailors out at sea used it as a landmark—not that it gave a thought to all the eyes that strained to make it out.

THE LAST DREAM OF THE
OLD OAK TREE

When the leaves were green, wood pigeons made their nests right at the top of the tree; in autumn, when the leaves turned to burnished copper, migrating birds rested there on their journey. But in the winter the tree was bare, and only crows and jackdaws rested in its branches, chattering about the lean times to come, with food so hard to find.

It was at the holy Christmastime that the oak tree dreamed its loveliest dream. It went like this.

In its dream, the tree knew that it was a special day. It could hear the church bells ringing, and it was a beautiful day, as soft and warm as summer. The tree unfolded its great crown, fresh and green, and let the sun play on its leaves and branches. The air was scented with herbs and flowers, and butterflies were playing hide-and-seek and mayflies were dancing as if the whole world had been made just for them to enjoy.

Everything that the tree had seen and known over its long life paraded by. It saw knights and ladies riding through the wood with feathers in their hats and hawks on their wrists. It heard the huntsman's horn and the barking of the hounds. It saw enemy soldiers pitch camp beneath its branches. The soldiers sang, and their weapons glittered in the light of the watch-fires. Then it saw two shy lovers carve their initials in its bark.

Once, many years ago, a wandering musician had hung his harp in the tree's branches. Now it was hanging there again, and playing in the wind. The wood pigeons cooed for pleasure, and the cuckoo called out all the days of summer.

The tree felt life surging through it like a wave, from the ends of its roots to the tips of its branches. It basked in the warmth. It felt itself growing stronger, and taller, growing up and up towards the blissful heat of the sun.

Now it was so tall that it rose high above the clouds, which swam below it like flocks of swans.

Each of its leaves could see, as if they were so many eyes. And

141

even though it was daytime, the bright stars came out, and winked at each other, so kind and calm they reminded the tree of the children and the lovers whose eyes had shone and sparkled beneath its boughs.

It was a moment of pure joy.

Yet something was missing. The tree wished that all the other trees and bushes and flowers could rise up too, and share its happiness. For the great oak tree could not enjoy its glorious dream to the full without the others. This wish quivered through it from top to toe, as strong as any human desire.

The tree craned down to look below. It smelled the woodruff, and then the strong scent of violet and honeysuckle. It even thought it could hear the cuckoo call.

Now the tops of the other trees broke through the clouds. They, too, were growing. The bushes and flowers were so eager in their flight that some of them pulled themselves right out of the earth. The birch soared past like a bolt of lightning. The whole forest was flying up into the sky—even the brown reeds. The birds were there, too, and a grasshopper who sat on a ribbon of grass, fiddling away on his shinbone. The songs of all the birds and insects lifted triumphantly up to heaven.

'But where are the little blue flowers from the stream?' asked the oak. 'They should be here. And the harebells, and the daisies!' For the oak wanted them all to come.

'Here we are! Here we are!' came the answer.

'And what about last summer's woodruff, and the lilies-of-the-valley from the summer before that—where are they? And the wild apples, with their lovely blossom? All the beauty of the forest over all the years—if only it could be here.'

'Here we are! Here we are!' came the response from up ahead.

'Oh, it's too good to be true!' cried the oak tree. 'They're all here, big and little—not one has been forgotten. How can such happiness be?'

'In heaven, it can be,' came the reply.

The tree felt its roots slip from the earth.

'That's right!' it shouted. 'Now there's nothing to hold me back. I can fly up into the light and the glory, and all that I loved is with me.'

'All!'

That was the oak tree's dream. And while it was dreaming on that Christmas Eve, a fierce storm raged over land and sea. The waves crashed against the cliff, and—just as the tree dreamed that its roots were loosening their hold—the wind tore the tree from the earth and it fell to the ground. Its three hundred and sixty-five years were now as a day is for the mayfly.

By Christmas morning the wind had fallen, and the sun was shining. Church bells were ringing out, and from every chimney—even from the poorest cottage—blue smoke was rising in thanksgiving like the tribute from a druid's altar. The sea grew calmer and calmer, and on board the big ship that had weathered the storm just off the coast, all the flags were being hoisted for Christmas.

'The tree is gone! The big old oak tree that we used as a landmark!' cried the sailors. 'It must have fallen in the storm. What ever shall we use now? There's not another like it.'

That was the old tree's funeral sermon—short, but heartfelt.

The tree itself lay stretched out on the snow beside the beach. Over it washed the sound of a carol from the ship, as the sailors sung of the joy of Christmas, and Christ who was born to give us eternal life.

Now let us of our blessings sing,

> *Alleluia, alleluia,*
> *Let the song to heaven ring,*
> *Alleluia, alleluia.*

So ran the old carol, and everyone on the ship was uplifted in his own way by prayer, just as the old oak tree was uplifted in its last, loveliest dream that Christmas Eve.

THE SHADOW

N THE HOT COUNTRIES, the sun really knows how to shine—it scorches down so hard it turns the people quite brown.

This story is about a clever young man—a philosopher—who came from the cold north to the hot south. At first he thought he could wander about just as if he were at home, but he soon learned better. During the day, he, like all sensible people, stayed in his room with the shutters closed. It was as if they were all asleep, or there was no one at home.

The worst of it was that the narrow street of tall houses in which he lived was open all day to the full glare of the sun. It was awful; the young philosopher felt as if he were sweltering in an oven. He really couldn't bear it. He began to waste away, and so did his shadow, for the blazing sun affected that too; it was much smaller here than at home. It was only after the sun went down that the man and his shadow began to revive.

That was a sight to see! As soon as the lamp was brought into the room, the shadow stretched itself right up the wall until it touched the ceiling; it had to stretch to get its strength back. The young stranger used to go out onto the balcony to have his stretch. As he watched the stars twinkling through the cool clear air, he felt the life tingling back into his veins.

All along the street, people were coming out onto their balconies to taste the air. Up on the balconies, and down on the street, the city came to life. Tailors and shoemakers moved out onto the street; chairs and tables were fetched outside, and lamps lit; some shouted, some sang; everywhere people were strolling, or driving in carriages; a tinkling *ting-a-ling-a-ling* sounded from the bells on donkeys' harnesses. Little boys were letting off fireworks; church bells were ringing; a funeral passed through the street— yes, it was all going on down there!

Only one house remained silent—the house directly opposite the young philosopher's. Yet someone must live there, because beautiful flowers grew on the balcony, and they would wither up in the hot sun if they weren't watered. Besides, in the evening the balcony door was left open, and although it seemed quite dark inside—certainly in the front room—the young man could hear music from within. He thought the music utterly beautiful—but then, he thought everything was wonderful in that hot country, except for the sun. He asked his landlord who lived there, but he didn't know; as for the music, the landlord thought it was an annoying racket: 'Just like someone playing the same piece over and over again, telling themselves, "This time I *will* get it right!" But they won't, however hard they try.'

One night the stranger woke up. He was sleeping with the balcony door open, and the curtain had been blown aside by the breeze. A light was shining from the balcony opposite, lighting up the flowers. In the heart of the glow stood a slim, graceful girl, with a beauty about her that dazzled the eyes. In a moment he was wide awake. He leaped from his bed and up to the curtain—but the girl was gone, the light was gone. Through the open door, music was drifting, music so soft and enchanting that it left him rapt in thought. It was a kind of magic.

Who could be living there? The young man couldn't even see where the entrance to the room was, for the whole ground floor was taken up with shops.

One evening, the stranger was sitting on his balcony with a lamp burning behind him. So naturally, his shadow fell upon the wall opposite; right among the flowers on the balcony. And when the stranger moved, the shadow moved, as shadows will.

'I believe my shadow is the only living thing over there,' said the young man. 'It looks really at home among the flowers. And the door is ajar—what a chance for the shadow to nip in and have a look-see; then it could come and tell me all about it.' He looked right at the shadow. 'Now then, look lively,' he said, only joking. 'Step inside! Well, aren't you going?' And he gave the shadow a nod, and the shadow nodded back. 'Off you go,' said the stranger, 'but mind you come back.' The stranger stood up, and the shadow stood up. The stranger turned round, and the shadow turned round. And anyone watching would have seen the shadow slip through the half-open balcony door, just as the stranger went back into his room, and closed the curtains behind him.

Next morning the philosopher went out to get a coffee and read the papers. 'What's this?' he exclaimed, as he walked into the sunshine. 'Where's my shadow? Don't say it really did go off exploring last night, and hasn't returned. What a bore.'

That evening, he went out once again onto his balcony, with the light behind him, knowing that a shadow always likes its master to act as a screen. But he couldn't fetch it back. He stretched and crouched, but no shadow fell. He stood and coughed meaningfully—*Ahem! Ahem!*—but it did no good.

It was all very irritating. But in the hot countries everything grows very fast. Only a week later, the stranger noticed, when he stepped into the sun, that he was growing a new shadow, from the roots of the old one. He was delighted. In three weeks, he had quite a respectable shadow again. He decided to return home, and as he travelled north, his new shadow kept growing, until it was bigger than he really needed.

So the young philosopher settled down in his cold homeland, and wrote books about all that is true and good and beautiful in the world. The days, weeks and years passed—many years.

One evening, when he was sitting in his study, he heard a discreet knock at the door. He called out, 'Come in,' but no one entered. So he got up and opened the door. The man who stood there gave him an uncomfortable feeling. He was so very thin. But he was dressed smartly, and was obviously a man of rank.

'Who are you?' asked the philosopher.

'I thought you wouldn't recognise me,' said the skinny visitor. 'I've filled out so much—in fact, I've become a man of substance. I dare say you never thought I'd do so well for myself. Don't you know your own old shadow? I can see you thought I'd gone for good. But here I am. I'll have you know I'm quite rich—I can buy my freedom, if it's necessary.' So saying he fingered the heavy gold chain he was wearing round his neck, and showed off the diamond rings that sparkled on his fingers. They were all real!

'You've taken my breath away!' said the philosopher. 'What does all this mean?'

'It is out of the ordinary,' replied the shadow, 'but then, you are by no means an ordinary man, and from our earliest memories I walked in your footsteps. When you thought I was able to make my own way in the world, I set out alone. I've done very well for myself, but nevertheless I've lately found myself longing to see you once more before you die—for you must die one day. Also, I wanted to revisit the land of my childhood. By the way, I see you've found yourself a new shadow. Do I owe you or it anything? Please let me know.'

'Is it really you?' said the philosopher. 'What a turn-up for the books! Who would have thought my old shadow would come knocking on my door?'

'Tell me what I owe you,' repeated the shadow. 'I don't like to be in anyone's debt.'

'Stop babbling about debts,' said the philosopher. 'You owe me nothing. You are as free as air; I'm just delighted to hear of your good fortune. Sit down, old friend, and tell me all about it— and first, tell me what happened that night in the house across the street.'

'Very well,' said the shadow, sitting down. 'But first promise me that you will not tell anyone in this town that I was once your shadow. I am thinking of getting married—I could support a family.'

'Of course I won't tell,' said the philosopher. 'My lips are sealed; I give you my word—and a man is only as good as his word.'

'So is a shadow,' came the reply.

It was amazing, really, how human the shadow had become. He was dressed all in black, but everything was of the finest quality, from his shining leather boots to his smart black hat. What with his gold chain and his diamond rings, the shadow was very well turned out; it was the clothes that made the man.

'Now I shall begin,' said the shadow, stamping his boots firmly down on the philosopher's new shadow, which was lying like a poodle at his feet. It may just have been pride; or maybe he was hoping the shadow would attach itself to him. The new shadow just lay there, quite still, hanging on every word: it wanted to learn how it might free itself, and be its own master.

'Who do you think it was living in that house?' asked the shadow. 'It was the fairest of all—it was Poetry! I was there for three weeks, and that's as good as living for three thousand years, and reading everything that was imagined or written in all that time. Believe me, it's true. I've seen all, and I know all!'

'Poetry!' cried the philosopher. 'Yes, often she lives a quiet life in the heart of the bustling city. I glimpsed her once, when I was still half-asleep. She dazzled my eyes, as she stood on the balcony, radiant as the Northern Lights. Go on, please. You were on the balcony, you slipped through the door, and then ... '

'I found myself in an entrance hall; that's what you were looking at all that time. There was no lamp; it was dark. But there was a long row of rooms leading off it, all lit by the glare from the innermost room, where Poetry lived. That was so bright it would have snuffed out a shadow, so I took my time approaching it—as everyone should.'

'Yes, yes, but get on with the story!' snapped the philosopher.

'I saw everything, and I will tell you about it,' replied the shadow, 'but first I must ask you to show me some respect. I'm not a snob, but I am a free man, and a man of learning, not to speak of my position in society, and I'll thank you to remember it.'

'You're right, sir,' said the philosopher. 'I was at fault, and I will bear what you say in mind. Now, please tell me everything you saw.'

'Everything?' said the shadow. 'I saw all, and I know all.'

'What did Poetry's inner room look like?' asked the philosopher. 'Like a grove of forest trees? Or a vaulted church? Or like the starlit heavens seen from a mountain top?'

'I didn't go right inside,' replied the shadow. 'I stayed in the twilit hall, and peered in from there. It was a good vantage point. I saw everything; I know everything. I have been in Poetry's entrance hall.'

'Yes, but what did you see? Did you see the ancient gods and heroes striding through those great halls? Did you see the children playing and telling each other their dreams?'

'I was there, I tell you, and I saw everything. What you would have made of it, I do not know, but it turned me into a man. I learned about my own nature and its inborn poetry. When I lived with you, I never thought of these things. When the sun rose and set, you will remember, I grew uncommonly tall—by moonlight, I was almost more plain to see than you. But I didn't understand, until I was standing there in Poetry's entrance hall, and then I realised—I was a man. I left the place transformed.

'By then, you had left for home. I was ashamed, as a man, to be seen about in my condition. I needed boots and clothes—all the outer trappings by which a man is judged. I hid—I can trust you not to put this in a book—under the skirts of a woman who sold cakes in the market; I didn't come out until nightfall. Then I ran along the street in the moonlight, and stretched myself up against the wall—it did my back good. I ran up and down, peeping into rooms, high and low. I peeped where no one else could peep; I saw what no one else could see—what no one ever should see.

'What a sorry world this is. I wouldn't want to be a man, if people didn't value it so. I saw ugly, unbelievable things done by husbands and wives, mothers and fathers, even by little children. I saw what no one should ever see, but everyone wants to see—people's dirty secrets. If I had published them in a newspaper, I should have had plenty of readers! But instead I wrote privately to each individual: that made them quake in their boots. Everywhere I went, I threw them into a panic. They feared me, so they fawned on me. The professors gave me an honorary degree, the tailors gave me new clothes—you see how well I dress—the bankers lent me money, all the women fell at my feet. And that's what made me the man I am today.

'I must be going. Here's my card. I live on the sunny side of the street, and am always at home when it rains.' And the shadow left.

'Strange,' said the philosopher. 'How strange!'

Days, years passed—the shadow came again.

'How are things?' he asked.

'I still write about the good, the true and the beautiful,' replied the philosopher, 'but no one seems to care. It makes me sick at heart, for these things mean the world to me.'

'I never think of them,' said the shadow. 'I've been concentrating on getting fat; that's what matters. You just don't understand the world, that's what's wrong with you. You should travel. I'm planning a trip abroad this summer; why not come with me? I would like a companion—you could come as my shadow! It really would be fun, and I would pay for everything.'

'That's a bit much,' said the philosopher.

'Not at all,' replied the shadow. 'It would do you the world of good to travel. If you went as my shadow, it wouldn't cost you a thing.'

'It's absurd!'

'Maybe it is, but so is the world, and it always has been.' And with that the shadow went away.

Things didn't go well with the philosopher. He was dogged by worry and grief. Whenever he talked about the true, the good and the beautiful, people looked at him like a cow that's just been offered a bunch of roses. In the end his health failed.

'You're a shadow of your former self,' his friends told him, and it sent a chill right through him.

'You should go and take a cure at a health spa,' said the shadow, when he dropped in one day. 'That's the thing for you. I'll take you with me for old time's sake and bear all the expenses. You can write an account of our travels and keep me amused on the journey. I want to go to a spa anyway, as my beard won't grow. That's just as much an illness as anything else—a man needs a beard. Do come with me.'

So they set off together, only this time the shadow was the master and the master was the shadow. Whether they were driving in a coach, riding or walking, the shadow always put himself in the master's place in the line of the sun; though the good-natured philosopher never noticed.

One day the philosopher said, 'I've been turning over in my mind what you said when we first met again, that I didn't show you enough respect. Since then, we've been formal with each other. But now that we are companions, and have known each other since childhood, I would like us to clasp hands and call each other friend, and be easy in our speech once more.'

'That's all very well,' said the shadow. 'You've been frank; I shall be so too. As a philosopher, you must know how fussy people can be. Some can't abide brown paper; others are set on edge when someone runs a fingernail down a pane of glass. That's how I feel when you talk to me in a familiar manner. It rubs me up the wrong way. It's as if you're reminding me of our former relations. I'm not a snob; it's just the way I feel. So I can't let you speak to me without showing respect; but I'm quite willing to meet you halfway, and talk to you without any respect at all.'

'This is a pretty pass,' thought the philosopher, 'that I must "Sir" him while he calls me names.' But he had to put up with it.

At last they came to the spa. There were plenty of people there taking the waters, among them a princess, whose problem was that she saw too clearly for comfort.

The princess noticed at once that the newcomer was different from all the others. 'They say he's here because his beard won't grow,' she said to herself, 'but really it must be because he can't cast a shadow.'

She was dying to know the truth, so when she saw him out walking, she went straight up to him, in the direct way princesses have, and said, 'Your trouble is that you have no shadow.'

'Your Royal Highness must be getting better,' he replied. 'I know that you were too clear-sighted, but you must be cured. I do indeed have a shadow, though an unusual one: that's him over there. Ordinary people have ordinary shadows, but I am not an ordinary person. Just as grand folk dress their servants in the finest livery, so I have decked my shadow out as a human being. If you look, you'll see I've even given him a shadow of his own. It was expensive, but worth it, for he's one of a kind.'

'Have I really been cured?' wondered the Princess. 'If so, the waters here must be miraculous. But even so, there's no need to hurry away, just as things are getting interesting. I do hope this man's beard doesn't grow too quickly.'

In the ballroom that evening, the princess danced with the shadow. She was as light as a feather, but he was lighter still; she had never had such a partner. She told him where she came from, and it turned out he had once visited the country, when she had

been abroad. He had peeped in at all sorts of windows, and seen all sorts of things. He told her some of these, and hinted at others, and quite amazed her. She thought he must know more than anyone else in the world.

By the second dance, she was in love. The shadow knew it, for she began to look right through him. During the third dance, she nearly told him, but she kept her head, remembering her duty to her country and her people. 'He knows the ways of the world,' she thought, 'and that's good. He's a beautiful dancer, and that's better still. But is he wise? That's the most important thing of all.' So she began to ask him hard questions, which she couldn't have answered herself.

The shadow's face clouded over. 'You can't answer!' she said.

'I could,' said the shadow, 'but these are children's riddles. I believe even my old shadow could answer them.'

'Your shadow,' said the princess. 'That would be remarkable.'

'I don't promise,' said the shadow, 'but I think he could. After all, he's been following me around all these years, and hearing everything I say. Yes—I think he could do it. But, a word to the wise, Your Highness, he is so proud of people taking him for a man; if you treat him as one, you'll get the best out of him.'

'It will be my pleasure,' said the princess.

So she joined the philosopher by the door, and quizzed him about the sun and the moon and human beings, inside and out, and his answers were both learned and wise.

'What a man this must be, when his shadow knows so much,' she thought. 'And what a blessing to my people and my country if I married him! I shall do it.'

The princess and the shadow soon came to an understanding, but they decided to keep it a secret until the princess got home. 'I won't even tell my shadow,' said the shadow; no doubt he had his own reasons for that.

At last they came to the princess's country.

'Now listen to me, friend,' said the shadow to the philosopher. 'I am now as rich and as powerful as a man can be, and I want you to share in my good fortune. You shall live with me in the palace, and ride with me in the royal coach, and be well paid for it. But you must let everybody call you "Shadow", and never tell anyone that you were once a man; and once a year, when I sit in the sun on the balcony to show myself to the people, you must lie at my feet like a good shadow. You know, I am marrying the princess this very evening.'

'It's wrong!' said the philosopher. 'I won't do it. You'd be cheating the people, never mind the princess. I'm going to tell the truth: that I am a man, and you are a mere shadow, just dressed like one.'

'It won't do any good,' said the shadow. 'No one will believe you. Do be sensible, or I'll have to call the guard.'

'I'm going straight to the princess.'

'But I'm going first,' said the shadow, 'and you're going to prison. Guard!'

And to prison he went, for of course the guard obeyed the princess's betrothed.

'You're trembling,' said the princess, when the shadow found her. 'Has something happened? You're not coming down with something, on our wedding day?'

'I've had a terrible shock,' said the shadow. 'It's my poor shadow; I can hardly believe it—I suppose it's all been too much for his shadow-brain—he's gone quite mad! He's convinced himself that he really is a man, and—if you can believe it—that *I* am his shadow.'

'How awful,' said the princess. 'I hope he's safely locked up.'

'For his own good. I fear he may never recover.'

'Poor shadow!' said the princess. 'How sad. Perhaps it would be a kindness to put him out of his misery. Now I think of it, I'm sure that would be the best course—just to put him to sleep without any fuss.'

'It seems hard,' said the shadow, 'for he was a faithful servant.' And he pursed his lips and made a sound like a sigh.

'You are noble,' said the princess.

That night the whole city was lit up. Cannons were fired— *Boom! Boom! Boom!* Soldiers presented arms. What a wedding it was! At the end the shadow and the princess came out onto the balcony, and the people cheered them to the skies.

The philosopher didn't hear it; for the shadow had taken his life.

IT'S PERFECTLY TRUE

HAT'S THE WORLD COMING TO?' asked a hen—who lived on the other side of town from where it all happened. 'The goings-on in that henhouse—it's quite shocking. It's just as well that there are so many of us roosting together; I wouldn't get a wink of sleep on my own.' And then she told them the story. It made the other hens' feathers stand on end, and the rooster's comb flop over. It's perfectly true!

But let's begin at the beginning. It was in the henhouse on the other side of town. The sun was setting, and the hens were settling on their roost. One of them was a stumpy-legged bird with white feathers; she laid an egg every day and was altogether a model of respectability. When she flew up to the roost, she plumed herself with her beak, and a little feather fell out.

'Let it go!' she said. 'The more I preen the lovelier I will grow.' All this was said in fun, for—despite being so respectable—she was a hen with a merry heart. And then she went to sleep.

It was dark; hen nestled up to hen; but the one next to the one who had lost a feather was not asleep. She had both heard and not heard what was said—as you must often do if you want a quiet life. But she couldn't keep what she had heard to herself. She said to the next hen along, 'Did you hear that? Naming no names, a certain hen in this roost means to pluck out all her feathers; it's the fashion. If I were a rooster, I wouldn't look twice at her.'

Right above the henhouse lived a family of owls. With their sharp ears they could hear every word that the hen said. The mother rolled her eyes and fanned herself with her wings. 'Don't listen! But I suppose you must have heard what she said? I could hardly believe my ears! One of the hens has so forgotten all decency that she is calmly plucking off all her feathers, in full view of the rooster!'

'*Prenez garde aux enfants!*' said the father owl. 'Not in front of the children!'

'But I must tell my friend across the way,' said the mother. 'She has to hear this.' And away she flew.

Tu-whit, tu-whoo! Tu-whit, tu-whoo! The mother owl and her friend hooted over the tale; and it carried right down to the dovecot. 'Have you heard the latest? *Tu-whit, tu-whoo!* A hen has plucked out all her feathers to please the rooster. She'll freeze to death, if she hasn't died already.'

'Where, where?' cooed the doves.

'In the yard over there. I as good as saw it with my own eyes. The story's scarcely fit to be told, but it's perfectly true!'

'True, true!' cooed the doves. 'Perfectly true!' And they took the story down to the henhouse in their yard. 'There's a hen—some say there were two of them—and they've plucked out all their feathers so that they'll stand out from the crowd and attract the rooster. But they're playing with fire, for it's easy to take a chill, and a chill can turn to a fever; in fact, they'll catch their death, the pair of them.'

That gave the rooster a jolt. 'Wake up! Wake up!' he crowed, and he flew up onto the fence post. His eyes were still full of sleep, but he crowed anyway: 'Three hens have died for love of a rooster! They plucked out all their feathers! It's a scandal—I won't hush it up—pass it on!'

'Pass it on! Pass it on!' piped the bats. 'Pass it on!' clucked the hens. 'Pass it on!' crowed the roosters. And so the story went from henhouse to henhouse, right round town, until it came back to the very spot where it started.

'There were five hens,' the tale now ran, 'who plucked off all their feathers, to show which of them had wasted away the most for love of a rooster. Then they pecked each other to death. It's a great shame for their family, and a serious loss for their owner.'

The hen that had lost just one little feather didn't recognise her own story. As she was a respectable hen, she said, 'I despise those hens! And there are others like them. Such things shouldn't be kept secret. I'm going to write to the papers about it, and then the whole country will hear about it—and serve those hens right, and their family too.'

The story was published in the newspaper and—as it was in print—it must be perfectly true!

'One little feather can become five hens!'

GRIEF

HIS STORY IS IN TWO PARTS. The first part's not really necessary, but it makes a good foundation, and that's always a help.

We were staying at a manor house in the country, and our host was away for the day. Along came a widow woman from the nearby town, with a pug dog under her arm. She said she'd come to sell shares in her tannery. She had all her papers with her. We told her to put them in an envelope and address it to the owner of the house, with all his titles: Commissary General, Sir and so on.

She put pen to paper, and then paused. She asked us to repeat the address, a bit more slowly. She started to write it out, but bang in the middle of the word 'Commissary' she got stuck. 'I'm only a woman!' she said.

The pug, which she had put down on the floor, started to growl. He had accompanied her on the outing for the sake of his health, but he hadn't bargained on being put on the floor. He was a podgy, snub-nosed pug.

'He won't bite,' said the woman. 'He's got no teeth. He's like one of the family. He's faithful, and if he's cranky, it's my grandchildren's fault. They tease him, making him be the bridesmaid when they play at weddings; he finds it all a strain, the poor old boy.'

Then she handed in her papers, picked up the pug and left.

That's the first part of the story, the part we could have left out.

The pug dog died—that's the second part.

It was about a week later. We were visiting the town, and staying at an inn. Our rooms looked over the back yard, which was

divided in two by a wooden fence. On one side, hides were hanging to dry; it was the widow's tannery.

The pug dog had died that very morning and been buried in the yard. The grandchildren—that's the widow's grandchildren, not the pug's, for the pug had never married—were putting the final touches to the grave. It was a fine grave—a pleasure to lie in.

It had an edging of broken pots, and it was covered with sand. For a tombstone there was a broken beer-bottle, neck upwards, though that didn't mean anything.

The children danced around the grave, and the eldest boy, a likely lad of seven, suggested that they should exhibit the grave to anyone in the street who would like to see it: admission, one trouser button. Every boy could afford that, and pay for a girl too. Everyone agreed.

All the children from the street, and the back alley too, came and paid their buttons. Quite a few trousers were in danger of falling down that afternoon, but it was worth it, to see the pug dog's grave.

Outside the yard, pressed up against the gate, stood a little, ragged girl. She was lovely, with curly hair and clear blue eyes. She didn't say a word, or shed a tear, but every time the gate opened she tried to peek in. She didn't have a button, so she had to stand outside while all the other children had their look at the grave. When the last one left, she sat down on the ground, put her head in her hands and sobbed her heart out; she was the only one who hadn't seen the pug dog's grave. That was grief, as heart-rending for her as any grown-up sorrow.

We watched from above. And from above, her trouble, like our own, might seem a joke.

That's the story. Anyone who doesn't understand it had better take shares in the widow's tannery.

FATHER'S ALWAYS RIGHT

OW I WANT to tell you a story I heard when I was a boy. It seems to have got better every time I've thought of it since. Stories are like many people—they improve with age, and that's a good thing.

Now you know what a real old farmhouse looks like, with a thatched roof all overgrown with moss and weeds, and a stork's nest on the ridge. The walls are all crooked, and the windows are tiny, and only one of them will open. The bread oven bulges out of the wall like a plump stomach; there's an elderberry hedge, and a little duck pond by the willow tree, with a duck and ducklings on it. In the yard there's an old dog on a chain who barks at anyone who goes by.

Well in just such a farmhouse, out in the country, there lived a farmer and his wife. They had little to spare, but one luxury they had was a horse, which they put out to graze by the side of the road. The farmer would ride it in to town every now and then, or lend it out to friends—and, of course, one good turn deserves another; but all in all, he felt it would be better to sell the horse, or trade it for something more useful. What that would be, he couldn't think.

'You'll know when you see it, Father,' said his wife. 'It's market day in town today. Why don't you ride in and sell the horse or exchange it for something. Whatever you do will be right.'

She tied on his necktie—she was better at that than he was—

and fastened it in a double bow; he did look spruce. She brushed his hat with the palm of her hand and gave him a kiss, and off he rode on the horse, to sell it or exchange it. Father knew what was what.

It was a sunny day without a cloud in the sky. The road was hot and dusty, and full of people going to market: some driving carts, some riding horses and some walking on their own two legs. It really was a scorching day, and there wasn't a scrap of shade on the road.

The farmer noticed a man driving a cow along the road—a very fine cow, too. 'I bet that cow gives lovely refreshing milk,' he said to himself. Then he called out, 'Hey! You with the cow! Can I have a word?' The man stopped, and the farmer continued, 'I suppose a horse is really worth more than a cow, but a cow is more use to me. Will you swap?'

'Yes!' said the man.

And that should be that. The farmer had done the deal, and he should have just turned round and gone home. But he'd been looking forward to the market and didn't want to miss it. So on he went with the cow.

He strode along, and soon he caught up with a man who was driving a sheep. It was a nice fat sheep, with a woolly coat.

'I like the look of that sheep,' thought the farmer. 'There's plenty of grazing by the side of the road for a sheep, and in winter it could come into the house. Really, a sheep would be better than a cow.' So he called out, 'Will you swap?' And of course the man with the sheep was very ready to do so.

The farmer went on with the sheep until he came to a stile, where he met a man with an enormous goose under his arm. 'That's a plump one you've got there,' said the farmer. 'There's plenty of flesh on that. It would look just right on our pond, and it would be something for Mother to give the vegetable peelings to. She's often said how she'd like a goose—and now she shall have one. Will you swap? I'll give you this sheep for your goose, and throw a thank you into the bargain.' The man didn't mind if he did, so they swapped, and the farmer got the goose.

As he came nearer to town, the road grew more and more crowded with animals and folk. They spilled right off the road onto the gatekeeper's potato patch, where he had tethered his hen so that she wouldn't get frightened and stray off. She was a smart short-tailed hen, and she winked her eye at the farmer and said, *Cluck! Cluck!* What she meant by it I don't know.

The farmer thought, 'My, that's a handsome hen, finer than the parson's best. I wish it were mine. A hen can always scratch for its own corn; they don't need much looking after.' And he called out, 'How about swapping your hen for my goose?' And the gatekeeper thought that was a very good idea, so they did.

The farmer had had a busy morning, and it was a hot day, so he was done in. He could do with a drink and a bite. So he went to the inn. Just as he was going in, he met a servant coming out, carrying a bulging sack.

'What have you got in there?' asked the farmer.

'Rotten apples,' said the servant. 'I'm taking them to the pigs.'

'A whole sackful! I wish Mother could see them. Last year we only got one apple off the old tree by the woodshed; so of course we kept it for a special occasion, and it lay on the chest of drawers until it rotted away. "It makes me feel quite rich," Mother used to say. Just think what she'd say to a whole sackful.'

'What will you give me for it?' asked the servant.

'This hen,' said the farmer. So they swapped.

The farmer made his way into the bar, and leaned his sack of apples up against the potbellied stove, without noticing that it was lit. There were a lot of strangers in the bar—horse-traders, cattle-dealers, even a couple of Englishmen, who were so rich that their pockets were bursting with gold coins. And being English, they would bet on anything.

S-s-s! S-s-s! What was that noise? It was the apples baking in their skins.

'Whose apples are these?' asked one of the Englishmen.

'Mine,' said the farmer, and he told the Englishmen the whole story of how he traded his horse for a cow, and right on down to the sack of rotten apples.

'You'll catch it hot from your wife when you get back,' said the Englishmen. 'She'll fly off the handle.'

'No she won't. She'll give me a kiss, and say, "Father's always right!"'

'What do you bet?' they asked. 'We'll give you a hundred gold coins against whatever you stake.'

'I've only got this sack of rotten apples,' said the farmer, 'but if I lose, you can have Mother and me too. You can't say fairer than that.'

'Done!' they said.

So the innkeeper fetched his cart, and the Englishmen and the farmer got in, with the rotten apples, and they went to the farmer's house.

'Evening, Mother.'

'Evening, Father.'

'I've done the deal.'

'And got the best of it, I'm sure.' The farmer's wife didn't mind the strangers, she went right up and gave her husband a big hug.

'I swapped the horse for a cow.'

'Thank goodness for the milk,' she said. 'Now we can make butter and cheese. What a good bargain.'

'Then I swapped the cow for a sheep.'

'Better still,' she replied. 'How clever of you. We've got just enough grazing for a sheep, and ewe's milk makes good cheese, and I can spin the wool into yarn and knit woollen socks and nightshirts—cow's hair wouldn't have been any good at all. You think of everything.'

'Then I swapped the sheep for a goose.'

'Oh Father, you dear man. Are we really going to have goose for the Martinmas feast? You're forever thinking of ways to please me. We can tether the goose and fatten it up for Martinmas.'

'Then I swapped the goose for a hen.'

'A hen! What a good exchange. Hens lay eggs, and eggs turn into chicks. I've always wanted to keep hens.'

'Then I swapped the hen for a sackful of rotten apples.'

'Now I really must give you a kiss; you dear heart! Now listen to me. While you were gone, I thought I must make you a special meal to come home to. I wanted to make you an omelette with chives. I had the eggs, but no chives. So I went to the school-master's; I know they grow chives. But when I asked to borrow some, his wife—the stingy old biddy—just snipped, "Borrow! Out of the question! Nothing grows in our garden. I couldn't lend you so much as rotten apple." And now I can lend her ten—a whole sackful, if she wants them! What a hoot, Father!' And she kissed him smack on the lips.

'That's the spirit,' said the Englishmen. 'Always downhill, but never downhearted. That was worth the money!' And they counted out a hundred gold coins to the farmer whose wife greeted him with kisses not blows.

Yes, it always pays for a wife to think that whatever Father does is for the best.

That's my story. I heard it when I was a boy; and now that you have heard it, too, you know that Father's always right.

THE SNOWMAN

T'S SO COLD I'm creaking with it,' said the snowman. 'It's lovely. The sting in this wind really lets you know you're alive. As for that shiner who thinks she's so bright'—he meant the sun—'she won't outface me. I've got all my bits and pieces under control.' For he had two three-cornered bits of tile for eyes, and an old rake for a mouth, with teeth too.

He had been born to the sound of boys' laughter, the jingle of sleigh bells and the cracking of whips.

The sun set and the moon rose, round and full, clear and calm in the blue night sky. 'Here she comes again, from the other direction,' said the snowman, who thought it was the sun coming back. 'At least I've taught her not to stare so. I don't mind if she wants to stay there and light me up. If only I could get the hang of moving, I'd be well set. First thing I'd do is go and slide on the ice, like the boys do. But I don't know how to run.'

Gr-off-off! barked the old watchdog on his chain. He'd got a sore throat; he'd had it ever since he was pushed outdoors, away from the warm stove. 'The sun will teach you how to run. I saw what happened to last year's snowman, and the one before that. Before I can say *gr-off-off*, you'll be gone.'

'What do you mean, friend?' asked the snowman. 'How can that so-and-so up there teach me how to run? I made her run fast enough when I returned her stare, though now she is trying to sneak back the other way.'

'You don't know anything,' said the watchdog, 'but then, they've only just put you up. That one is the moon; the one that

172

went away is the sun. She'll be back tomorrow, and she'll show you how to run all right—all the way to the pond! This weather won't last—I can feel it in my back legs; a change is on the way.'

'I don't know what he's getting at,' said the snowman, 'but I've got an inkling it's not very nice. That one who stared at me and then went away—he called her the sun—is no friend of mine, that's for sure.'

Gr-off-off! barked the watchdog; he turned himself round three times, and lay down in the kennel to sleep.

The weather did change. By morning, the whole landscape was smothered in a thick, clammy fog. Then an icy wind got up, and the frost bit hard. But what a sight it was when the sun came out! The trees and bushes were covered with hoarfrost, like a forest of white coral; every branch was covered with glittering blossom. In summer, the leaves hide the tracery of branch and twig, but now you could see it clearly, like delicate lace, radiant with whiteness. The birch tree swayed in the wind, as full of life as a tree in summer. It was so lovely. And when the sun shone down everything glinted as if it were covered with diamond dust—and the snow itself sparkled like a carpet of diamonds, or thousands of tiny candles, burning whiter than white.

'Isn't it just beautiful?' said a young girl, who was walking in the garden with a young man. 'Even lovelier than in summer.' And her eyes, too, sparkled.

'And you'd never meet a fellow like this in summer,' said the young man, pointing to the snowman. 'He's splendid.'

The girl laughed, and nodded to the snowman; then she and the young man danced back across the snow, which crunched beneath their feet as if they were walking on starch.

'Who were those two?' the snowman asked the watchdog. 'You've been here longer than I have; do you know them?'

'Of course I do,' said the watchdog. 'She's patted me, oh, many's the time, and he's given me bones; I wouldn't bite *them*.'

'But what are they doing here?' asked the snowman.

'Ccc-courting!' said the watchdog. 'Soon they'll be moving into a kennel of their own, and gnawing bones together. *Gr-off-off!*'

'And are those two as important as you and I?' asked the snowman.

'Well, they're part of the family,' replied the watchdog. 'You were only born yesterday, so can't be expected to know these things; I've got the knowledge of experience, I have; I know what's what on this farm. I wasn't always chained up here in the cold. *Gr-off-off!*'

'There's nothing wrong with the cold,' said the snowman. 'I love it. But tell me more—only please stop rattling your chain, it makes me feel queasy.'

Gr-off-off! barked the watchdog. 'I was a puppy once. "Oh! Isn't he sweet!" they used to say. I slept indoors on a velvet chair, or even curled up on the mistress's lap. She kissed me on the nose, and wiped my paws with an embroidered handkerchief, and called me "diddums" and "dear little puppy-wuppy". But then I got too big for that, and they gave me to the housekeeper, and I went to live in the basement. You can see right into the very room from where you're standing: that was my domain. It wasn't so fine and luxurious as upstairs, but it was more comfortable. The housekeeper gave me just as good food, and more of it; and I wasn't being constantly petted, or chased by the children. I had my own cushion, and then there was a stove. There's nothing like a stove at this time of the year. I used to crawl right underneath it. Oh, I still dream about that stove. *Gr-off-off! Gr-off-off!*'

'Is a stove nice to look at?' asked the snowman. 'Does it look like me?'

'It's exactly the opposite of you. It's coal-black, with a long neck and a brass collar. It eats logs and breathes flame. Until you've lain near it—or better still right underneath it—you've no idea what true comfort is. I'm sure you can see it through the window from where you are.'

And the snowman looked, and sure enough he saw a shiny black thing with a brass collar and the gleam of fire. The snowman felt a strange feeling that he couldn't understand—he was thrown off balance in a way all people are sometimes, unless they're made of ice.

'Why did you leave her?' he asked—for he was sure that the stove must be a girl. 'How could you bear to?'

'I had no choice,' said the watchdog. 'They turned me out of doors, and chained me up here, and all because I bit the youngest son in the leg. He took the bone I was gnawing—so, "a bone for a bone", thought I. But they didn't see it my way, and from that day I've been chained up, and that was that. It's ruined my voice. *Gr-off-off!* You can hear how hoarse I am.'

The snowman had stopped listening. He was gazing into the housekeeper's room in the basement, where the stove stood on its four iron legs; it looked much the same size as the snowman himself.

'I can feel a strange creaking inside,' he said. 'Shall I ever get into that room? It's an innocent wish, and innocent wishes must surely come true. It's all I wish for, and I wish it with all my heart; so it would be very unfair if it weren't granted. I must get in, and lie beside her, even if I have to break the window.'

'You'll never get in,' said the watchdog. 'And if you did, you'd soon go off, *gr-off-off!*'

'I'm as good as off,' said the snowman. 'I feel I'm breaking apart.'

All day long the snowman stared through the window. In the evening, the room looked even more inviting. The stove shone with a soft, warm light that neither the sun nor the moon can make—only a stove. Every time the stove door was opened to feed it, flames leaped out; the snowman's white face blushed red, and the blush went right down to his chest.

'It's more than I can bear,' he said. 'How beautiful she is when she puts out her tongue!'

The night was long, but not for the snowman. He was happy thinking his own beautiful thoughts and freezing until he crackled.

In the morning the basement windows were frozen over, frosted with the loveliest ice-flowers any snowman could wish for—but they hid the stove. The ice on the panes just wouldn't thaw, so he couldn't see her. Everything crackled and crunched, it was perfect weather for a snowman, but he couldn't enjoy it. He should have been happy, but he wasn't. He was love-sick for the stove.

'That's a serious problem for a snowman,' said the watchdog. 'I've suffered that way myself, but I got over it. *Gr-off-off!* The weather's on the change.'

And the weather did change. There was a thaw. And the more the weather thawed, the more the snowman thawed. He didn't say anything—not a word—and that's a sure sign.

One morning he collapsed. Where he had been, there was something sticking up, like the handle of a broom; that's what the boys had built him round.

'Now I understand his love-sickness,' said the watchdog. 'The snowman had a stove rake in his body; that's what set him off. Well, now he's over it. *Gr-off-off!*'

And soon winter was over with too.

Gr-off-off! barked the watchdog, and the little girls on the farm sang:

>*Now the flowers shall shoot and sprout;*
>*Willow, hang your mittens out.*
>*Lark and cuckoo, soar and sing.*
>*And help us welcome in the spring.*

And no one gave a thought to the snowman.

THE SNAIL AND
THE ROSE TREE

ROUND THE GARDEN ran a hazel hedge, on the far side of which were fields and meadows dotted with cows and sheep. But in the heart of the garden was a rose tree in bloom, and under the rose tree was a snail, snug and smug in his shell.

'My time will come,' said the snail. 'I shall do something more than just grow roses or hazelnuts, or give milk or wool.'

'I can't wait,' said the rose tree.

'Well, you will have to,' said the snail. 'I'm going to take my time. Where's the sense in haste? Anticipation is half the fun.'

Next year the snail took up the same position in the sun beneath the rose tree, which unfolded its fresh new roses from the bud. The snail crept halfway out of his shell, stretched out his horns and said, 'Just the same as last year. Not the slightest variation. More roses!'

Summer passed, autumn passed, and still the rose tree budded and bloomed—until the snow came. Then the weather turned raw and blustery. The rose tree bent to the ground, and the snail burrowed into the earth.

Then another spring arrived, and the roses came out and so did the snail.

'You are growing old,' he told the rose tree. 'You should be thinking of going—you've given the world all you had to give. Whether it was worth the bother is another question. You never

gave a thought to your inner development, and soon you will be a dry old stick and it will be too late. Do you know what I'm saying?'

'You're frightening me,' said the rose tree.

'Did you never even wonder why you flowered—what your motivation was?'

'No,' said the rose tree. 'I flowered for sheer joy. I couldn't help myself. I drank the dew and the rain, I drew strength from the earth and the sun—I breathed, I lived! I felt so happy I just had to flower. It was my life.'

'A very lazy life,' said the snail.

'Yes,' agreed the rose tree. 'I've been given everything I could want. But you've been even more fortunate. You can think! With your gifts, you will astound the world one day.'

'Astound the world!' said the snail. 'What do I care for the world? My thoughts are mine—I don't need to share them.'

'But shouldn't we all share the best of ourselves with others? I know I've only given roses—but you, what have you given? What will you give?'

'What have I given? What will I give? I spit on the world. What's the good of it? You grow your roses if you like—it's all you're good for. Let the hazels bear their nuts, the cows give their milk and the sheep their wool. Each of them has their admirers, and I have mine—me! I am snug and smug in my shell, and the world outside it means nothing to me.' And with that the snail withdrew into his house and sealed it up.

'What a shame!' said the rose tree. 'But I can't retreat into myself, even if I wanted to. I've got to unfurl my roses. Their petals drop off and are carried away by the breeze. I saw one pressed inside a mother's prayer book, and another pinned at a young girl's breast. One was kissed by a child out of sheer joy in being alive. That was a rare blessing—I'll remember it all my life.'

The rose tree went on innocently blooming, and the snail slumbered in his shell, for the world meant nothing to him.

The years went by. The snail passed on—earth to earth. The rose tree passed on—earth to earth. But in the garden new rose trees bloomed, and new snails crept into their shells and spat at the world, which meant nothing to them.

Should I try that story again, from the beginning? It wouldn't be any different.

'SOMETHING'

WANT TO DO SOMETHING!' said the eldest of five brothers. 'I want to be of use to the world. It doesn't matter if I'm not important, so long as I'm useful—that will be something. I shall make bricks—people can't do without them—and then I shall have done something!'

'Something, but not much,' said the second brother. 'Unskilled work, that could be done by a machine. I shall be a builder—that's really something. There's even a Builders' Guild, with a banner and a guildhall. If all goes well, I shall have workmen under me who call me "Master". That will be something!'

'That is nothing!' said the third brother. 'A builder is just a labourer putting on airs. It's a trade, not a profession. I shall be an architect, and belong to the world of art and ideas. I shall have to start at the bottom of the ladder, as a mere carpenter's apprentice—fetching and carrying for the journeymen. I shall have to put up with their teasing and their practical jokes. I shall pretend it's all make-believe, and my flat cap is really a silk top hat. Then when I've served my time I shall be on my way, and never think about it again. I shall go to the Academy and learn to draw, and then I shall be an architect. That's something! I will have letters after my name—and in front of it, too—and people will call me "Sir". That's my idea of "something".'

'It may be something, but it's not much,' said the fourth brother. 'What's the point of just doing what other people have already done? I want to be a genius—cleverer than the whole lot of you put together! I shall invent a whole new style of building for this country, with new materials and new techniques—and on the top of the tallest building that can be built I shall add an extra floor, just to prove my genius.'

'But what if the buildings fall down?' asked the fifth brother. 'That would be a bad business. And anyway what is new today looks tired tomorrow. Novelty! What is it? Just the affectations of sensation-seeking youth. It's clear none of you will come to anything, whatever you think. But carry on, don't let me stop you. Just don't think I will follow in your footsteps. No, I intend to stand aside, and criticise what others do. Nothing's perfect, and I shall be the one who points out all the faults—that really will be something!'

He did just what he said, and everyone said of him, 'He really is something. He lives on his wits, and he knows how to make something out of nothing.' And there's always a place in the world for someone who can do that.

That's not much of a story so far—but it's not over yet.

The eldest brother, who made bricks, found that from every brick he made he got a little copper coin. When he added enough copper coins together, he could change them for a silver one—and then he could knock at the door of the butcher, the baker or the tailor, and they would open up for him. That's what he got from the bricks.

Some of the bricks broke in two, but even those could be used. The eldest brother had a kind heart, and he gave the broken bricks to old Mother Margaret, a poor woman who longed to build herself a little house up on the sea wall.

Mother Margaret built the house with her own hands. The house was cramped, the window was crooked, the door was too low and the thatch was a mess—but it was her own house, and it had a wonderful view of the sea. When the sea rose in fury against the sea wall, it would spatter the house with salt spray, but the house kept it out, and when the brickmaker died, it was still standing.

The second brother—the builder—did his training, and then packed his knapsack and set off into the world to ply his trade. And as he walked he sang a cheerful song.

He put money in his purse, and when he came home he set up as a master builder, and built house after house—whole streets of them. And the profit from those streets built a little house just for him. It was a modest house, with a plain earth floor, but he danced around it with his bride, and their dancing feet gave it a polish. It seemed to them that every brick of their home was as precious as a flower, and they needed no fancy decorations, for they were truly happy. Outside the house he hung the banner of the Guild, and all the journeymen and apprentices sang, 'For He's a Jolly Good Fellow'. That was something. And in due course he died—that was something, too.

Now we come to the third brother—the one who started as a lowly carpenter's apprentice, pretending his cap was a top hat. He graduated from the Academy and became an architect, and everyone called him 'Sir'. And the profits from the houses he designed built him a mansion, and they even named a street after him. That was something, and he was something—with letters after his name, and before it too. His children were the children of a gentleman, and when he died his wife was the widow of a gentleman—and that's something! His name can still be read on the street sign, and that too is something.

Then there was the fourth brother—the genius. With his new techniques, he built the tallest house that could be built, and then built an extra floor on top of that. But the extra floor fell down, and he fell with it and broke his neck. But he had a flowery obituary in the newspaper and a fine funeral, with banners and a band, and three speeches, each one longer than the last, which would have pleased him, because he liked being talked about. A monument was put up over his grave. It was only one storey, but still—it was something.

So four of the brothers had died, but the fifth—the critic—outlived them. He had the last word, and that was important to him. He was the brainy one—everyone said so. But his time came too, and he died and stood at the gate of heaven. They always enter that gate in twos, so he had to wait for another soul to arrive. And it was Mother Margaret, who built the house on the sea wall.

'I suppose it is for the sake of the contrast that this wretched creature and I must arrive here together,' he thought. And then he asked, 'Who are you? Do you want to go in?'

Mother Margaret did her best to curtsey—she thought he must be St Peter himself. 'I'm only a poor old woman, without any family. Old Margaret from the house on the sea wall.'

'And what have you done down below?'

'Done? Why, nothing. Nothing that would open this gate for me. It will only be God's grace that will let me in.'

'And what made you leave the world?' he asked—just to pass the time, because it was boring waiting there.

'I can't hardly say,' she answered. 'I have been so poorly for the last few years, with barely enough strength to crawl out of bed. And this winter was a hard one. You'll remember the two bitterly cold days we had. The sea froze over as far as you could see. The whole town went out on the ice, dancing and skating. There was a band playing, and people eating, drinking and having fun. The noise rang so clearly across the ice, I enjoyed listening to it as I lay in bed.

'It was just growing dark, and the moon was up, but not shining at full strength. My bed was by the window, so I could look out over the sea. Where the sea and the sky met I saw a strange white cloud. I lay there watching it, and saw that the black spot in the middle of it was getting bigger and bigger. I knew what *that* meant. I've watched the weather all my life, and it's not often you see it. But I recognised it, and it filled me with dread.

'Twice before I've seen the same sign in the sky. I knew that

185

with the spring tide would come a terrible storm. All those poor people out frolicking on the ice would be caught, and it would be all over with them. The whole town was out there, young and old. What if none of them knew what that white cloud with the black spot meant? Who would warn them?

'I was so frightened it gave me the strength to pull myself out of bed and stumble to the window. I couldn't go any further. But I managed to open the window. I could see all the people skating on the ice. The boys and girls were screaming and shouting, and the young men and women were singing. They were having no end of fun.

'The white cloud with the billowing black centre was rising higher and higher. I called out, but nobody heard me—I was too far away. Soon the storm would burst, the ice would break and they would all be swept away. If only I wasn't so weak! If only I could bring them to the shore!

'Then God gave me the idea of setting fire to the straw mattress on my bed. It was better to let my house burn down than for all those people to be drowned. So I set a match to it. When the flames had taken, I managed to crawl out of the door, and there I laid—it was all I could do.

'The flames flickered out of the door and the window, and up onto the thatched roof. The whole house went up in flames. They saw it from the ice, and they all came running to help me, thinking I must be burning to death inside. Not one of them stayed behind.

'I heard them coming, and I also heard the air thrumming with the rumble of thunder. Then the spring tide lifted up the ice and it shattered with a terrible sound like cannons firing. But all the people had reached the sea wall, where the air around me was dancing with fiery sparks. I had brought them all to safety.

'But I think it must have all been too much for me, what with the shock and the cold—so here I am, at the gate of heaven. They tell me it will even open for a poor creature like me. I don't even have a little house any more, down there; though that doesn't give me any right to come in here.'

Just then the gate of heaven opened, and an angel came to lead the old woman inside. As her skirt brushed against the gate, a straw fell from it. It was one of the straws from her bed, the one she set fire to in order to save the people on the ice. The straw had turned to pure gold.

The angel picked it up. 'This is what the old woman brought,' the angel said to the critic. 'Now show me what you have brought. I know you have never made anything—not so much as a brick. If only you could go back and bring even that, even if it was badly made, it would still be something. But you can't go back, so I can do nothing for you.'

The poor old woman, Mother Margaret, pleaded for him. 'His brother gave me all his broken bricks to build my house. They meant so much to me. Couldn't all those bits and pieces count as one brick for him? It would be an act of mercy, and this is the home of mercy, isn't it?'

'Your brother, whose honest work you thought so inferior, now buys you a second chance. You shall not be turned away. You shall stand outside here and meditate on your life below. But you shall not come in until you have done one good deed—it doesn't matter what it is, but it must be something.'

'I could have phrased that much better,' thought the critic. But he didn't say it aloud, so that was already something.

THE FIR TREE

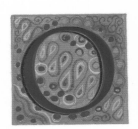

UT IN THE FOREST there was a pretty little fir tree. It had room to grow and fresh air, and all the sun it could want, and plenty of bigger companions, both firs and pines. But the little fir tree was in such a tearing hurry to grow that it took no notice of the warm sunshine or the fresh air, and didn't give a second glance to the village children gathering wild strawberries or raspberries. Sometimes when they had gathered the fruit they would sit down by the tree and say, 'What a sweet little tree!' But the tree had no time to listen to idle chatter.

By the next year the tree had grown taller, and the year after that it was bigger still—you could tell how old it was by counting the rings on its stem.

'Oh, if only I were as tall as the others,' sighed the little fir tree. 'Then I could spread my branches out and look out from my top over the wide world. The birds would nest in my branches, and when the wind blew I could bow my head just as grandly as the others.'

It took no pleasure in the sunshine, or the birds, or the rosy-tinted clouds that drifted overhead, morning and evening.

When winter came, and the sparkling snow lay all around, a hare might come bounding along and jump right over the little tree—it was so vexing! Two winters passed, and by the third, the tree was too tall, and the hares had to run round it. Oh, to grow, to grow, and become tall and old—that was the only joy in life, thought the tree.

In the autumn the woodcutters used to come and fell some of the largest trees. It happened every year, and the young fir tree,

now it was growing up, used to shudder when the mighty trees came crashing to the ground. With their branches lopped off you could hardly recognise them, they looked so thin and bare. They were loaded onto wagons and hauled away by horses.

Where were they going? What was going to happen to them?

In the spring, when the swallows and the stork arrived, the tree asked them, 'Do you know where they've been taken? Have you seen them?'

The swallows didn't know anything, but the stork nodded wisely and said, 'I think I know. As I flew here from Egypt, I saw a lot of new ships, with splendid tall masts, and I daresay that was them—they certainly smelled of pine. You'd have been proud of them, they were standing so straight.'

'Oh, I wish I were old enough to sail over the sea!' said the little tree. 'By the way, what is the sea?'

'It's too big to explain,' said the stork, and walked away.

'Enjoy your youth,' said the sunbeams. 'Have fun while you're growing up, and the fresh sap is rising in you. Rejoice in life!' And the wind caressed the tree and kissed it, and the dew wept tears over it, but the little fir tree didn't understand why.

As Christmas drew near, some younger trees were cut down—some of them no bigger than the restless little fir tree, who so longed to be up and doing. These young trees—always the very handsomest ones—kept their branches. They too were loaded onto wagons and hauled away by horses.

'Where have they gone?' asked the fir tree. 'They were no bigger than I am—in fact one was much smaller. Why did they keep their branches? Where will they end up?'

'We know! We know!' twittered the sparrows. 'We peeped in at the windows in the town. We know where they are. Oh, you can't imagine the glory and fame! They've been planted in the middle of a warm room, and garlanded with beauty—golden apples, honey-cakes, toys and hundreds of candles! We saw it.'

'And then?' asked the fir tree, trembling in every branch. 'And then? What happens then?'

'That's all we saw. But it was wonderful.'

'I wonder if I will take that golden road,' said the excited tree. 'That would be even better than sailing on the sea. Oh, I wish Christmas would come again soon. I'm just as tall and branchy as the ones that were chosen. I wish I were on the wagon now, or standing in a warm room in all my glory. And then—then there must be something even more beautiful to come. Why else would they decorate me? Something even bigger and better will happen—but what will it be? Oh, I can't bear the waiting! I'm all of a fluster.'

'Enjoy yourself with us,' said the air and the sunshine. 'Enjoy your youth and freedom.'

But the fir tree couldn't be happy. It was in such a hurry to grow. It stayed dark green through the winter and summer, and people passing by would say, 'What a handsome tree!'

That Christmas it was the first to be felled. The axe cut deep into its pith, and the tree fell to the earth with a sigh. It felt faint with pain and quite forgot to be happy. It just felt sad at leaving its home, where its roots were. Never again would it see its friends, the bushes and flowers—perhaps not even the birds. There was no joy in such a parting.

The tree didn't come to itself until it was unloaded in a yard with the other trees and heard a man say, 'What a beauty—that's the one for us!'

Then two servants in full livery came and carried the tree into a grand room. There were portraits hanging on the walls, and by the big tile stove stood two enormous Chinese vases with lions on their lids. There were rocking-chairs, silk-covered sofas, and big tables covered with picture books and toys worth ever so much money—or so the children said. The tree was planted in a barrel filled with sand—but you couldn't see that it was a barrel because it was draped with green baize and standing on a patterned rug. How the tree trembled! What was going to happen?

Then the servants and the young ladies of the family came to decorate it. On the branches they hung little nets cut out of fancy paper and filled with sweets; golden apples and walnuts that hung down as if they grew there; and over a hundred red, blue and white candles were fastened to the branches. Perched here and there were little dolls that looked just like people. And right at the top was a golden star made out of tinsel. It was glorious—quite glorious!

'Just wait for tonight,' they all said. 'Tonight it will really sparkle.'

'If only it were tonight now,' thought the tree. 'If only the candles were lit. What will happen then? Will the trees come from the wood to admire me? Will the sparrows peep through the windows? Will I take root here, and keep my decorations winter and summer?'

That's what the fir tree thought. It gave itself a barkache from sheer longing—and a barkache for a tree is as nasty as a headache is for us.

At last the candles were lit. How they blazed! It made the tree tremble, so that one of the candles set fire to a branch. Oh, that hurt!

'Heavens!' cried the ladies, and put out the fire.

Now the tree didn't dare tremble—what a strain that was! But it was afraid of losing its decorations. It was quite dazed by all the brilliance.

Then the big doors opened, and the children came rushing in, as if they meant to knock the tree over. The adults followed more quietly, with the littlest ones, who stood quite silent for a moment, before shouting in delight and running round the tree. One by one the presents were taken down.

'What are they doing?' thought the tree. 'What's going to happen now?'

When the candles had burned down, they were snuffed out, and then the children were allowed to plunder the tree. They rushed in so eagerly they made the branches creak—and if the tree hadn't been fixed to the ceiling at the top, where the gold star was, it would have toppled over.

The children danced round with their precious toys, and nobody took any notice of the tree, except their old nurse, who searched among the branches in case she could find an apple or a fig that the others had missed.

'A story! Let's have a story!' shouted the children, and they dragged a little fat man over to the tree. He sat down beneath it, saying, 'Now we're in the wood—and besides, the tree might like to hear the story too. Now I'm only going to tell one, so which shall it be—Ivedy-Avedy or Klumpy-Dumpy, who fell downstairs yet still came to the throne and married the princess?'

Some of them shouted, 'Ivedy-Avedy!' and some, 'Klumpy-Dumpy!' There was a lot of screaming and shouting. Only the fir tree was silent, and it was thinking, 'Is there something I should be doing?' But it had already done everything it was meant to do.

The little fat man told the story of Klumpy-Dumpy, who fell downstairs yet still came to the throne and married the princess. The children clapped their hands, and shouted, 'Tell us another!' They wanted Ivedy-Avedy, too, but they only got Klumpy-Dumpy.

The fir tree just stood still, deep in its own thoughts. The birds in the forest had never told a story like that of Klumpy-Dumpy, who fell downstairs, yet still came to the throne and married the princess. 'That's the kind of thing that happens in the world,' thought the fir tree, who believed every word, because the storyteller was such a nice man. 'Ah, who knows? Perhaps I'll fall downstairs too, and marry a princess!' And it looked forward to being decorated again next day with candles, toys, tinsel and fruit.

'I shan't tremble tomorrow,' it thought. 'I'll enjoy it all. And

I'll hear the story of Klumpy-Dumpy again, and maybe the one about Ivedy-Avedy, too.' The tree spent all night wrapped in such thoughts.

Next morning the maids and servants came in.

'Now everything will begin again,' thought the tree. But instead, they dragged it out of the room, up the stairs and into the attic, where they stowed it away in a dark corner where the sun never shone.

'What's the meaning of this?' the tree asked itself. 'What will I do here? What will I listen to?' And it leaned up against the wall, and stood there, thinking and thinking. It had plenty of time, as the days and nights passed by. No one came up there, and when at last someone did, it was only to put some old boxes up there. The tree was out of sight, and out of mind—utterly forgotten.

'It's winter now outside,' thought the tree. 'The ground will be hard and covered with snow. Of course they can't plant me now, so I shall have to shelter here until spring. How thoughtful people are! If only it weren't so dark and lonely up here. There's not even a little hare. Those were good times, out in the forest, with the snow on the ground, and the hare bounding along—yes, even when he jumped right over me, though I didn't like it at the time. Up here it's so lonely.'

Squeak! Squeak! said a little mouse, creeping along the floor, with another one behind it. The two mice sniffed at the fir tree, and clambered in and out among its branches. 'It is dreadfully cold,' they said. 'But otherwise this is a fine place to be. Don't you think so, old tree?'

'Less of the "old",' said the fir tree. 'There are lots of trees older than I am.'

'Where do you come from?' asked the mice. 'What do you know?' They were full of questions. 'What's the most beautiful place on earth? Have you been there? Have you ever been to the larder, where the shelves are stacked with cheeses, and the ceiling is hung with hams—where you can dance on the tallow candles, and go in thin and come out fat?'

'Never heard of it,' said the tree. 'But I know the wood, where the sun shines, and the birds sing.' And the tree told them all about its young days. The mice had never heard anything like it. They listened closely and said, 'What a lot you've seen! How happy you must have been!'

'Me?' said the fir tree, and thought about what it had been saying. 'Yes, I suppose they were good times.' But then it told them about Christmas Eve, when it had been hung with sweets and candles.

'Ooh!' said the mice. 'You have been a lucky old tree!'

'Less of the "old",' said the fir tree. 'I've only this winter left the wood. I'm in my prime; it's only that I'm not growing just at the moment.'

'What lovely stories you tell,' said the little mice, and they came back the next night with four more mice who wanted to hear the fir tree tell stories. The more it told them, the more clearly it remembered everything, and thought, 'Those really were good times—and they'll come again, they'll come again. Klumpy-Dumpy fell downstairs, yet still came to the throne and married the princess—perhaps I'll marry a princess, too.' And then the fir tree thought of a little birch tree growing out in the forest, that was as pretty as a princess.

'Who's Klumpy-Dumpy?' asked the little mice. So the fir tree told them the whole story. It could remember every single word. The little mice could have jumped to the top of the tree they were so happy. The next night, many more mice came, and on Sunday, even a couple of rats—but they said the story wasn't up to much, which made the mice sad, for now they didn't like it so well, either.

'Is that the only story you know?' asked the rats.

'The only one,' replied the tree. 'I heard it on the happiest night of my life, though at the time I didn't realise how happy I was.'

'It's very boring! Don't you know any about bacon, or tallow candles? One about the larder?'

'No,' said the tree.

'Then thanks for nothing,' said the rats, and they went back home.

After that, the little mice stayed away too, and the tree sighed, 'It really was fun when they all sat round me, those perky little mice, and listened to what I had to say. Now that's over too. I must remember to enjoy myself when I'm taken out of here.'

But when would that happen? It was one morning, when people came up and rummaged in the attic. The boxes were pulled aside, and the tree was discovered. One of the men dragged it roughly down stairs and into the daylight.

'My life's beginning again!' thought the tree. It could feel the fresh air, the sunshine—now it was out in the yard. Everything happened so quickly that the tree forgot to look at itself, there was so much else to see. The yard opened on to a garden where everything was in bloom. The sweet-smelling roses were rambling over a trellis, the lindens were in blossom and the swallows were flying about, crying, '*Kvirre-virre-vit*—my husband's home!' But they didn't mean the fir tree.

'This is the life!' The tree shouted for joy and tried to stretch out its branches. But all its needles were withered and yellow.

The tree had been thrown into a corner among the nettles. But the gold tinsel star was still fixed to its top, and it glittered in the bright sunshine.

Playing in the yard were some of the happy children who had danced around the tree at Christmas and had so much fun. One of the youngest ran up and tore off the golden star.

'Look what I've found on that horrid old Christmas tree!' he shouted, stamping on its branches so that they snapped under his boots.

And the tree looked at the fresh garden and the beautiful

flowers, and then at itself, and wished that it had stayed up in the dark attic. It thought of its young days in the wood, of that joyous Christmas Eve, and of the little mice who had listened so happily to the story of Klumpy-Dumpy.

'It's all over, all over!' said the poor tree. 'I should have enjoyed myself while I had the chance. It's all over, over and done with!'

And a servant came and chopped the tree into small pieces, until there was quite a pile. It made a fine blaze in the kitchen, and it groaned so loudly that every groan sounded like a pistol shot. That brought the children in from the yard: they sat around the fire, shouting 'Bang! Bang!'

As it sighed and groaned, the tree thought of a summer's day in the forest, and a winter's night when the stars are shining. It thought of Christmas Eve and Klumpy-Dumpy, the only story it had ever heard or knew how to tell—and so the tree was burned to ash.

The children went back to the yard to play, and the littlest had on his chest the gold star that the tree had worn on the happiest night of its life. That was all over now, and it was all over with the tree, and the story too. All stories must come to an end.

THE TINDERBOX

EFT, RIGHT! LEFT, RIGHT!
A soldier came marching down the road. He had a pack on his back and a sword at his side. He was coming home from the wars.

On the way he met an old witch. She was so ugly, her lower lip hung right down to her chest. 'Good evening, handsome,' she said. 'I can see from your pack and your sword that you are a real soldier. How would you like to be rich?'

'I'd like it very much, old witch,' said the soldier.

'Do you see that big tree over there?' said the witch, pointing to a tree nearby. 'It's quite hollow inside. If you climb to the top, you can get in and lower yourself to the bottom. I'll tie a rope around your waist so I can pull you back up when you call.'

'Why should I do that?' asked the soldier.

'To fetch the treasure!' said the witch. 'Now, listen. When you get to the bottom you will find yourself in a wide passage lit by over a hundred lamps. You will see three doors, with keys in the locks. If you go through the first door you will see a large chest, guarded by a dog with eyes as big as saucers. But don't worry about him! I'll lend you my blue-and-white checked apron. Just spread it on the floor, and lift the dog down off the chest and onto the apron. Then you can open the chest and take out as many coins as you like. But they're only coppers. If you want silver, you'll have to go through the second door.

'Behind that is a dog with eyes as big as soup plates. But don't mind him! Just put him on the apron and take the money.

'Or if you'd prefer gold, go through the third door. The dog in

200

there is a bit of a caution—eyes as big as cartwheels! But don't worry. Just put him on the apron and he won't hurt you. Then you can take as much gold as you can carry.'

'That's all very well,' said the soldier, 'but what do you get out of it, witch? I've no doubt you'll want your cut.'

'No,' said the witch, 'I won't take a single penny. All I want is an old tinderbox, for its sentimental value. My granny left it behind by mistake last time she was down there.'

'Let's get on with it then,' said the soldier. 'Tie the rope around my waist.'

'There you are,' said the witch, 'and here is the apron.'

So the soldier climbed the tree and lowered himself down the hole in the trunk, until he came to the wide passage lit by over a hundred lamps, just as the witch had promised.

He opened the first door. *Oh!* There was the dog with eyes as big as saucers, glaring at him.

'Good dog!' he said. He set it down on the witch's apron, opened the chest and took as many copper coins as he could cram into his pockets. Then he shut the chest and lifted the dog back onto it.

He opened the second door. *Ah!* There was the dog with eyes as big as soup plates. 'Don't stare at me like that!' said the soldier. 'You'll strain your eyes.' And he set the dog down on the apron. When he saw all the silver coins in the chest, he threw away the copper ones and filled his pockets and his pack with silver.

He opened the third door. *Ugh!* There was the dog with eyes as big as cartwheels—and they were spinning round in his head!

'Good evening,' said the soldier, and he saluted, for he had never seen such a dog in his life. For a while the soldier just stood there looking at him, but then he said to himself, 'Enough of this!' and lifted the dog down onto the apron.

When he opened the chest—my goodness what a lot of gold there was! Enough to buy up the whole city of Copenhagen, and

all the gingerbread men and tin soldiers and rocking horses in the world. There was an absolute fortune.

So the soldier cast aside the silver coins and filled his pockets and his pack with gold instead, he even stuffed it down his boots and in his cap. He could hardly move—but he was rich!

He put the dog back on the chest, slammed the door behind him, and called up through the hollow tree, 'Pull me up, you old witch!'

'Have you got the tinderbox?' asked the witch.

'No,' said the soldier, 'I'd clean forgotten it.' He went back to fetch it, and then the witch hauled him up. Then he was standing back on the road, with his pockets and his pack, his boots and his cap filled with gold.

'What's so special about the tinderbox?' he asked.

'Mind your own business,' snapped the witch. 'You've got your money. Just give me the box.'

'Stuff and nonsense!' said the soldier. 'Tell me what it's for or I'll cut off your head.'

'No!' said the witch.

So he cut off her head. There she lay!

The soldier bundled up all his gold in the witch's apron and slung it over his shoulder, tucked the tinderbox in his pocket and set off to town.

It was a fine town, and the soldier checked into the finest hotel in the place. He stayed in the best rooms and ordered the choicest things on the menu, because now he was a rich man with money to burn.

The servant who cleaned his boots did think it was odd that such a wealthy man should have such shabby shoes—for the soldier hadn't had time to buy anything yet. But next day the soldier kitted himself out with smart clothes and new boots, and then he really looked the part of a fashionable gentleman. Everyone wanted to know him. They boasted to him about their town, and about their king and his beautiful daughter.

'I'd like to see her,' said the soldier.

'No one can see her,' they answered. 'She lives in a copper castle surrounded by walls and towers. The king doesn't let anyone in to see her, because it was foretold that she will marry a common soldier, and the king doesn't like that idea at all.'

'Wouldn't I like to get a look at her!' thought the soldier, but it was no use dreaming of that.

His life now was a merry one. And when he went to the theatre, or out riding in his carriage, he gave away lots of money to the poor, because he remembered when his own pockets had been empty.

Now that he was rich and well dressed, he had many friends. They all told him how generous he was, and that this was the mark of a true gentleman, and the soldier liked that. But as he was spending money like water and never earning any more, he was soon down to his last two coppers. He had to leave his fine suite and move to a poky little room in the attic. Now he had to polish his own boots and darn his own clothes. None of his new friends ever came to see him; they said there were too many stairs to climb.

One evening he was sitting in the dark, without even a candle, when he remembered that he had seen a candle stub in the tinderbox when he fetched it out of the tree for the old witch. So he got out the candle stub, and struck a spark from the tinderbox.

As soon as he had done so, the door sprang open, and there was the dog with eyes as big as saucers, saying, 'What is your command, master?'

'What's going on here?' thought the soldier. 'This is a funny sort of tinderbox. Can I have whatever I want?' And he said to the dog, 'Bring me some money!' It was gone and back in a flash, and when it returned it was carrying a big sack of copper coins in its mouth.

Now the soldier began to appreciate what a special tinderbox it was. If he struck it once it summoned the dog who guarded the copper coins, twice, the dog who guarded the silver; three times, the dog who guarded the gold.

So the soldier was able to move back into his old rooms and buy more fine clothes, and all his friends remembered him and took up with him just where they had left off.

One night he was sitting by himself and thinking about the princess. 'It's a shame that no one can see her. It doesn't matter how lovely she is if she's kept hidden away in that copper castle. If only I could see her!' And then he thought, 'Where's that tinderbox?'

He struck a spark, and the dog with eyes as big as saucers came. 'I know it's the middle of the night,' the soldier said, 'but all the same I'd like to see the princess, if only for a minute.'

Away went the dog, and before the soldier could think things over he had returned with the sleeping princess lying on his back. Anyone could see she was a true princess, she was so beautiful. The soldier kissed her. He couldn't help himself—he was a real soldier.

The dog ran straight back to the copper castle with the princess. At breakfast next morning she told her father and mother about the strange dream she had had. 'I was riding on a dog's back, and a soldier kissed me.'

The queen pursed her lips. 'A nice kind of dream that is!' she said. And she insisted that one of her ladies-in-waiting must watch over the princess that night, just in case.

The soldier longed to see the princess again, and so that night he sent the dog to fetch her. And although the dog was very fast, the old lady who was watching over the princess had just time to pull on her boots and run after it. She saw the dog go into a big house. *Aha!* she thought. She chalked a white cross on the door, so that she would be able to find it in the morning. Then she went home to bed.

When the dog carried the princess back to the castle, he noticed the white cross on the soldier's door. So the dog took some chalk and put a cross on every door in town. It was a clever thing to do, because now the lady-in-waiting would never find the right door.

The next morning the king and the queen, the old lady-in-waiting and all the court went out to see where the princess had been.

'Here it is!' exclaimed the king, when he saw a door with a cross in it.

'No, it's here, dear,' said the queen, who had seen another door with a cross.

'Here's one!'

'Here's another!'

Wherever they looked, every door had a cross. So they gave up.

But the queen had quick wits; she was good for more than just riding around in a carriage. She took her gold scissors and cut out some silk and sewed it into a pretty bag, which she filled with fine white flour. That evening, she tied the bag to the princess's waist and then made a tiny hole in it with her scissors, so that if the princess moved, flour would leak out.

That night the dog came once more to fetch the princess. The soldier loved her so. How he wished he were a prince so that he could marry her.

The dog never noticed the flour, which made a trail all the way from the castle to the soldier's room. So in the morning the king and queen could see where their daughter had been taken. They had the soldier arrested and thrown into prison.

And there he sat in the dark, with nothing to do but listen to them saying, 'You'll be hanged tomorrow!' It wasn't much fun. And what's worse, the tinderbox had been left behind at the hotel.

In the morning, the soldier looked through the iron bars of his cell and watched the people going out of town to the place where the gallows had been set up. The royal guards marched past to the sound of drums. Everyone was in a hurry to see him hanged.

Last of all was a shoemaker's apprentice, in his leather apron and slippers. As he rode along, one of his shoes fell off, and he stopped to put it back on right outside the window of the soldier's cell.

'Hey!' shouted the soldier. 'Apprentice! Not so fast! They can't start without me. If you will go to my room and fetch me my tinderbox, and be quick about it, I'll give you four coppers.'

The shoemaker's apprentice was very glad of the chance to earn four coppers, so he sprinted off at the double to fetch the tinderbox and bring it back to the soldier.

And now you shall hear what happened then.

The gallows had been set up outside the town gates, and all the guards and the people were standing around it. The king and the queen were sitting on their thrones opposite the judge and the whole council.

The soldier had climbed the ladder, and the executioner was just about to fasten the noose around his neck. Then the soldier spoke up. He said it was the custom to grant a condemned man's last request; all he wanted was to smoke one last pipe of tobacco.

The king couldn't say no to that. So the soldier took his tinderbox and struck it—once, twice, three times! And there stood all three dogs: the one with eyes as big as saucers, the one with eyes as big as soup plates, and the one with eyes as big as cartwheels.

'Help me now. I don't want to be hanged!' shouted the soldier.

And the dogs fell on the judge and the councillors, tossing them high into the air—so high that when they fell back to the ground, they broke into pieces.

'Not me!' shrieked the king, but the biggest dog picked up both the king and the queen and flung them up into the air like the others.

The royal guards were frightened out of their wits, and the people shouted, 'Little soldier, you shall be our king, and marry the princess!'

The soldier sat in the king's carriage, and the three dogs danced in front of it and barked, 'Hurrah!' The guards presented arms, while little boys whistled through their fingers.

So the princess married the soldier and became his queen, which was better than being locked up in a copper castle. The wedding feast lasted for a week, and the dogs sat at the table, staring about them with their great glaring eyes.

LITTLE IDA'S FLOWERS

'Y POOR FLOWERS are nearly dead!' said little Ida. 'Only last night they were so beautiful, and now they are withering.'

She showed them to the student who was sitting on the sofa. She was very fond of him, because he used to tell her wonderful stories and could cut amazing pictures out of a piece of paper—hearts with little dancers in them, flowers and great castles with doors that opened. He was a lighthearted young man.

'Why are they drooping so?' she asked.

'Don't you know?' replied the student. 'They've been dancing all night. They are exhausted; that is why they are hanging their heads.'

'But flowers can't dance,' said Ida.

'Oh yes they can,' said the student. 'After dark, when we are all tucked up in our beds, the flowers hop around quite gaily. They hold a ball nearly every night.'

'Can the little ones go to the ball too?' asked Ida.

'Yes, both the daisies and the lilies-of-the-valley can go.'

'And where do the loveliest flowers dance?'

'Do you remember the flower garden of the king's summer palace, where you go to feed bread to the swans? That's where the grand ball is held.'

'I went there yesterday with Mother,' said Ida. 'But there wasn't a leaf on the trees, and there were no flowers at all. Where can they have gone? There are so many in the summertime.'

'The king and queen move to the city for the winter, and as soon as they have gone, the flowers move into the palace and have a wonderful time. You should see them! The two loveliest roses go and sit on the throne and act the king and queen. The red cockscombs line up along both sides and bow, like gentlemen of the court. Then all the most beautiful flowers come in, and the grand ball begins. The blue violets are young naval cadets, and they dance with the hyacinths and crocuses, whom they call Miss. The tulips and the big yellow lilies are like old dowagers, and they keep an eye on things and make sure there's no hanky-panky.'

'But,' interrupted Ida, 'surely the flowers aren't allowed to hold a ball in the king's palace.'

'Nobody knows anything about it,' said the student. 'Once in a while the old night watchman who looks after the castle walks through it, but he carries a great bunch of keys, and when they hear the keys rattling, all the flowers hide. Sometimes the night watchman sniffs the air and thinks to himself, "I'm sure I can smell flowers", but he has never seen them.'

'Oh, what fun!' said little Ida, and she clapped her hands. 'But could I see the flowers?'

'Of course,' said the student. 'Next time you are there, just peep through the windows, and you'll be sure to see them. Only today I saw a long yellow daffodil reclining on a sofa, pretending to be a lady-in-waiting.'

'What about the flowers in the botanical garden—could they go to the ball? It's a long way.'

'Yes, they could. If flowers really want to, they can fly. That's what butterflies are—flowers that jumped off their stems, flapped their petals and flew away. Some of them never go back to their stems but grow real wings and flutter about all day. You must have often seen it.

'It may be that the flowers in the botanical garden have never heard what goes on in the palace. Next time you are there, lean

over and whisper to one of the flowers, "There's a grand ball at the summer palace tonight", and then just wait and see. Flowers can't keep a secret; they'll whisper it from one to another, and at nightfall they'll all fly away. The professor who looks after them will go into the garden and find all the flowers gone. That will give him something to think about!'

'But how can the flowers tell each other about the ball? They can't speak.'

'Not in words,' said the student. 'They communicate by mime. You must have seen them nodding and swaying in the breeze. They can understand each other just as well as we can by talking.'

'Does the professor understand them?' asked Ida.

'He most certainly does! Why, one morning he went into the garden and saw a hulking great stinging nettle rustling its leaves at a pretty little red carnation. It was saying, "Be mine!" Now the professor doesn't like that kind of talk, so he rapped the nettle over its fingers—its leaves, you would call them. But the nettle stung him, and ever since the professor has been afraid to touch a nettle.'

Ida laughed. 'What fun!'

But the grumpy old councillor who was also sitting in the room said, 'Fancy filling a child's head with such rubbish!' He didn't like the student one bit. When the student made one of his funny papercuts—it might be of a man hanging from a gallows with a heart in his hand, who had been condemned for stealing hearts, or an old witch riding on a broomstick, with her husband balanced on her nose—the councillor would always mutter, 'Such rubbish to put into a child's head! What tomfoolery!'

But Ida thought what the student had said was very funny, and she kept on thinking about it. She was sure that the flowers were hanging their heads because they were tired out from dancing all night. She took them over to the little table where her playthings were, and where her doll Sophie was sleeping in her cradle. Ida said, 'You must be a good doll, Sophie, and let the flowers sleep in your bed tonight, for they are ill and need to be made better. You can sleep in the drawer.' Sophie never said a word, but she looked cross at having to give up her bed to the flowers.

Ida laid the faded flowers in her doll's bed, tucked them in and told them to lie quiet while she made them a cup of tea. 'You'll feel much better in the morning,' she said. Then she drew the curtains around the bed so that the sun wouldn't shine in their eyes.

All that evening she kept thinking about what the student had told her. At bedtime, she went to the window and peeped behind the curtains at her mother's tulips and hyacinths in their pots, and whispered, 'I know where you are going tonight.' The flowers acted as though they hadn't understood; they never stirred a leaf. But Ida knew what was what.

Once she was in bed, Ida lay awake thinking how lovely it would be to see the beautiful flowers dancing in the king's palace. 'I wonder if my flowers have really been there?' she thought, and then she was asleep.

In the middle of the night, she woke; she had been dreaming about the flowers, and how the councillor had scolded the student for filling her head with rubbish. It was very quiet in her bedroom; the night-light was burning on the table beside her; her mother and father were asleep.

'I wonder if my flowers are still lying in Sophie's bed,' she thought. 'I would love to know!' She sat up in bed and looked through the open door to the room in which the flowers were. She thought she could hear a piano playing, soft and sweet.

'Now all the flowers are dancing. Oh! If only I could see them!' But she didn't dare get up, for fear of waking her mother and father.

'If only they would come in here!' she wished. But the flowers never came, though the beautiful music kept playing. She couldn't bear it any longer. She crept out of bed, tiptoed to the door and looked into the next room.

There was no night-light, but it wasn't dark, because the moon was shining through the window onto the floor. It was nearly as bright as day. All the tulips and hyacinths were standing in two long rows on the floor; they had left their flowerpots behind on the windowsill. The flowers danced so prettily on the floor, holding on to each other's leaves and swinging each other around.

A tall yellow lily was playing the piano. Ida remembered seeing it in the garden that summer, because the student had said, 'It looks just like Miss Lena!' And although everyone had laughed at him then, Ida now thought that the flower did look just like Miss Lena; it had the same trick of turning its face from side to side as it played, and nodding in time to the music.

None of the flowers noticed little Ida.

Now a tall blue crocus leaped right up onto the table and drew back the curtains from the cradle where the sick flowers were lying. They looked quite well again, and they wanted to join in. The old porcelain chimney sweep with the chipped chin stood up and bowed to them, and then they were swept off into the dance.

Something fell from the table with a crash. It was a bundle of sticks tied together with ribbons, which had been given to Ida for a carnival parade. It thought it was a flower too; and it did look fine, with its ribbons flying. It had three legs, and it could dance the mazurka, which none of the flowers could do because they couldn't stamp.

Now there was a little wax doll tied to the top of this bundle of sticks, wearing a wide-brimmed hat just like the councillor's. All at once, this doll seemed to swell up, and it boomed, 'Fancy filling a child's head with such nonsense! What tomfoolery!' It really did look just like the councillor, and Ida couldn't help laughing.

The bundle kept dancing all this time and whipping at the wax doll with its ribbons, so that the doll had to dance too, until the soft-hearted flowers begged it to stop.

Then came a knocking from the drawer. The little porcelain

chimney sweep managed to open it a crack, and Sophie the doll poked her head out. 'Is there a ball going on? Why wasn't I told?'

'May I have the pleasure of this dance?' asked the sweep.

'You? Dance with me?' said Sophie, and she sat down on the open drawer with her back to him. She thought that one of the flowers would ask her to dance; but none of them did. The chimney sweep had to dance on his own, and he didn't do badly at all.

Sophie coughed—*ahem! ahem!*—but still none of the flowers noticed her. So she let herself fall to the floor. She landed with a crash, and all the flowers ran up to her to ask whether she had hurt herself; Ida's flowers were especially concerned. But Sophie wasn't hurt in the slightest. Ida's flowers said thank you for the loan of the bed, and Sophie said they were quite welcome, and she was perfectly happy in the drawer. Then all the flowers danced around her in the middle of the floor, where there was a great splash of moonlight.

Sophie told the flowers they could keep her bed, but they replied, 'Thank you, but we shan't need it. We don't live long; we shall be dead by the morning. Ask Ida to bury us in the garden, where the canary is buried. Next year we shall come to life again, and be even prettier.'

'You mustn't die,' said Sophie, and she kissed the flowers.

At that moment the door of the drawing room opened, and a troop of lovely flowers came dancing in. Ida could not think where they could have come from, if not from the king's palace. Two beautiful roses wearing crowns led the way. They were the king and queen. Behind them came the stocks and carnations, bowing to the company. There was even a band—poppies and peonies blowing on the pods of sweet peas until they were red in the face, and bluebells tinkling like real bells. It was a funny sort of orchestra.

At the end of the throng came all the dancing flowers—violets, daisies and lilies-of-the-valley. It was lovely to see how they kissed each other at the end of the dance.

At last they said goodnight to one another, and little Ida crept back to bed, to dream of everything she had seen.

Next morning when she woke, she ran straight to the doll's cradle to see if the flowers were still there. They were, but they had withered and died. Sophie was still in the drawer; she looked very sleepy.

'Do you have something to tell me?' asked Ida; but Sophie just looked stupid and didn't say a word.

'You're very naughty,' said Ida, 'and yet all the flowers danced with you.' Then she took a cardboard box with a picture of a bird on it and laid the flowers in it, saying, 'When my cousins come from Norway, we shall bury you in the garden, so that you will come up again next year.'

Ida's cousins were two lively boys called Jonas and Adolph. Their father had given them new bows and arrows, and they brought those with them to show Ida.

She told them all about the poor dead flowers, and the two boys came to the funeral. They walked in front, with their bows slung over their shoulders, and Ida followed with the dead flowers in their pretty coffin. They dug a hole in the corner of the garden. Then Ida kissed the flowers, and she laid them in the ground in their box. As they didn't have a gun or a cannon, Jonas and Adolph shot arrows over the grave.

THE LITTLE MERMAID

AR OUT TO SEA the water is as blue as the petals of the loveliest cornflower and as clear as the purest glass; but it is deep, deeper than any anchor can reach. Countless church steeples would have to be piled one on top of the other to stretch to the surface from the seabed. That's where the sea folk live.

Now you mustn't imagine that the bottom is just bare white sand; not at all. Wonderful trees and plants grow down there, with stems and leaves so sensitive that they curl and sway with the slightest movement of the water, as if they were living creatures. Fish, large and small, flit through the branches just like birds in the air up here.

At the very deepest point lies the palace of the Sea King. Its walls are of coral, and the long, pointed windows are of the clearest amber. The roof is made of cockle shells that open and shut with the play of the waves. It's lovely to see, because nestling in each shell is a shining pearl, any one of which would be the pride of a queen's crown.

The Sea King had been a widower for many years, but his old mother kept house for him. She was a wise old lady, but rather too proud of being royal; that's why she always wore twelve oysters on her tail, when the rest of the nobility were only allowed six. Aside from that she was a praiseworthy sort, and she took very good care of her granddaughters, the little sea princesses.

217

THE LITTLE MERMAID

There were six of them, all beautiful, but the youngest was the loveliest of them all. Her skin was pure and clear as a rose petal, and her eyes were as blue as the deepest lake. But like all the others, she had no legs—her body ended in a fish's tail.

All the livelong day they would play down there in the palace, in its spacious rooms, where living flowers grew from the walls. When the great amber windows were open, the fish would dart in and out, just as swallows do up here, and they would eat out of the princesses' hands and let themselves be petted.

Outside the castle was a great park with trees of deep blue and fiery red; their fruits shone like gold, and their flowers glowed like flames among the flickering leaves. The earth was of the finest sand, but blue as burning sulphur. Everything was suffused with blue, so that you might think you were high up in the air, with sky above and below you, rather than down at the bottom of the sea. When the sea was calm, you could glimpse the sun up above, like a crimson flower from which light came streaming down.

Each little princess had her own patch of garden, where she could plant whatever she fancied. One made a flowerbed in the shape of a whale; another in the shape of a mermaid like herself. But the youngest princess made hers into a circle and filled it with flowers that shone red like the sun. She was a strange child, quiet and thoughtful. Her sisters' gardens were full of oddments salvaged from shipwrecks, but she had only the statue of a handsome boy in hers. It was carved from clear white marble, and it had sunk to the bottom of the sea when the ship that was carrying it was lost. Beside this statue she planted a rose-red weeping willow, which soon grew tall enough to shade the statue with its overhanging branches. In the play of violet shadows on the blue sand, it looked as if the statue and the tree were embracing.

The princesses liked nothing more than to listen to stories of the world above. The old grandmother had to tell again and again everything she knew about ships, and towns, and people, and

219

animals. The youngest princess was particularly taken with the idea that in the world up above flowers were scented, for at the bottom of the sea they had no smell at all. She also liked to hear about the green forest, and how the fish that swam among the branches could sing so beautifully. Her grandmother called birds 'fish'—otherwise the princesses wouldn't have understood, for they had never seen a bird.

'When you turn fifteen,' their grandmother would say, 'you too will be able to swim to the surface and sit on rocks in the moonlight to watch the great ships sailing by. If you dare, you can swim close enough to the shore to see woods and towns.'

The following year the oldest of the sisters would be fifteen. The others were each spaced about a year apart, so that the youngest would have to wait another five whole years before she was allowed to swim up from the seabed and take a look at us. But each sister promised the others she would come back after her first day on the surface and tell of all the exciting things she had seen. For their grandmother didn't tell them nearly enough—there was so much they wanted to know.

None of them was so full of yearning as the youngest—the one who had the longest time to wait, and who was so quiet and thoughtful. Many a night she stood at the open window and gazed up through the dark blue water. She could make out the moon and the stars, though they were pale and blurry beneath the sea. If a black cloud passed over, she knew it must be either a whale swimming overhead or else a ship sailing along the surface; the passengers and crew never dreaming that a lovely mermaid stood in the depths below them and stretched her white hands out to them.

Now the oldest sister was fifteen, and free to swim up to the surface. When she came back she had hundreds of things to tell. The loveliest thing of all, she said, was to lie in the moonlight on a sandbank when the sea was calm and look across to a seaport town, with its lights twinkling like stars and music playing, and all the clatter of carts and people; she loved to watch and listen, and to see the church spires and hear the bells ringing. She longed to go there, though she knew she never could.

The youngest princess hung on her every word. Late in the evening, as she stood dreaming at the open window and gazing up through the water, she thought so hard about the town that she imagined she could hear the church bells chime.

Next year the second sister got her freedom. She surfaced just as the sun was setting, and the sight was so ravishing she could barely describe it. The whole sky had been a blaze of gold, she said, and as for the clouds—she couldn't find words to capture their beauty as they sailed over her head, streaked with crimson and violet. A flight of wild swans had flown into the setting sun, as if drawing a white veil across the water. She had swum after them, but as the sun sank, so the vision of sea, sky and cloud had faded.

The third of the sisters was the most daring of them all. She swam right inland up a broad river. She saw green hills covered with vines, distant castles, and farms hidden in the forest. She heard the birds singing, and the sun was so hot that she was often forced to dive back under water to cool her burning face. In a small cove she had come upon a group of human children splashing in the water, quite naked; but when she tried to play with them, they ran off in alarm. Then a little black animal—it was a dog, but she didn't know that—had come and barked at her so furiously that she took fright and headed out to sea. But she would never forget those magnificent woods and green hills, and those sweet little children who tried to swim in the water even though they had no tails.

The fourth sister was not so bold. She stayed well away from shore, and she said that there wasn't anything more beautiful than the open sea, with nothing for miles around and the sky above like a great glass bell. She had seen ships, but so far away they looked like seagulls. She had swum with the dolphins, who had turned

somersaults for her, and the huge whales had sprayed jets of water into the air, like so many fountains.

The fifth sister's birthday fell in winter, so she saw something none of her sisters had seen. The sea looked quite green, and great icebergs were floating in it. They looked like pearls, yet each one was larger than a church tower. They had the strangest shapes, and they sparkled like diamonds. She had seated herself on one of the largest, and all the sailors had steered away in fear as they sailed past the iceberg where she sat with her long hair streaming in the wind. By evening a storm was blowing. The dark waves lifted the icebergs high up, and lightning flashed red on the ice. The ships had furled their sails and waited out the storm in terror, while she sat calmly on her iceberg and watched the blue lightning zigzag into the glittering sea.

The first time any of the sisters was allowed to go to the surface she was always delighted to see so many things that were new and beautiful. But when they were older and could go any time they liked, they soon lost interest; they wanted to be back home. To them, the bottom of the ocean was the most beautiful place of all.

Still, many an evening the five sisters would link arms and rise to the surface together. They had lovely voices—more hauntingly beautiful than any human voice—and when a storm was blowing and they thought ships might be wrecked, they would swim in front of them and sing about all the wonders waiting at the bottom of the sea. Their song told the sailors not to be afraid of coming down— but the sailors could not make out the words in the howling storm. Nor did they ever see any of the delights of which the princesses sang, for when the ship sank the crew were drowned, and they came only as dead men to the palace of the Sea King.

When the sisters floated up to the surface like this, arm in arm, their little sister stayed behind all alone. As she watched them go she would have cried, but a mermaid has no tears, and so she suffers all the more.

'If only I were fifteen!' she sighed. 'I know that I shall love the world up there, and the people who live in it.'

And then at last she *was* fifteen.

'There now! We're getting you off our hands at last,' said her old grandmother. 'Let me dress you up like your sisters.' She set a garland of white lilies in her hair; each petal was half a pearl. Then she made eight big oysters pinch fast onto her tail, to show that she was a princess.

'Ow! That hurts,' said the little mermaid.

'One must suffer to be beautiful,' said her grandmother.

The little mermaid would have gladly swapped her heavy garland of pearls for some of the red flowers from her garden, which suited her much better, but she didn't dare.

'Goodbye,' she said, and she floated up through the water as lightly as a bubble.

The sun had just set when she lifted her head above the water. The clouds still gleamed rose and gold, and in the pale pink sky the evening star shone clear and bright. The air was soft and fresh, and the sea was perfectly calm. A large three-masted ship lay close by. Only one sail was set, because there wasn't a breath of wind. The sailors were sitting idly in the rigging; below on the deck there was music and singing, and as the evening grew dark hundreds of lanterns were lit, like so many flags.

The little mermaid swam to a porthole and the waves lifted her up so that she could see the smartly dressed people inside. The handsomest of all was a young prince with jet-black eyes. This was his sixteenth birthday, and that was the cause of the celebrations. The sailors were dancing up on the deck, and when the young prince appeared, a hundred rockets shot up into the sky and turned the night back into bright day.

The little mermaid was scared and ducked back beneath the water, but she soon surfaced again. It felt as if the stars were falling out of the sky. She had never seen such fireworks. Great

suns were spinning around, fiery fish were darting about the blue air, and all this glitter was reflected back from the clear mirror of the sea. The deck of the ship was so brightly lit that you could see every rope. How handsome the young prince was! He was laughing and smiling and shaking hands with everyone, while music rang out into the night.

It grew late, but the little mermaid could not take her eyes from the ship, and the handsome prince. The lanterns were put out; the rockets were finished; no more cannons were fired. Yet deep beneath the sea there was a murmuring and grumbling. Still the mermaid rocked up and down on the waves to look into the cabin.

The ship gathered speed; more sails were unfurled. The waves became choppy, and clouds began to mass; in the distance there were flashes of lightning. A storm was brewing.

The sails were taken in, and the ship was tossed about by the huge waves that rose like black mountains high above the masts. The ship was like a swan diving down into the troughs of the waves and riding high on their crests. The little mermaid watched it all with glee—she thought it was great fun. But it was no joke for the sailors. The ship creaked and cracked, and its stout timbers shivered as the raging sea pounded against them. Suddenly the main mast snapped like a stick, and then the ship keeled over on her side as water poured into the hold.

Now the little mermaid could see that the sailors were in danger; she herself had to watch out for planks and bits of wreckage that were floating in the water. For a moment it was so dark she couldn't see a thing; then lightning flashed and she could make out the desperate figures on board. It was every man for himself. She looked frantically for the young prince, and caught sight of him just as the ship broke up and sank into the sea. For a split second she was filled with joy. Now he was coming to her! But then she remembered that men cannot live in the water, and that he could only come to her father's palace as a corpse.

'No! He must not die!' She flung herself forward, heedless of the drifting beams that threatened to crush her, and plunged into the turbulent waves again and again until she found the prince. He was barely able to keep afloat in that heaving sea; his arms and legs were tired out. He closed his beautiful eyes, and he must certainly have drowned if the little mermaid had not come to him. She held his head above water and let the waves carry the two of them where they would.

By morning the storm was over. Not a trace of the ship remained. The sun rose up red and glorious from the waves, and it seemed to bring a touch of life to the pale face of the prince, though his eyes remained shut. The mermaid kissed his forehead and stroked his wet hair. She thought he looked like the marble statue in her garden. She kissed him again and wished with all her heart that he might live.

Now she could see dry land ahead and high blue mountains with snow-covered peaks. Down by the shore there were green woods and a little whitewashed church or monastery, the little mermaid didn't know which. Orange and lemon trees grew in the garden, and by the gate were tall palms. There was a little bay with deep water right up to the shore, and the mermaid swam into it with the handsome prince and laid him on the white sand in the sun, taking care that his head was out of the water.

Now bells rang out from the building, and some young girls came out to walk in the garden. So the little mermaid swam out to some foam-flecked rocks and hid behind them, so that she could wait for someone to come and help the poor prince.

Quite soon a young girl came by. She seemed startled to see the half-drowned figure, but only for a few seconds; then she went and fetched help. The mermaid saw the prince revive and smile at those around him. He didn't smile at her; he didn't even know that she had rescued him. She felt empty. After he had been taken into the white building, she dived down into the water and returned sorrowing to her father's palace.

She had always been quiet and thoughtful; now she was even more so. Her sisters asked her what she had seen on her first visit to the surface, but she wouldn't say.

On many evenings, and many mornings, she went back to the place where she had left the prince. She saw the fruits in the garden grow ripe and be harvested. She saw the snow melt from the mountaintops, but she never saw the prince, and so she always went home even sadder than before.

Her one comfort was to sit in her little garden with her arms wrapped around the beautiful marble statue that reminded her so much of the prince. She never tended the flowers, and they grew wild and tangled, climbing and interweaving until they shut out all the light from the garden.

At last she could bear it no longer and told one of her sisters her story; so before long all the sisters knew about it—but nobody else, except for a few mermaids who only told their closest friends. And it was one of these who found out who the prince was. She too had seen the birthday party on the ship, and she knew where he came from and where his kingdom lay.

'Come on, little sister,' said the other princesses, and with their arms twined around each other's shoulders they rose up through the sea to surface outside the prince's palace.

The palace was built of pale yellow stone, with great flights of marble steps, one of which stretched right down to the sea. Gilded domes capped the roof, and between the pillars around the building were lifelike marble statues. Through the clear glass of the high windows you could see right into the state rooms with their precious hangings and tapestries and wonderful paintings. In the middle of the biggest room a great fountain played, splashing its water right up to a glass dome in the roof. The sun shone down through the glass onto the fountain and the beautiful plants that grew in it.

Now that she knew where he lived, she went there many an

evening and many a night. She swam closer than any of the others dared—right up the narrow canal into the shadow cast by the prince's marble balcony. There she would gaze at the young prince, who believed himself all alone in the moonlight.

Often in the evening she saw him sailing in his fine boat, with its banners flying and music playing. She peeped from behind the reeds on the shore, and if anyone caught sight of her long silver veil when it was caught by the breeze, they only thought it was a swan spreading its wings.

Many a time, late at night, when the fishermen were casting their nets by torchlight, she heard them speaking well of the young prince, and that made her glad, for she had saved his life when he lay drifting half-dead on the waves. She remembered how his head had rested on her breast, and how fiercely she had kissed him. But he knew nothing about that; he never dreamed she existed.

She became fonder and fonder of human beings, and longed to join them. Their world seemed so much larger than hers. They could sail across the oceans in ships and climb mountains high above the clouds. Their lands with their fields and forests seemed to stretch forever. There was so much she wanted to know; questions her sisters couldn't answer. So she quizzed her old grandmother for everything she knew about the upper world, as she called the countries above the sea.

'If human beings are not drowned do they live forever?' she asked. 'Or do they die, as we do in the sea?'

'Yes,' said the old lady, 'they must die. And their lives are far shorter than ours. We can live for three hundred years, but at the end we just turn to foam on the water—we do not even have a grave down here among our loved ones. We do not have immortal souls; there is no new life for us. We are like the green reeds—once they are cut, they will never be green again. But human beings have a soul which lives forever, even after their body has turned to dust. The soul rises through the air to the bright stars. Just as we rise up out of the sea and gaze on the upper world, so they rise up to unknown glorious regions that we shall never see.'

'Why have we no immortal soul?' the little mermaid asked sadly. 'I would give all my three hundred years if I could live as a human being for one single day and share in that heavenly world.'

'You must not think of such things,' said her grandmother. 'We are happier and better off down here than they are up there.'

'So I shall die, and drift as foam upon the ocean,' said the little mermaid, 'and never hear the waves again, or see the lovely flowers and the red sun. Is there nothing I can do to gain an immortal soul?'

'No,' said the old lady. 'Only if a human loved you more than his father and mother, and thought only of you, and let a priest take his right hand and put it in yours, while he promised to be true to you for all eternity, then his soul would flow into you, and you would share in human happiness. He would give you a soul, yet still keep his own. But that can never be. For what we think beautiful down here—your tail—is thought ugly up there. They prefer two clumsy props, called legs.'

The little mermaid glanced down at her fishtail and sighed.

'We must be content with what we have,' said the old lady, 'and make the best of our three hundred years. We should dance and be happy; for it's a long sleep after. Tonight, let's hold a court ball!'

It was a magnificent affair, the like of which has never been seen on earth. The walls and ceilings of the great ballroom were made of glass—quite thick, but perfectly clear. Several hundred enormous shells, rose red and grass green, were ranged as lamps on either side, and their blue flames lit up the whole room. Light spilled through the glass walls into the sea outside, where countless fish could be seen swimming about, their scales glowing purple, silver and gold.

Through the middle of the ballroom flowed a broad swift stream, on which the sea folk danced to their own sweet songs. No humans have such lovely voices, and the little mermaid sang most beautifully of all. The others clapped their hands for her, and for a moment she felt a thrill of joy, for she knew that she had the most beautiful voice of anyone on land or sea. But her thoughts soon returned to the world above, for she could not forget the handsome prince and her grief that she did not, like him, have an immortal soul. So she crept out of her father's palace, and while everyone else danced and sang, she sat alone in her gloomy little garden.

From up above she heard the sound of a horn echoing through the water. 'There he is,' she thought, 'sailing so far beyond my reach, though I love him more than my father and mother, though he is always in my thoughts, though I would place my life's happiness in his hands.

'To win his love, and gain an immortal soul, I would dare anything! While my sisters are dancing in the palace, I will go to the sea witch, though I have always feared her, and ask her to help me.'

And so the little mermaid left her garden and swam to the place where the sea witch lived, on the far side of a raging whirlpool. She had never gone that way before. No flowers grew there; no sea grass; nothing but bare sand until she reached the fearsome whirlpool, which was twisting and turning like a millwheel, dragging everything it could clutch down into the deep. She had to brave those roaring waters to reach the sea witch's domain. Once through the whirlpool, the path lay over a swamp of hot, bubbling mud, which the sea witch called her peat bog. Beyond this lay the witch's house, deep in an eerie forest.

The trees and bushes in this forest were all what they call polyps—half beast and half plant. They looked like hundred-headed snakes growing from the ground. Their branches were long slimy arms with fingers like wiggling worms; they never stopped moving, from root to tip, and whatever they touched they wound round, never to let go.

THE LITTLE MERMAID

The little mermaid paused at the edge of this wood. She was so frightened she thought her heart would stop beating. She almost turned back. But then she thought of the prince and her longing for a human soul, and that gave her courage. She bound up her long flowing hair, so that the polyps could not snatch at it. Then she folded her hands together and dived forward, darting as fast as the fastest fish, in and out of the gruesome branches, which reached out their waving arms after her. She noticed that every one of them was holding tight to something it had caught: white skulls of drowned men, ships' rudders and seamen's chests, skeletons of land animals and—most horrible of all—a little mermaid whom they had taken and throttled.

Now she came to a swampy clearing in the wood, where enormous eels were writhing about, exposing their horrible white underbellies. Here the witch had built her house from the bones of shipwrecked men, and here she sat, letting a toad feed out of her mouth, just as some people do with a pet canary. She called the vile, slimy eels her little chickabiddies and pressed them close to her great spongy chest.

'I know what you're after,' she cackled, 'and you're a fool. But you shall have your wish, though it will only bring you misery, my pretty princess. You want to be rid of your fishtail and have two stumps instead, like humans have, and then the prince will fall in love with you, and you will marry him and win an immortal soul— isn't that so?' And the sea witch gave such an evil laugh that the toad and the eels fell away from her and lay there sprawling in the slime.

'You've come in the nick of time,' said the witch. 'Tomorrow I couldn't have helped you for another year. I shall prepare you a potion. Tomorrow morning go to the shore and drink it before the sun rises. Then your tail will split in two and shrink into what humans call "pretty legs". But it will hurt. It will be like a sharp sword slicing through you. Everyone who sees you will say you are the loveliest girl they have ever seen. But though you will move with a dancer's grace, every step you take will be like treading on a sharp knife—a blade that cuts to the bone. Will you suffer all this? If so, I can help you.'

'Yes,' said the little mermaid, though her voice trembled. She fixed her thoughts on the prince, and the prize of an immortal soul.

'Don't forget,' said the witch, 'when once you have taken a human shape, you can never again be a mermaid. You can never dive down to your father's palace, or to your sisters. Yet if you do not win the prince's love, so that he forgets his father and mother and thinks only of you, and lets the priest join your hands as man and wife, then you will get no immortal soul. On the morning after the prince marries another, your heart will break and you will be nothing but foam on the water.'

'My mind is made up,' said the little mermaid, as pale as death.

'Then there's the matter of my fee,' said the witch. 'I won't do it for nothing. Yours is the most beautiful voice of all the sea folk; I expect you think to use it to charm the prince. But that voice you must give to me. You must pay for my potion with the most precious thing you possess. For in return I must shed my own blood, to make the potion as sharp as a two-edged sword.'

'But if you take my voice,' said the little mermaid, 'what will I have left?'

'Your beauty, your grace and your speaking eyes,' said the witch. 'These are enough to win a human heart. Well? Have you lost your courage? Put out your little tongue, and I shall cut it off in payment, then you shall receive my precious potion.'

'Let it be so,' said the little mermaid.

The witch put a cauldron on the fire to prepare her potion. 'Cleanliness is a good thing,' she said, wiping out the cauldron with some eels that she had tied into a knot. Then she scratched her breast and let black blood drip into the cauldron. The steam that arose was full of terrifying shapes. Every moment the witch threw some horrible ingredient into the brew. When it came to

the boil, it shrieked like a crying crocodile. But when the potion was ready, it looked like the clearest water.

'There you are!' said the witch, and she cut off the little mermaid's tongue. Now she had no voice, and she could neither sing nor speak.

'If the polyps give you any trouble on the way back,' said the witch, 'just throw one single drop of this potion at them, and they will split apart.' But there was no need for that. When the polyps saw her, they shrank back in terror from the bright vial shining in her hand like a star. So the little mermaid passed safely back across the wood, the swamp and the roaring whirlpool.

She could see her father's palace. The lights were out in the great ballroom, everyone must be asleep. She didn't dare go and look, now that she had lost her voice and was going to leave them for ever. She felt her heart would break from grief. She crept into the garden and took one flower from the flower beds of each of her sisters, then she blew them each a farewell kiss, and rose up through the deep blue sea.

The sun had not yet risen when she reached the prince's castle and made her way up the marble steps. The moon shone bright and clear. The little mermaid drank the bitter, burning drink, and it was as if a two-edged sword had been thrust through her delicate body. She fainted away with the pain.

When the sun's rays touched her she awoke. The pain was still as sharp, but there in front of her stood the young prince. He fastened his jet-black eyes on her, and she cast her eyes down—and then she saw that her fishtail was gone. Instead she had the prettiest, slenderest legs that any girl could wish for. But she was quite naked, so she wrapped herself in her long flowing hair.

The prince asked who she was and how she had come there, but she could only look at him with her sweet, sad eyes—she could not speak. He took her by the hand and led her into the palace. Just as the witch had warned her, every step was like treading on a knife-edge. But she welcomed the pain. With her hand in the prince's, she felt she was walking on air. Everyone who saw her was charmed by her grace of movement.

She was given a lovely dress of silk and muslin, and everyone agreed she was the most beautiful girl in the palace. But she was mute, and could neither sing nor speak.

Beautiful girls dressed in silk and gold came and performed for the prince and his parents. One of them sang more prettily than the rest, and the prince clapped his hands and smiled at her. It made the little mermaid sad, for she knew that she had once sung far more beautifully. And she thought, 'Oh! If only he knew I had sacrificed my voice in order to be with him!'

Next the girls did a delightful dance. When they had finished, the little mermaid lifted her arms and stood on the tips of her toes. Then she began to float across the dance floor, with a grace that had never been seen before. There was such beauty in her movements, and her eyes were so full of feeling, that everyone was enchanted—especially the prince. He called her his little foundling. So she danced on and on, though every time her foot touched the floor she felt she was treading on sharp knives. The prince declared she must never leave him, and she was given a place to sleep outside his door on a velvet cushion.

The prince had a boy's velvet suit made for her, so that she could ride out with him on horseback. They rode through the sweet-smelling woods, where green branches brushed their shoulders, and the little birds trilled from among the cool leaves. She climbed high hills by the prince's side, and though her delicate feet bled for all to see, she only laughed, and followed him until they could see the clouds sailing beneath them like a flock of birds setting off for distant lands.

At night in the palace, while the others slept, she would go down the marble steps and cool her poor burning feet in the cold water. Then she would think of her sisters, down in the deep sea.

One night they came, arm in arm, singing the saddest song. She waved to them, and they recognised her at once. They told her how unhappy she had made them all. After that, they visited every night. Once she saw her old grandmother, far out to sea, and once her father, the Sea King, with his crown on his head. They stretched out their hands to her, but they did not venture near enough to speak.

Day by day the prince grew more fond of her. But he loved her only as a dear, good child—he never thought of making her his wife. And she had to become his wife, or she could never win an immortal soul. On the day he married another, she would dissolve into foam on the sea.

'Don't you love me best?' her eyes would plead, when he took her in his arms and kissed her lovely brow.

'You really are the dearest creature,' the prince would say, 'because you have the kindest heart. You are so devoted, and you remind me of a young girl I met only once, and shall probably never see again. I was on a ship that was wrecked, and the waves carried me to land close to a convent, which was home to many young maidens. The youngest of them all found me on the beach and saved my life. I saw her but twice, no more, yet I know she is the only one I could ever love, and you are so like her that you almost take her place in my heart. She belongs to the convent, but good fortune has sent you to me—we shall never be parted!'

'Ah! He does not know that I was the one who saved his life,' thought the little mermaid. 'He does not know that I was the one who carried him through the waves to the convent, or that I waited in the foam to see if anyone would come, and saw the pretty girl whom he loves better than me.' She gave a deep sigh, for she did not know how to cry. 'The girl belongs to the convent, so she will never come out into the world. I am with him every day. I will care for him and love him, and give up my life to him.'

But now people said that the young prince was to be married.

He was fitting out a fine ship to go and see the country of another king, but everyone said, 'It's not the country, it's the princess he's going to inspect.' The little mermaid just shook her head and smiled a secret smile, for she knew the prince's thoughts, and they didn't.

'I shall have to go,' he told her. 'My parents insist. But they cannot make me marry this princess, however pretty she is. I cannot love her. She will not remind me of the beautiful girl in the temple, as you do. If ever I chose a bride, I should choose you first, my silent foundling with the speaking eyes!' And he kissed her rose-red mouth, played with her long hair, and laid his head so near her heart that she was filled with dreams of human happiness and an immortal soul.

'Have you no fear of the sea, my silent child?' he said, as they stood on the deck of the splendid ship that was to take him to the nearby kingdom. He told the little mermaid how the sea could turn in a moment from calm to storm, and of the rare fish in the deep, and the strange sights divers had seen down there. And she smiled at his tales, for she knew better than he what lay beneath the waves.

In the moonlit night, when everyone but the helmsman at the wheel was asleep, she sat on the ship's rail and stared down through the clear water. She thought she saw her father's palace. On the topmost tower her grandmother was perched, with a silver crown on her head, staring up through the swift current at the passing ship. Then her sisters came to the surface, wringing their white hands, and looking at her with despair. She waved to them and smiled, she wanted them to know that all was well with her. But just then the cabin boy came out, and her sisters dived down; all he saw was foam on the water.

Next morning the ship sailed into port. Church bells rang out, and soldiers stood to attention with glittering bayonets. Banners were flying; everyone was on holiday. The prince was invited to one ball or party after another; but nothing was seen of the princess. It was said that she was being educated at a convent, learning how to be royal.

At last she arrived. The little mermaid was waiting for her, eager to judge her beauty. She had to admit that it would be hard to find a lovelier human girl. Her skin was so clear and delicate, and behind long dark lashes she had a pair of baby blue eyes.

'It is you!' cried the prince. 'You who saved me when I lay half dead on the shore.' And he clasped the blushing princess in his arms.

'Now I am too happy,' he told the little mermaid. 'My dearest wish—all I ever dared hope for—has been granted. You, whose heart is so true, will share my happiness.' And the little mermaid kissed his hand and thought her heart would break. His wedding morning would bring her death; she would be nothing but foam on the sea.

All the church bells rang, and heralds rode through the streets to announce the wedding.

On the altar, silver lamps burned rare oils. The priests swung censers with burning incense. The prince and princess gave each other their hands, and the bishop blessed them. The little mermaid, dressed in silk and gold, held up the train of the bride's dress. But her ears did not hear the music, and her eyes did not see the sacred ceremony. This night would bring her death, and she was thinking of all she had lost.

That evening, the bride and bridegroom went on board ship; cannons were fired, and banners flew. Right on the main deck, a sumptuous tent of scarlet and gold had been set up, with the softest cushions on which the happy pair would rest on that calm, cool night.

The sails swelled in the breeze, and the ship glided across the clear water.

As darkness fell, bright lamps were lit, and the sailors danced jigs and reels on the deck. The little mermaid remembered the first

time she had come to the surface, and had spied on just such a scene. Now she, too, whirled in the dance, gliding and soaring as a swallow does when it is pursued. How everyone cheered and clapped! Never before had she danced with such abandon. Sharp knives sliced her tender feet, but she scarcely felt the pain beside the raw wound in her heart. This was the last time she would see him—the handsome prince for whom she had given up her beautiful voice, turned her back on her home and family, and day after day endured pain without end. He had never noticed any of it. This was the last time she would breathe the same air as he, or look upon the deep sea or the starry sky. An everlasting night, without thoughts, without dreams, awaited her—for she had no soul, nor any hope of one.

The merrymaking lasted long into the night. The little mermaid danced and laughed, with the thought of death heavy in her heart. Then the prince kissed his lovely bride, she caressed his dark locks, and arm in arm they retired to their magnificent tent.

The ship was hushed and still, there was only the helmsman standing at the wheel. The little mermaid leaned her white arms on the rail and looked eastward for the first pink of dawn. The first ray of sun, she knew, would kill her.

Then she saw her sisters rising out of the water. Their faces were pale and grim, and their long lustrous hair no longer streamed in the wind—it had been cut off.

'We have given our hair to the sea witch, so that she would help us to save your life. She has given us this knife. See how sharp it is! Before the sun rises you must plunge it into the prince's heart. When his warm blood splashes over your feet they will join together into a fishtail, and you will be a mermaid once more. You can come down to us and live out your three hundred years before you melt into the salt sea foam. Hurry! Either he or you must die by sunrise. Our old grandmother is grieving; her white hair has fallen out through sorrow, just as ours fell before the scissors of the witch. Kill the prince, and come back to us! Hurry! Do you not see the red streak in the sky? In a few minutes the sun will rise, and then you must die.' And with a strange, deep sigh they sank beneath the waves.

The little mermaid drew aside the purple curtain of the tent and saw the beautiful bride asleep, with her head on the prince's breast. She stooped and kissed his handsome brow, glanced into the sky where the red light of dawn was glowing ever stronger, and looked back to the prince. In his sleep he was calling his bride by name; she alone filled his thoughts. The knife trembled in the mermaid's hand.

She flung it far out to sea. There was a glimmer of red as it fell, as if red drops of blood were splashing up from the water. One last glimpse of the prince through eyes half glazed by death, and she threw herself into the sea; she felt her body dissolving into the foam.

And now the sun came rising from the sea. It rays were so gentle and warm on the cold foam that the little mermaid did not feel the hand of death. She saw the bright sun and, hovering above her, hundreds of bright transparent creatures—she could see through them to the white sails of the ship and the pink clouds in the sky. Their voices were pure melody—so pure that no human ear could hear it, just as no human eye could see them. They had no wings—they were lighter than air. The little mermaid saw that she had become like them, and was floating free above the foam.

'Who are you?' she asked, and she had a voice again—a voice like theirs, so heavenly that no music could ever capture it.

'We are the daughters of the air!' they replied. 'A mermaid has no immortal soul, and she can never gain one unless she wins the love of a mortal. Her only chance of eternal life depends upon another. We daughters of the air are not given an immortal soul either, but by good deeds we can make our own soul. We fly to the hot countries, where plague gathers in the sultry air, and blow cool

breezes to dispel it. We carry the healing fragrance of flowers to the sick. If for three hundred years we do nothing but good, then we win an immortal soul, and a share in mankind's eternal happiness. You, poor little mermaid, have striven with all your heart. You have suffered, and endured, and have raised yourself into the world of the spirits of the air. Now, by three hundred years of good deeds, you can make yourself an immortal soul.'

And the little mermaid raised her translucent arms to the sun, and for the first time she shed a tear.

She heard life and movement from the ship. The prince and the princess were searching for her; they were gazing sadly into the foam, as if they guessed she had flung herself into the sea. Unseen, she kissed the bride's forehead, gave a smile to the prince, and then with the other daughters of the air she ascended to a rose-pink cloud that was sailing by.

'In three hundred years I shall rise like this into the kingdom of heaven,' she whispered.

'Maybe even sooner,' said one of the others. 'We enter unseen into human homes where there are children. Whenever we find a good child, who makes its parents happy and repays their love, it makes us smile with joy, and a year is taken from the three hundred. But if we see a mean and naughty child, then we must weep tears of sorrow, and every tear adds another day to our time of trial.'

THE EMPEROR'S
NEW CLOTHES

ANY YEARS AGO there was an emperor who was so mad about fashionable new clothes that he spent all his money on dressing up. He never inspected his army, or went to the theatre or drove through the countryside, unless he had a new outfit to show off. He had different clothes for every hour of the day, and at any time when you might say of another king, 'His Majesty is in the council chamber,' you could always say of him, 'The emperor's in his dressing room.'

The emperor's city was a hive of activity, and there were always strangers coming and going. One day a pair of swindlers turned up, claiming to be weavers. Their cloth, they boasted, was not just of the finest quality and design, but had the virtue of being invisible to anyone who was stupid or not fit to hold his job.

'What wonderful cloth!' thought the emperor. 'If I wore it, I would be able to find out which of my courtiers are unfit for their posts, and also be able to tell the clever ones from the stupid. Yes, I must have a suit made at once!' He handed over a large sum of money to the swindlers, so that they could start work straight away.

So the swindlers set up a loom and pretended to be weaving, though in fact there was nothing at all on their loom. They coolly demanded the finest silks and costliest gold thread, which they stuffed into their own packs, and then carried on working at the empty loom into the night.

'I wonder how they're getting on with my cloth,' thought the emperor. But there was one thing which made him feel uneasy, and that was that a man who was stupid or unfit for his job would not be able to see the cloth. Not that he had anything to fear, but all the same he thought it might be best to send someone else first to see how things were going. Everyone in the city had heard about the special virtue of the cloth, and they were all agog to find out how stupid or incompetent their friends were.

'I will send my honest old prime minister to the weavers,' thought the emperor. 'He'll be the best judge of the cloth, for he's got brains, and he's good at his job.'

So the honest old prime minister went to the room where the two swindlers were working away. 'Good Lord!' thought the old man, as he goggled at the empty loom. 'I can't see a thing!' But he kept that to himself.

The swindlers begged him to be so good as to come closer and tell them what he thought of the cloth. 'Do you like the design?' They pointed to the empty loom, but though the poor old man stared and stared he couldn't see a thing. 'Oh dear!' he thought. 'Does this mean that I am stupid? I never had an inkling, and no one else must either! Or perhaps I am unfit for my job? Whatever, no one must find out that I cannot see the cloth.'

'Now, do you like it or not?' asked one of the weavers.

'Oh, it's charming, absolutely delightful,' said the old prime minister, peering through his spectacles. 'What a gorgeous pattern! I shall tell the emperor that I am most pleased with it.'

'You're too kind,' said the swindlers. And then they described the pattern in detail, and the old prime minister listened carefully so that he could repeat it all to the emperor—which he duly did.

The swindlers now asked for more money, to buy silk and gold thread in order to finish the cloth. But it all went straight into their own pockets. Not a single thread was put on the loom—they just carried on weaving air.

Before long, the emperor sent a second official to see how work was progressing, and find out when the clothes would be ready. The same things happened to him as to the prime minister. No matter how hard he looked, he could not see anything on the empty loom.

'It's really beautiful, isn't it?' asked one of the swindlers.

'I'm not stupid,' thought the official, 'so I must be unfit for my job. If people found out, I'd be a laughing stock.' So he too praised the material which he couldn't see, and said how pleased he was with its subtle shades and beautiful design.

'It's quite exquisite,' he told the emperor.

The wonderful material was the talk of the town. At last, the emperor decided he must go and see it for himself while it was still on the loom. He took along a number of courtiers, including the two honest officials who had already described the cloth, to see the two swindlers working busily at their empty looms.

'Isn't it *magnifique?*' said the two honest officials. 'Just look at the pattern, Your Majesty.' And they pointed to the empty loom, sure that everyone else could see the cloth.

'What's this?' thought the emperor. 'I can't see anything! Am I stupid? Or am I unfit to be emperor? This is too awful for words.'

'Oh! It's wonderful!' he said. 'It is everything I hoped for.' And he gave a satisfied nod at the empty loom. He wasn't going to admit he couldn't see a thing.

All the others who were there were in the same boat. They could see nothing, but they all said what the emperor said: 'Oh! It's wonderful!' They told him he should have some clothes made from the magnificent material in time to wear them at the great procession that was soon to take place. 'Magnificent! Wonderful! Superb!' were the words on everyone's lips. They were all delighted. The emperor gave each of the swindlers a knighthood, with a medal to wear in his buttonhole, and the title 'Knight of the Loom'.

The swindlers sat up all night before the procession, with more than sixteen candles burning, so that people could see how hard they were working on the emperor's new clothes. They pretended to take the cloth off the loom, made cuts in the air with huge scissors, and sewed with needles that had no thread, and finally they announced, 'Look! The emperor's clothes are ready!'

The emperor came with his courtiers, and the weavers held out their arms as if they were carrying something, and said, 'Here are the trousers! Here is the jacket! Here is the cloak!' and so on. 'The whole suit is as light as a spider's web. You'll feel as if you've got nothing on; that's the beauty of the cloth.'

'Yes indeed!' said all the courtiers; but they couldn't see anything, for there was nothing to see.

'If Your Majesty would graciously take off the clothes you are wearing, we shall think it a privilege to help you into the new ones in front of the great mirror.'

So the emperor took off all his clothes, and the swindlers went through the motions of fitting him with his new suit, even pretending to fasten the train around his waist. The emperor turned this way and that, preening in the mirror.

'How elegant Your Majesty looks! What a perfect fit!' everyone exclaimed. 'What a triumph!'

Then the master of ceremonies announced, 'The canopy which will be carried above Your Majesty in the procession is waiting outside.'

'I am ready to go,' said the emperor. 'See how well my new clothes fit!' And he did a final twirl in front of the mirror, pretending to admire his fine clothes.

The chamberlains, who were to carry the emperor's train, fumbled on the floor looking for it. They didn't dare admit they couldn't see anything, so they pretended to pick the train up, and as they walked they held their hands in the air as if they were carrying it.

So the emperor marched in procession under the beautiful canopy, and all the people lining the streets or standing at their windows exclaimed, 'The emperor's new clothes are the best he's ever had! What a perfect fit! And just look at the train!' For no one wanted people to think that he couldn't see anything, and so was a fool or unfit for his job. Never had the emperor's clothes been such a success.

'But he hasn't got anything on!' said a little child.

'Listen to the little innocent!' said the father.

But the whisper passed through the crowd: 'He hasn't got anything on! There's a little child who says he hasn't got anything on!' And at last the people shouted with one voice, 'He hasn't got anything on!'

The emperor had the uncomfortable feeling that they were right. But he thought, 'I must go through with it now.' So he drew himself up to his full height and walked proudly on, and the chamberlains walked behind him carrying the train that wasn't there.

THE STEADFAST
TIN SOLDIER

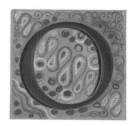NCE THERE WERE twenty-five soldiers, all brothers, because they were all made out of the same old tin spoon. They stood up straight with their muskets on their shoulders, very proud in their red and blue uniforms. The very first thing they heard in the world, when the lid of their box was taken off, was 'Tin soldiers!' It was a little boy who shouted it, with a clap of his hands. They were a birthday present, and he paraded them on the table.

All the soldiers were exactly alike, except one. He'd only got one leg, because he was made last, and the tin had run out. But he stood just as firm on his one leg as the others did on two, and he's the one this story is about.

There were plenty of other toys on the table where the tin soldiers were set out, but the one that really caught your eye was a paper castle. You could see through its little windows right into the rooms. Outside, tiny trees stood beside a little mirror, which was meant to be a lake. Wax swans swam on it, admiring their own reflections. It was a lovely scene—and loveliest of all was the girl who stood in the castle's open door. She too was cut out of paper, but her skirt was made of finest muslin, and as a shawl around her shoulders she wore a narrow sky-blue ribbon, fastened with a gleaming star the size of her face. She stretched out her arms, for she was a dancer, and kicked one leg so high that the tin soldier couldn't see it and thought she'd only got one leg, like him.

'That's just the wife for me,' he thought. 'But she's so grand. She lives in a castle. I have only a box, and there are twenty-five of us in that. There's no room for her. Still, I'll try to get to know her.' So he hid behind a snuff box that was on the table, where he had a good view of the charming dancer, poised with such perfect balance on one leg.

When night came, the other tin soldiers were put back in their box, and the children went to bed. Now it was time for the toys to play. They paid each other visits, waged wars and even held a ball. How the tin soldiers rattled in their box, trying to join in! But they couldn't get the lid off. The nutcracker turned somersaults, and the slate pencil kept score on the slate. They made such a row they woke the canary, and it started speechifying—in verse, too!

Only two never moved. The little dancer stayed on tiptoe with her arms outstretched, and the tin soldier stood steadfast on his single leg, and his eyes never left her for a moment.

And then the clock struck twelve, and *crash!* up jumped the lid of the snuff box. There wasn't any snuff inside, oh no. Out sprang a little black goblin. It was a jack-in-the-box.

'Tin soldier!' said the goblin. 'You keep your eyes to yourself.' But the tin soldier pretended not to hear.

'All right,' said the goblin. 'Just you wait till tomorrow.'

And whether it was the goblin's doing or just the wind, no one can say, but next morning, when the children got up, and the little boy put the tin soldier on the windowsill, the window flew open and the tin soldier fell out, head over heels, from three floors up. It was a fearful drop. He landed on his head with his leg in the air and his bayonet trapped between two cobblestones.

The maid and the little boy went to look for him there and then, but even though they nearly trod on him they didn't see him. If only he had called out, 'Here I am!' they would have found him, but he didn't think it right to make a commotion when he was wearing his uniform.

Now it began to rain, heavier and heavier till it was a real storm. And when it was over, along came two boys.

'Look!' said one. 'Here's a tin soldier! Let's sail him.'

So they made a boat out of newspaper and put the tin soldier in it, and away he sailed down the gutter, with the boys running by his side clapping their hands. Heavens above! What waves, what tides there were in that gutter. It had been a real downpour.

The boat plunged up and down and whirled round and round till the tin soldier was quite dizzy. But he stood fast. He never flinched, but looked straight ahead with his musket on his shoulder.

Suddenly the boat ducked into a gutter pipe. It was as dark in there as in his box at home.

'Where am I going now?' he wondered. 'Oh, it's all that goblin's fault. But if only the little dancer was by my side, I wouldn't care if it was twice as dark.'

Just then a huge rat, who lived in the pipe, darted out. 'Passport!' said the rat. 'Where's your passport?'

The tin soldier kept quiet and gripped his musket. The boat sailed on and the rat gave chase. *Ugh!* How he gnashed his teeth, screeching to floating bits of straw and wood, 'Stop him! Stop him! He's not paid the toll! He hasn't shown his passport!'

But the current swept faster and faster. The tin soldier could already spy daylight at the end of the pipe, but he could also hear a terrible roaring fit to frighten the bravest of men. Think of it: at the end of the pipe, the water gushed out into a great canal. It was as risky for him as it would be for us to plunge down a mighty waterfall.

He was so near there was no stopping. The boat raced out, and the poor tin soldier braced himself as stiffly as he could—no one could say he so much as blinked.

The boat spun round three or four times and filled with water to the brim. It had to sink. The tin soldier was in the water up to

his neck. Down, down sank the boat. The paper turned to mush, and the water closed over the tin soldier's head. He thought of the lovely little dancer whom he would never see again, and the words of an old song rang in his ears:

> *March on, march on to victory—*
> *Tomorrow you must die.*

The boat fell to bits, the soldier fell through—and at that very moment was swallowed up by a great fish.

Oh my! How dark it was in there! It was even worse than the gutter pipe, and a tighter fit, too. But the tin soldier was steadfast. He lay there, flat out, with his musket over his shoulder. Round and about swam the fish, with all sorts of twists and turns. Then it was still.

Suddenly a bolt of lightning seemed to flash through it. It was the clear light of day, and someone was exclaiming, 'A tin soldier!' For the fish had been caught and taken to market, and sold, and now it was in the kitchen where the cook had cut it open with a big knife.

She picked up the tin soldier round the waist and carried him between her finger and thumb into the living room. Everyone wanted to see the remarkable character who had voyaged inside a fish. But the tin soldier didn't let it go to his head.

They stood him on the table and—the world is full of wonders—there he was, back in the very room he'd set out from.

Here were the same children, the same toys on the table, the beautiful castle, the graceful little dancer. Still she balanced on just one leg, with the other held high in the air. She, too, was steadfast. The tin soldier was touched to the quick. He could have wept tin tears, if he hadn't been a soldier. He looked at her, and she looked at him, but they never said a word.

Suddenly, the little boy took the soldier and flung him into the stove. Why, he couldn't say. No doubt the goblin in the snuff box was at the bottom of it.

The tin soldier stood in a blaze of light. Whether he burned from the heat of the fire or the heat of his love he did not know. All his paint was worn away; whether from the hardships of his journey or the bitterness of his grief, no one could tell.

He looked at the little dancer and she looked at him. He felt himself melting away, but he was steadfast, with his musket on his shoulder. Then the door opened, a draft caught the dancer and she flew into the stove to the tin soldier. She flared and was gone. And then the tin soldier melted back into a lump of tin.

Next morning, when she raked out the ashes, the maid found him, shaped like a little tin heart. Of the dancer nothing remained, save the star from her breast, and that was burned as black as coal.

THE FLYING TRUNK

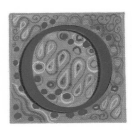NCE THERE WAS a merchant who was so rich that he could have paved the whole street with silver. But he didn't actually do that because he had other ideas about what to do with his money. Before he spent a copper coin, he made sure he would get a silver one back. That's the sort of merchant he was. A merchant he lived, and a merchant he died.

All his money now went to his son, who had a high old time with it. He went dancing every night, made paper kites out of folding money and skimmed gold pieces over the lake instead of stones. That's the way the money goes, and it went. Soon he had nothing left but four pennies, a pair of slippers and an old dressing gown. His friends wouldn't have anything more to do with him; they didn't want to be seen with him on the street. But one of them, in a friendly spirit, sent him an old trunk, with the advice, 'Get packing!'

A fat lot of good that was—he didn't have anything to pack. So he packed himself.

It was a strange trunk. As soon as you pressed the lock, it took off into the air. And that's what it did now! Up it flew, with the young man in it, up the chimney, through the clouds and off into the wide blue yonder.

The bottom of the trunk kept creaking, and the young man was scared it would fall to bits—and then, heaven help him, he'd have had to learn some fancy acrobatics fast. But at last he landed in Turkey.

He hid the trunk in the woods and walked into town. He felt right at home, as the Turks all went around just like him in dressing gowns and slippers. Then he met a nurse with a baby. 'Nurse,' he said, 'what is that big palace over there, with the high windows?'

'That is where the princess lives,' she replied. 'It has been foretold that she will be unlucky in love, so no one is allowed to visit her unless the king and queen are there.'

'Thank you,' said the merchant's son, and he went back to the wood, got into his trunk, flew up to the palace roof and crept in at the princess's window.

She was lying on her sofa asleep. She was so lovely that the merchant's son couldn't stop himself from kissing her. This woke her up, and she was scared out of her wits until he told her he was a god, who had come down to her from the sky. That cheered her up.

They sat side by side on the sofa, and he told her stories about her eyes. They were like dark deep lakes, he said, in which her thoughts swam like lovely mermaids. He told her about her forehead—it was like a snowy mountain, with wonderful caves full of treasure. And he told her about the stork, which brings dear little babies. Oh, he said wonderful things. So when he asked her to marry him, she said yes.

'Come back on Saturday,' she said, 'and have tea with the king and queen. They will be so proud when I tell them that I am going to marry a god. They love stories, so you must be sure to have a good one to tell them. My mother likes high-class stories with a proper moral, and my father likes funny ones that makes him laugh.'

'I shall bring a story as my wedding gift,' he said. Before they parted, the princess gave him a sword decorated with gold coins—those would come in useful!

So he flew off and bought himself a new dressing gown, and then he settled down in the woods to make up a fairy tale for the king and queen. It had to be finished by Saturday, and that's not as easy as it seems.

But at last the story was done, and Saturday had come.

The king and the queen and the whole court were at the princess's for tea; and the merchant's son was most gracefully received.

'Now you must tell us a story,' said the queen. 'One that is both profound and instructive.'

'And funny,' said the king.

'I'll try,' said the merchant's son.

This is the story he told. Listen to it carefully.

Once upon a time there was a bundle of matches, who were very proud because they came of such noble stock. Their family tree—of which each of them was but a chip—had been a huge old fir tree in the forest. So now, as they lay on a shelf between a tinderbox and an old iron pot, they reminisced about their glory days.

'Yes,' they said, 'those were the days. We were at the very top of the tree! Diamond-tea—that is to say, dew—every morning and evening, non-stop sunshine from dawn to dusk, and all the little birds eager to tell us their stories. We were so rich we could afford to wear our best green clothes all year round, while other trees spent the winter in rags and tatters. But at last the revolution came—that is to say, the woodcutter—and we were laid low. The family was split up. The tree trunk got a job as a mainmast on a schooner that can sail right round the world if it wants to; the branches had business here and there; and we were entrusted with the task of spreading light among the common people—that's what gentlefolk like us are doing down here in the kitchen.'

'It's not been like that for me,' said the iron pot which was next to the matches on the shelf. 'From the moment I came into the world I've been scrubbed and put on to boil—I've lost count of the times! My job's the foundation of the home—so I'm the most important one in it. My only respite is to sit on the shelf after I've been scoured clean and enjoy a little after-dinner conversation with my friends.

But apart from the bucket, which does get out to the well every so often, we're all real stay-at-homes. Of course the shopping basket does bring us all the gossip, but she's a regular firebrand, always jabbering on about the government and the people. Why, the other day her wild talk gave one old jug an a fit, and he fell down and broke into pieces.'

'You do rattle on,' said the tinderbox. 'Can't we just enjoy ourselves?' And he struck his steel against his flints so that the sparks flew.

'Yes,' said the matches. 'Let's discuss which of us is the most distinguished.'

'No, I don't like to talk about myself,' said an earthenware bowl. 'Let's tell each other stories. I will begin with a story of everyday life, something we can all relate to.'

And the bowl began, 'On the shores of the Baltic, where the Danish beech trees grow …'

'What a beautiful beginning!' exclaimed the plates. 'We're going to enjoy this!'

'There I spent my youth,' continued the bowl, 'in a quiet household where the furniture was always polished, the floors always scrubbed and we had clean curtains every fortnight.'

'How interestingly you put it,' said the feather duster. 'Your story has a woman's touch, there's something so pure and refined about it.'

'I feel that too!' said the water bucket, and she gave a little jump of pleasure, so that some of her water splashed onto the floor.

Then the earthenware bowl carried on with her story—and the middle and the end were just as exciting as the beginning.

The plates all rattled with joy, and the feather duster took some parsley and crowned the bowl with a garland. She knew that would make the others jealous, but she thought, 'If I crown her today, she'll crown me tomorrow.'

'I feel like dancing,' said the fire tongs—and what a dance!

When she kicked one leg up high, the old chair cushion split his seams. 'Don't I get a crown?' wheedled the tongs, and she did.

'Vulgar riffraff,' thought the matches.

Then someone called for a song from the tea urn, but the urn said it had caught a cold and could only sing if it was brought to the boil. But it was just giving itself airs, it never would sing unless it was at the table with the master and mistress.

Over on the windowsill was an old quill pen that the maid used. There was nothing remarkable about her except that she'd been dipped too far into the inkwell, which made her rather stuck-up. 'If the tea urn doesn't want to sing, she needn't,' said the pen. 'There's a nightingale in a cage outside, it can sing. Of course its voice is untrained, but we won't hold that against it this evening.'

'I don't think it's right,' said the tea kettle, which was a singer itself, and half sister to the urn, 'for us to listen to a foreign bird. Is it patriotic? I think the shopping basket should decide.'

'This makes me sick,' said the shopping basket. 'Sick to my stomach. What goings on! Isn't it about time we reformed the whole house and established a new order? That really would be something! I'll take full responsibility.'

'That's it, let's have a riot!' they all shouted—but just at that moment the door opened. It was the maid. They all stood still, no one made a sound. But there wasn't one of them who wasn't thinking, 'I really am superior to the others; if it had been left to me, this evening would have gone with a swing.'

Then the maid took the matches and lit the fire with them. My goodness, how they sputtered and blazed! 'Now everyone can see that we are the best,' they thought. 'How bright we are! How brilliant!'

And then they burned out.

'That was lovely!' said the queen. 'I really felt I was right there in the kitchen with the matches. You must certainly marry our daughter.'

'Absolutely,' said the king. 'Let's fix the wedding for Monday.'
Already they regarded the young man as one of the family.

On the evening before the wedding, the whole town was
illuminated. Cakes and buns were distributed to the crowd; and all
the little boys shouted 'Hurrah!' and whistled through their
fingers. It was wonderful.

'I suppose I'd better do my bit,' thought the merchant's son. So
he bought some rockets and whizzbangs and every sort of firework
he could lay his hands on, and flew up into the air with them.

Whoosh! They went off with a bang! Such a glorious spectacle
had never been seen before. The crowd nearly jumped out of their
skins, and they did jump out of their slippers. Now they were sure
it really was a god who was going to marry the princess.

As soon as the trunk came to earth, the merchant's son left it
in the woods and returned to town to hear what people were
saying about his performance—and that was only natural.

Everybody was talking about it. They all had their own views,
and they were all fired up about it.

'I saw the god himself,' said one. 'He had eyes like sparkling
stars, and a beard like a foaming torrent.'

'He wrapped himself in a cloak of fire,' said another, 'with
cherubs nestling in the folds.'

What wonderful things he heard—and the next day would be
his wedding day.

Now he went back to the woods to climb back into his trunk—
but where was it? A spark from the fireworks had set it on fire,
and the trunk was burned to ash. So the merchant's son could
never fly again, and he had no way of getting to the princess.

She waited for him on the roof all day, and she is waiting still.

As for him, he goes around the world telling stories—but they
are not so lighthearted as the one he told about the matches.

THE SWEETHEARTS

 WHIPPING TOP AND A BALL were lying in a drawer along with some other toys. The top said to the ball, 'Shouldn't we be sweethearts? After all, we are lying right next to each other in the drawer.' But the ball, who was made of morocco leather, thought herself too much of a lady even to notice such a comment.

Next day, the little boy whose toys they were came and painted the top red and yellow and hammered a brass nail into its middle, so the top looked really splendid when he spun around.

'Look at me!' he said to the ball. 'What do you say now? Shouldn't we be sweethearts? We'd be so good together—you leaping and me dancing. No one would be happier than us.'

'That's your opinion,' said the ball. 'You don't seem to realise that my mother and father were a pair of morocco slippers, and that I have a cork inside me.'

'Yes,' said the top, 'but I am made of mahogany. The mayor himself turned me on his own lathe, and he was very pleased with me.'

'Oh yes?' said the ball. 'And I'm supposed to believe that?'

'May I never be whipped again, if I spoke a word of a lie,' said the top.

'You speak very well for yourself,' replied the ball, 'but I can't accept you—for I am as good as half engaged to a swallow. Every time I go up in the air, he pops his head out of his nest and says, "Will you? Will you?" and I have made up my mind to say yes—and that's as good as half engaged. But I do promise that I shall never forget you.'

'Much good that will do me,' said the top, and after that they had nothing more to say.

The next day the ball was taken out. The top watched as she flew up in the air like a bird, until she was out of sight. Every time she hit the ground she bounced back up again—which was due either to her natural high spirits, or to the cork she had inside her.

The ninth time the ball went up, she didn't come down again. The boy searched all over for her, but she was gone.

'I know where she is,' sighed the top. 'She's in the swallow's nest. She's going to marry the swallow.'

The more the top brooded on this, the more he longed for the ball. Because he couldn't have her, he loved her more than ever. How could she choose another? It was a real puzzle. The top spun and whirled around, and all the time he was thinking about the ball. In his imagination she grew prettier and prettier. The years went by, and she became his lost love.

The top wasn't young anymore—but then one day he was painted all over with gold. He was better than new; for now he was a golden top. He whizzed around and sprang into the air for joy. That was something! But then he jumped too high and was gone.

They looked for him high and low, but they couldn't find him.

Where on earth was he?

He had jumped into the dustbin, where there was all kinds of rubbish—cabbage stalks, floor sweepings and the contents of the gutters.

'This is a fine mess I've landed myself in,' thought the top. 'My gilding won't last long in here. What a lot of riffraff.' He glared at a long cabbage stalk that was poking too near him, and at a strange round thing like a rotten apple. But it wasn't an apple, it was an old ball, that had lain for years in the sodden ooze of the gutter.

'Thank goodness! Someone to talk to at last!' said the ball, looking at the golden top. 'I am made from morocco leather and was sewn by a fine young lady, and I have a cork inside me—

though you might not think so to look at me. I was going to marry a swallow, but I fell into the gutter, and I have been lying there for the past five years in the ooze. And you know, that's a long time for a young girl.'

The top didn't reply. He thought of his old sweetheart, and the more he heard, the more he felt that this was she.

Then the maid came to throw something away. 'Hey! Here's the golden top!' she shouted.

And the top was brought back into the house, where he was greeted with delight. No one spoke of the ball, and the top never mentioned his lost love again.

That's how it goes, when your sweetheart has lain five years in the gutter. You don't know her when you meet her in the rubbish.

'SHE WAS NO GOOD'

HE MAYOR STOOD by the open window. He was in his shirt-sleeves and feeling very pleased with himself, even though he had cut himself shaving. He had stuck a bit of newspaper on the cut to stop it bleeding.

'Hello, lad,' he called.

It was the washerwoman's son who was passing by. The boy respectfully doffed his cap and stuffed it in his pocket. His clothes were shabby but clean. He stood by the open window as if he were in the presence of the king himself.

'You're a good lad,' said the mayor. 'Is your mother washing clothes in the river? I expect you're taking her drink. How much is it this time?'

'Only a half bottle,' whispered the boy.

'It's a shame about your mother,' said the mayor. 'But she's no good. Tell her she should be ashamed of herself! And don't you become a drunkard—though I suppose you will. Poor boy! Run along.'

And the boy went. He kept his cap in his pocket, and the wind played in his yellow hair. He turned out of the street down an alley that led to the river. There he found his mother, up to her knees in the water, rinsing clothes. The river was flowing fast.

'I'm just about done in,' she said. 'I'm glad you've come. I need a little something to help me. It's so cold in this water, and I've been standing here for six hours. What have you got for me?'

The boy handed her the bottle, and the mother took a long swig from it.

'Ah! That's what I needed. It warms me up! It's as good as a hot meal, and it doesn't cost so much. Take a swallow, son—you look so pale, you must be freezing too. Autumn is here. How cold the water is! I hope I don't get ill. But why should I? Give me the bottle back, it's my turn. And now you—but only a sip. Don't get too used to it, my poor child.'

She climbed up onto the bank and stood by her son, water dripping from her skirt. 'I work my fingers to the bone,' she said, 'but that doesn't matter, so long as I can bring you up respectably.'

Just then an older woman appeared—poor soul, she walked with a limp, and she had a great curl of false hair hanging over her face to try to hide a missing eye, but it only drew attention to it. 'Lame Maren with the curl,' people called her. She was a friend of the washerwoman's.

'Poor thing,' she said, 'slaving away in the cold water. If anyone needs a sip of something strong to keep them warm, it's you. But still people make a fuss about it.' And Maren told the washerwoman everything the mayor had said to the boy, which she had overheard. 'As if he has any right to point the finger,' she said, 'with his fine wines and his fancy dinners.'

'Did he really say that you, my boy?' the washerwoman asked, with a tremble in her voice. 'Did he say your mother is no good? Well, he may be right. But he had no business saying so to her child. Still, it's not the first insult I've had to swallow from that house.'

'Weren't you in service there, ages ago, when the mayor's father and mother were alive?' asked Maren. 'We've eaten a heap of salt since then—no wonder we're thirsty!' Maren laughed. 'There's going to be a big dinner party there tonight. They wish they could cancel, but they can't, because all the food's been cooked. The mayor had a letter an hour ago saying his younger brother in Copenhagen is dead. I heard it from one of the servants.'

'Dead!' said the washerwoman, and all the colour drained from her face.

'No need to take it to heart,' said Maren. 'Though I suppose you must have known him when you were in service.'

'So he is dead! The best man I ever knew. God doesn't make many like him.' Tears ran down the washerwoman's cheeks, and she began to sway. 'I feel dizzy,' she said. 'I shouldn't have emptied that bottle. I don't feel well.' And she steadied herself against a fence.

'You are ill,' said Maren. 'I'll take you home.'

'But my washing …'

'I'll see to that. The boy can stay and mind it till I get back.'

The washerwoman could hardly walk. 'I've been standing too long in the water. I've had nothing to eat since early morning. I think I'm running a fever. O Jesus, help me! My poor child!' And she burst into tears.

The two women tottered up the lane. The boy sat alone on the riverbank with the sodden laundry and wept.

When the women reached the mayor's house, the washerwoman's legs gave way, and she collapsed on the pavement. A little crowd gathered to gawp at her.

Maren knocked at the door of the house to ask for help. The mayor and his guest looked out of the window. 'It's the washerwoman,' he said. 'Drunk again! She's no good. It's a shame for that lad of hers. I feel sorry for him—his mother is no good.'

The washerwoman was helped back to the hovel where she lived, and put to bed. Maren gave her warm beer to drink, with butter and sugar in it, which was her remedy for all ills. Then she went back to the river to finish the washing. She meant well, but she didn't do much more than dunk the linen in the water and then pull it out again.

That evening, Maren sat by the washerwoman's bedside. The cook at the mayor's had spared her some potatoes and a piece of ham, which made a good supper for Maren and the boy. The washerwoman was too sick to eat, but she said the smell of the food was doing her good.

The boy settled down for the night. He slept across the foot of his mother's bed, covered in an old rag rug.

The washerwoman was feeling a little better. The warm beer had strengthened her. 'You're so kind,' she said to Maren. 'When the boy's asleep, I'll tell you the whole story. I believe he's gone off already. How sweet he looks! He has no idea what his mother has suffered. God grant he never knows!

'I was in service with the mayor's parents when the youngest son came home after he finished school. I was full of the joys of spring in those days—but I was a good girl, I swear to God. The young son was so bright and cheerful—and kind, too. There wasn't a drop of bad blood in him. He was the young master, I was just a maid. But still we fell in love.

'It was all very innocent—there's nothing wrong with a kiss between two people who love each other. Before he went away, he gave me a gold ring. He told his mother all about it—he worshipped her, he thought she was so wise and good. And after he went, she sent for me. She spoke to me as solemnly as the Lord himself. She showed me what a gap there was between him and me. "Now he sees how pretty you are," she said, "but beauty fades. What then? You have no education, you won't be able to discuss things with him—you are just not his equal. I respect the poor—no doubt in heaven, God may set them higher than the rich—but here on earth we each have to keep our carriage travelling along the tracks in which it has been set. Otherwise, it will overturn. That is what would happen with you two—you would overturn. Now, I know that Eric the glover would marry you. He is a respectable widower, with no children. He would suit you very well."

'Every word she said cut me to the quick—because I knew she was right. I went to my room, flung myself on my bed and cried my heart out. All through the night I was in a torment of doubt.

Next day was Sunday, and I went to church to pray to the Lord for guidance. As I came out of church, I ran into Eric the glover. It was fate. I liked him well enough, and we came from the same station in life. He was even quite well-to-do. I walked straight up to him and asked him, "Do you want to marry me?" "Yes," he said. "Even though I honour and respect you, but I don't love you?" I said. "That may come," he said. So we clasped hands.

'I was wearing the gold ring the young master had given me around my neck. I could only wear it on my finger at night. That night I kissed the ring until my lips bled, and the next morning I gave it to the mistress and told her that Eric and I were to be married. She took me in her arms and kissed me. She didn't say I was no good. Perhaps I was better then—I didn't know how hard life is. And after that we were married. The first year went well enough. Eric employed a journeyman and an apprentice—and you, Maren, came to look after us.'

'You were such a kind mistress,' said Maren. 'I'll never forget it.'

'Yes, that was a good year. All we lacked was a child. I didn't see the young master again. Well, I did see him once, but he didn't see me. He came home for his mother's funeral. I saw him at the graveside. He looked so pale and sad—but that was for his mother. When the father died, he was abroad, and he didn't come back. He hasn't been back since. He never married—that much I do know. I think he became a lawyer. I'm sure he forgot all about me. He wouldn't have recognised me if he had seen me—I've grown so ugly. And that's probably for the best.'

She told about the hard years that followed. Bad luck seemed to haunt them. They bought a house and pulled it down, then couldn't afford to build a new one. The money they borrowed from Copenhagen was on a ship that sank. And then, just after their son was born, Eric fell ill. For nine months she nursed him; he was so weak she had to dress him and undress him. All the time, they were getting deeper and deeper into debt. And then he died.

'I had nothing. And since then I've slaved and toiled for my boy's sake. I've scrubbed floors and washed clothes—all kinds of rough work. It wasn't God's will for me to be comfortably off. Soon he'll let me go, I expect, and then He will have to provide for the boy.'

And she fell asleep.

In the morning she was a bit stronger, so she went back to work. But as soon as she stepped into the cold water she began to feel faint. She turned around, and a spasm ran through her. She reached out with her hands, clutching at the air. Her legs gave way and she fell, with her body in the river and her head on the bank. Her wooden clogs—each padded with a wisp of straw—slipped from her feet and floated away down the river.

That's how Maren found her, when she brought her some coffee.

The mayor sent a message that the washerwoman was to come and see him at once, for he had something to tell her. But it was too late. The washerwoman was dead.

'She has drunk herself to death,' said the mayor.

He had been sent a copy of his brother's will—it bequeathed a large sum of money to the glover's widow who had once been in service to his parents.

'There was some foolishness at one time between my brother and her,' said the mayor. 'It's a good thing she's out of the way. Now the boy will get the money. I'll place him with a good family, and in time he may make a good craftsman.'

He sent for the boy and told him what he proposed. 'It's as well for you your mother is dead,' he said. 'She was no good.'

The washerwoman was taken to the churchyard and buried in the corner reserved for paupers. Maren planted a rose tree on the grave, and the little boy stood beside her.

'My dear Mother!' he said. 'Is it true she was no good?'

'No,' said Lame Maren. 'She *was* good. I knew her for years and was with her on the last night of her life. I know she was good. God in heaven knows it too. So let the world say, "She was no good."'

THE BELL

T SUNSET, when the clouds glowed gold between the chimneys, the narrow streets of the city would be filled with a strange sound like the tolling of a church bell. People would hear it for a moment, and then the rumbling of the carts and the general hubbub would drown it out. 'That's the evening bell,' people said. 'The sun's going down.'

On the outskirts of the city, where the houses were spaced apart and had gardens and fields around them, the sunset was even lovelier, and the tolling of the bell was much louder. It seemed to come from a church in the heart of the still, fragrant forest. People would look in that direction and feel quiet and thoughtful.

As time passed, one person would say to another, 'Is there a church in the woods? The bell has such a strange, lovely sound. Why don't we go and look for it?'

The rich people drove in their carriages, and the poor people walked, and to all of them the road seemed very long. When they finally came to a clump of willows that grew on the edge of the forest, they sat down under the trees. Looking up into the branches, they thought they were right out in the wilds. A baker from town pitched a tent and began to sell cakes; soon there were two bakers, and the second one hung a bell over his tent. It was covered in tar to protect it from the weather, and it had no clapper.

When the people got back to town they said it had all been very romantic; and that was worth the effort, even without the tea party. Three of them said that they had gone right to the other side of the forest. They could still hear the bell, but now it seemed to be coming from the city. One wrote a whole poem about it. He said the bell was like a mother's lullaby to her child; no melody could be sweeter than that bell's song.

At last the emperor heard about it, and he promised that whoever could find out where the sound came from should have the post of 'Ringer of the World's Bell', even if it turned out not to be a bell at all.

So more and more people went looking for the bell, for they wanted the title. Only one came up with an explanation. He hadn't been much further into the wood than the rest, but he claimed that the bell sound came from a great owl in a hollow tree. It was the owl of wisdom, and it kept knocking its head against the trunk. He just wasn't sure whether the sound came from the bird's head or from the tree trunk. So he was made Ringer of the World's Bell, and every year he published an essay on the owl, without leaving anyone the wiser.

And now it was Confirmation Sunday. The priest had spoken so well and sincerely that the young people were all deeply moved. This was a big day for them, the day they became grown-ups. Their child-souls had to become adult and sensible.

It was beautifully sunny outside, and after the service the children who had been confirmed walked out of the city. From the forest came the powerful tolling of the big, unknown bell. They were filled with the desire to go and look for it—all except three. One of them was a girl who had to hurry home to try on her ballgown, for it was because of the dress and the ball that she had been confirmed that day; otherwise she wouldn't have come. Another was a poor boy who had borrowed both his suit and his shoes from the landlord's son, and had to take them back straight away. The third said he never went to strange places unless his parents were with him, and as he had always been a good boy, he was going to carry on being one even after he was confirmed. That's nothing to make fun of—but they all did.

So three of them stayed behind, but the others went on. The

sun shone, the birds sang, and the young people sang, too. They walked hand in hand, for as they hadn't taken their places in the world yet, they were still children in the eyes of heaven.

Soon two of the smallest grew tired and turned back to town, and two girls sat down to make wreaths of wild flowers. When the rest arrived at the willow trees where the bakers had their tents, they said, 'Well, here we are! Now we can see that there isn't really a bell. People just imagine it.'

Just then, from deep in the woods, the bell rang out, pure and true. Five of the children made up their minds to carry on into the forest. It was hard going, for the trees grew so thickly, and the flowers grew so tall. Flowering bindweed and brambles trailed in long garlands from tree to tree; the nightingale sang, and the sunbeams played. Oh, it was beautiful; but it was no place for girls, for their dresses would be torn to bits.

They came to some great boulders covered in different kinds of moss. A fresh spring was gurgling up, *glug, glug.*

'I wonder if that might be the bell,' said one of the five, lying down to listen. 'This needs looking into.' So he stayed behind and the others went on.

They came to a cottage made of branches and bark. A huge crab-apple tree was leaning over it, and roses were growing up it and over the roof. From one of its branches hung a little bell. Was that the bell they had heard? They all agreed it was, except for one boy who said that this bell was too small and delicate to be heard so far away, and that its tinkling tones could never touch the heart so deeply. But he was a king's son, and the others said, 'His kind always has to know better than everyone else.'

They let him go on alone. As he went on, his heart was more and more filled with the loneliness of the forest. He could still hear the little bell that the others were so pleased with, and even, when the wind was in the right direction, the sound of singing from the bakers' tent. But the tolling of the great bell sounded ever

louder; it reverberated like an organ, and it came from the left, where the heart is.

There was a rustling in the bushes, and there before the king's son stood a boy wearing wooden clogs and a jacket with sleeves so short that you couldn't help noticing his bony wrists. They recognised each other; it was the boy who couldn't join the others after the confirmation service because he had to return his suit and shoes to the landlord's son. Now he had followed alone in his clogs and old clothes, so strong was the pull of the deep-tolling bell.

'Let's go on together,' said the king's son. But the poor boy tugged at his sleeves and stared at his clogs. He mumbled that he was afraid he wouldn't be able to keep up. Besides, he thought that the bell should be looked for on the right, where everything great and glorious is.

'Then we shan't meet again,' said the king's son, nodding to the poor boy, who disappeared into the densest part of the wood, where brambles and thorns would tear his old clothes to shreds and scratch his face, hands and feet until they bled. The king's son, too, got scratched, but his path lay in the sunshine. We'll follow him, for he was a bold lad.

'I will find the bell,' he said, 'if I have to go to the ends of the earth.'

Hideous monkeys up in the trees bared their teeth in a grin and chattered to each other, 'Shall we pelt him? Shall we pelt him? He's the son of a king.'

But he kept on walking deeper and deeper into the forest. There, the most wonderful flowers grew: lilies like white stars, with blood-red stamens; tulips as blue as the sky, that sparkled in the wind; and apple trees with fruit like shining soap bubbles. How those trees must have shone in the sun! He passed green meadows where deer roamed on the grass beneath oak and beech trees, and every crack in the tree bark was filled with grass and moss. There were also woodland glades with peaceful lakes on which swans swam gracefully and flapped their wings. Often the king's son stopped to listen, thinking that the sound of the bell might be coming from one of these deep lakes, but no, it was from yet deeper in the wood that the tolling came.

Now it was sunset. The sky was red as fire, and the forest grew so still that the boy flung himself to his knees. He sang an evening hymn, and said, 'I'll never find what I'm looking for. The sun is setting, and night is coming; soon it will be dark. But perhaps if I climb up those rocks, which are higher than the tallest trees, I may get one last glimpse of the round, red sun.'

By catching hold of roots, he pulled himself up the wet rocks, past writhing snakes and toads that seemed to bark at him.

He reached the top just as the sun set. Oh, what magnificence! The sea, the boundless sea, stretched out before him, dashing its waves against the shore. Over where the sea met the sky stood the sun, like a great, shining altar. Everything fused together in the golden glow. The forest sang, the ocean sang, and his heart sang, too. All nature was a great holy cathedral. The trees and the floating clouds were the pillars; the flowers and grass were the woven altar cloth; and heaven itself was the dome.

The glory faded as the sun went down, but millions of stars were kindled, like so many diamond lamps. The king's son spread out his arms to it all: sky, ocean, forest. At that moment, from the right, came the poor boy in his outgrown jacket and wooden clogs. He had arrived almost as quickly, by going his own way.

The two boys ran to each other. They stood together, hand in hand, in the great cathedral of nature and poetry, and the sacred invisible bell tolled its joyful hallelujah above them.

THE LITTLE
MATCH GIRL

T WAS BITTER COLD and snowing hard, and it was almost dark; the last evening of the old year was drawing in. But despite the cold and dark, one poor little girl was still astray in the streets, with nothing on her head and nothing on her feet. She had slippers on when she left home, but they were her mother's and too big for her, and they dropped from her feet when she scampered across the road between two carriages. One slipper just disappeared and the other was snatched away by a little boy who wanted it as a doll's cradle.

So the little girl walked on, and her bare feet turned blue and raw with the cold. In her hand she carried a bundle of matches, and there were more in her ragged apron. No one had bought any matches the livelong day; no one had given her so much as a penny. And so she walked on, shivering and starved, poor girl.

The snowflakes fell on her long blonde hair, which curled so prettily on her shoulders. But she was not thinking of her beauty, or of the cold, for lights were winking from every window and the smell of roast goose was in the air. It was New Year's Eve, and that was what the girl was thinking of.

She sat down in a sheltered corner and snuggled her feet under her, but it was no use. She couldn't get them warm. She didn't dare go home, for she had sold no matches and not earned so much as a penny. Her father would beat her, and anyway her home was nearly as cold as the street. It was an attic, and despite the straw and rags stuffed into the worst holes in the roof, the wind and snow still whistled through.

Her hands were numb with cold. If only she dared strike a single match, perhaps that would warm them. She took one out and struck it on the wall. Ah! The flame was bright and warm, and she held her hands to it. It burned for her with a magic light, until it seemed as if she were sitting by a great iron stove, with a lovely fire burning in it. The girl stretched out her feet to warm them too, but oh! The flame died down. The stove was gone, and the little girl was frozen and alone, with the burnt match in her hand.

She struck a second match against the wall. It flamed, and wherever its light fell the wall thinned to a veil so that the little girl could see into the room within. She saw a table spread with a snow-white cloth all set with fine china, and a piping hot roast goose stuffed with apples and plums. Best of all, the goose— with the knife and fork still in its breast—jumped down from the dish and waddled along the floor right up to the poor child. Then the match burned out, and the girl was left alone beside the cold, thick wall.

She kindled another match. Now she was sitting under a lovely Christmas tree, far bigger and more beautifully decorated than the one she had peeped at through the glass doors of a rich merchant's house at Christmas. A thousand candles were glimmering in the branches, and little painted figures such as she had seen in shop windows were looking down at her from the tree. The girl reached out her hand toward them, and the match went out. But still the Christmas candles burned higher and higher; she could see them twinkling like stars in the sky. Then one of them fell, leaving a trail of fiery light.

'Now someone is dying,' said the little girl, for her grandmother, who was the only person who had been kind to her, but who was now dead, had told her that when a star falls, a soul is going to God.

She struck another match against the wall. It lit, and there, clear and bright in its glow, stood her old grandmother, as gentle and loving as ever.

'Grandmother!' shouted the little girl. 'Take me with you! I know you will leave me when the match goes out. You will vanish like the warm stove, the delicious roast goose and the beautiful big Christmas tree!' Feverishly the little girl struck all the rest of the matches in her bundle, to keep her grandmother there. The matches blazed like radiant bright sunshine. Never had grandmother looked so beautiful and so tall. She lifted the little girl in her arms, and they flew together in glory and joy, higher and higher, beyond cold, beyond hunger, beyond fear, to God.

They found her in the early morning, sitting in the corner of the wall with rosy cheeks and a smile on her lips, frozen to death on the last night of the old year. The new year's sun rose over the little body, sitting with her bundle of matches all burned out. 'She was trying to warm herself,' people said. But no one knew what beautiful visions she had seen, nor how gloriously she and her grandmother were seeing in the glad new year.

THE COLLAR

HERE WAS ONCE a man-about-town whose only belongings were a bootjack and a comb. But he had the smartest shirt collar you ever saw, and it is the collar that this story is about.

The collar was about old enough to start thinking of taking a wife, when by chance he met a lady's garter in the wash.

'Oh!' gasped the collar. 'You're the sweetest thing I've ever seen—so slim, so delicate, so pretty. What's your name?'

'I shan't tell you,' snapped the garter.

'Where do you live?' asked the collar.

But the garter, who had a shrinking nature, thought this was a rather personal question, so she didn't answer.

'You must be some kind of undergarment,' said the collar. 'A girdle, perhaps. I can see that you must be as useful as you are decorative, my dear.'

'How dare you talk to me like that!' said the garter. 'I never gave you permission to.'

'Beauty like yours gives its own permission,' said the collar.

'Keep away!' squealed the garter. 'You're too … masculine.'

'It's true I am a man-about-town,' said the collar. 'I own a bootjack and a comb.' But it wasn't true—he was just boasting. It was his master who owned the bootjack and the comb.

'Don't come so near!' the garter fluttered. 'I'm not used to it!'

'Hoity-toity!' said the collar.

Then he was lifted out of the wash. He was starched, hung to dry over a chair in the sun and laid on the ironing board, at the mercy of the hot iron.

THE COLLAR

'Madam,' said the collar, 'dear widow lady. You're getting me all hot. You're making a new man of me, you're smoothing out all my kinks. I feel I'm on fire. Oh! Be my wife!'

'Rag!' said the scornful iron, and she trundled back and forth over the collar, imagining she was a steam train. 'Rag!'

The collar was a bit frayed at the edges, so the big scissors came along to trim the threads.

'Oh!' said the collar. 'You must be a ballet dancer! Nobody could do the splits with more charm and grace.'

'I know,' said the scissors.

'You deserve to be a countess,' said the collar. 'I am just a man-about-town, though I have my own bootjack, and a comb. If only I were a count!'

'The nerve!' said the scissors. 'To propose to me!' And she gave him such a nasty cut that he would have to be thrown away.

'There's nothing for it, I shall have to propose to the comb,' thought the collar. 'It's extraordinary, my dear,' he said, 'how you still have all your own teeth. Have you ever thought of getting married?'

'Didn't you know?' simpered the comb. 'I'm engaged to the bootjack.'

'Engaged!' said the collar.

Now there was no one left to propose to, which put him off the whole idea.

A long time passed, and then the collar found himself in the rag pile at the paper mill. There was quite a crowd of rags, but the fine ones kept their distance from the common ones, just like in life. They all had a lot to say, especially the collar, who was such a braggart.

'I had my pick of the girls,' he said. 'They just wouldn't leave me alone. I was a real man-about-town in those days—starched to the nines! My own bootjack and comb, which I never used! Those were the days! You should have seen me.

'I shall never forget my first love. She was a girdle—so delicate, so sweet, so pretty. She threw herself into a washtub for my sake.

'And then there was the widow. She really turned on the heat! But I snubbed her and it was she who got scorched.

'Then there was the ballet dancer. She had an artistic temperament; I still bear the scars to this day.

'My own comb was in love with me. I broke her heart, and all her teeth fell out.

'The stories I could tell! But I'm sorriest for the garter—I mean the girdle—who flung herself into the washtub. I've got a lot on my conscience. I deserve to be turned into blank paper.'

And that is what happened. All the rags were pulped and made into blank paper, and the collar was made into this very page, with his own story printed on it. That's because he bragged so much afterwards about things that weren't true.

If we don't watch out, the same thing might happen to us. We'll end up in the rag pile, to be turned into blank paper and have our life story printed on it for the whole world to read—even the secret bits. Then we'll have to run around repeating it all, just like the collar.

291

THE GOBLIN AT THE GROCER'S

HERE WAS ONCE a typical student who lived in the attic and didn't own a thing, and a typical grocer who lived downstairs and owned the whole house. There was a goblin, too, and the goblin moved in with the grocer, because every Christmas Eve the grocer gave him a big lump of butter. The grocer could easily afford it, and so the goblin stayed in the shop, as you can well understand.

One evening the student came in by the back door to buy a candle and a piece of cheese; he had to run his own errands. He made his purchases and exchanged a 'Good evening' nod with the grocer and his wife—a woman who could do more than just nod, for she had what they call the gift of the gab. As the student nodded, his eye fell on the piece of paper wrapped round the cheese. It was a page torn from an old book, a book that ought never to have been torn up—a book of poetry.

'There's more of that book if you want it,' said the grocer. 'I gave an old woman some coffee beans for it. I'll let you have it for a few pennies.'

'Thanks,' said the student. 'I'll take the book instead of the cheese. Plain bread will do me fine, and it would be a shame for the rest of the book to be torn up. You are a good man, and a practical one, but you've as much sense of poetry as that barrel!'

That was a rude thing to say—especially about the barrel—but both the grocer and the student laughed, because after all it was only said in fun. But the little goblin was annoyed that anyone should dare to speak like that to a grocer who owned the whole house and sold the best butter.

So that night, when the shop was shut and everyone but the student had gone to bed, the goblin sneaked into the bedroom and borrowed the grocer's wife's gift of the gab; she didn't need it while she was asleep. The goblin could lend the gift of the gab to anything and it would be able to speak its mind as well as you or me; but only one thing could have it at a time, which was just as well, or they'd all have spoken at once.

First the goblin lent the gift of the gab to the barrel where the grocer kept old newspapers for wrapping paper. 'Is it really true,' he asked, 'that you have no sense of poetry?'

'Of course not,' said the barrel. 'I know all about it. It's the sort of thing they use to fill out the bottom of the page in a newspaper, and then people cut it out. I'm sure there's more poetry in me than in the student, and I'm only a humble barrel compared with the grocer.'

Then the goblin lent the gift of the gab to the coffee mill—what a clatter!—the butter cask and the till. They all agreed with the barrel, and the views of the majority have to be respected.

'Now for that student!' said the goblin, and he crept up the staircase to the attic where the student lived. The goblin peeked through the keyhole and saw the student reading the old book by the light of the candle.

How bright it was in there! A shaft of light was rising from the book, like a great shining tree which sheltered the student with its branches. Its leaves were a luminous green, and each flower was the head of a lovely girl—some with dark flashing eyes, and some with clear blue ones. Each fruit was a shining star which rang and sang with beautiful music.

The little goblin had never dreamed of such wonder. So he stood there on tiptoe, enraptured, until the light in the attic went

out. The student must have blown out the candle and gone to bed. But still the goblin lingered, listening as the fading echoes of the music lulled the student to sleep.

'That was amazing!' said the goblin. 'I never expected that! I think I'll stay with the student.' He thought it over long and hard, and then he sighed, 'But the student hasn't got any butter!' So he went—yes, he went back down to the shop, and it was just as well he did, for the barrel had nearly worn out the gift of the gab, telling all the news that was inside it from one angle, and then turning round and telling it all over again from another.

The goblin took the gift of the gab back to the grocer's wife. But from then on, the whole shop, from the till to the firewood, deferred to the barrel. They held it in such high regard that in future, when the grocer read out articles from the newspaper, they thought he must have learned it all from the barrel.

But the little goblin wasn't satisfied anymore to sit and listen to the talk downstairs, however wise and well informed it was. As soon as the light glimmered down from the attic, it seemed to draw him to it by invisible cables. He just had to go and look through the keyhole.

Whenever he did, a sense of unutterable grandeur surged through him—the kind of feeling you get when God rides his storm clouds across the thundering sea. The goblin would burst into tears. He couldn't have said what he was crying for, but it comforted him. How wonderful it would be to sit with the student under that tree! But it was not to be—he had to make do with the keyhole.

He stood there on the chilly landing, but he never noticed the cold until the light went out and the music had faded away into the wind. Then he shivered! He was glad to get back to his warm corner downstairs, where he was so snug. And there was the Christmas butter to look forward to. Yes—the grocer was the one!

But in the middle of the night the goblin was woken by a terrible commotion. People in the street were banging on the shutters, and the watchman was blowing his whistle. 'Fire! Fire!'

The whole street was lit up by flames. But where was the fire? Here, or next door? Everyone panicked. The grocer's wife was so flustered that she took off her gold earrings and put them in her pocket, to be sure of saving something. The grocer hunted frantically for his share certificates, and the maid ran to fetch the silk scarf she had saved up to buy. Everyone wanted to save the thing they cared about most.

The goblin was no different. He sprang up the stairs into the attic room, where the student was standing quietly looking out of the window at the fire across the road. The goblin grabbed the precious book from the table, wrapped it in his red cap and held onto it with both hands. The house's greatest treasure was safe!

Off he ran, up to the roof and onto the highest chimney pot. And there he sat, cradling the book in his hands, while the fire over the way lit up the sky. He knew now where his heart lay, and where he really belonged.

When the fire was put out, the goblin had time to reflect.

Yes! 'I'll divide my time between them,' he said. 'I can't forsake the grocer—because of the butter.'

And that was very human! Because we, too, have to go to the grocer—for the butter.

In a Thousand Years' Time

WRITTEN IN 1853

ES, IN A THOUSAND YEARS' TIME people will fly across the ocean on wings of steam. The young citizens of America will come to pay their respects to old Europe. They will come to see our monuments and decaying cities, just as today we tour the crumbling glories of South Asia.

In a thousand years' time, they will come.

The Thames, the Danube and the Rhine will still be rolling on; Mont Blanc will still be wearing its cap of snow; the northern lights will still play across the northlands. Generation after generation will have come to dust. The great men of our day will be as forgotten as the Viking chieftain whose funeral mound some prosperous farmer has turned into a viewpoint where he can sit and gaze out over his waving fields of corn.

'To Europe!' cry the young Americans. 'To the land of our fathers, to the wonderful land of memories and dreams—to Europe!'

Here comes the airship. It will be crowded, for it is much faster to fly than to sail. The electro-magnetic cable under the ocean has already telegraphed ahead the passenger list of this air caravan.

The coast of Ireland is reached first; but the passengers are still asleep; they are not to be woken until they arrive in England. There they will set foot in the land of Shakespeare, as the cultured

297

ones call it; the others call it the land of Democracy, or the land of the Industrial Revolution.

The tourists will devote a whole day to England and Scotland; then their journey continues through the Channel Tunnel to France, the country of Charlemagne and Napoleon. Some of them have heard of Molière, too, but the arguments of the classical and romantic schools are all in the past; the names on the tourists' lips are of celebrities, poets and scientists of whom our age has never heard—they have yet to be born, in that cradle of Europe, Paris.

The airship will then fly over the country from which Columbus sailed, where Cortés was born, and where Calderón composed his dramas in flowing verse. Beautiful dark-eyed women still live in its fertile valleys, and their folk songs still name El Cid and the palace of Alhambra.

Through the air once more, to Italy, where the Eternal City of Rome once stood. It has been wiped out. The Campagna is a desert; one wall of St Peter's is still standing, but there are doubts whether it is genuine.

Then to Greece, to spend a night in the luxury hotel on Mount Olympus—just to say that they have been there. Next stop is the Bosporus, for a few hours' rest on the site of Byzantium. A handful of poor fishermen spreading their nets still remember old tales of the harems that stood here in days gone by.

Then the airship flies along the Danube, allowing glimpses of ruined cities below, cities our age never knew. Every now and then the ship will land to allow the tourists to admire some monument that belongs to their past, but our future.

Then the airship is aloft again. Below lies Germany, which was once crisscrossed by railroads and canals—Germany, the land where Luther spoke and Goethe sang, and Mozart made his music. But when they speak of science and the arts, their talk will be of names we do not know.

One day is given to Germany, and one to the whole of Scandinavia—the homelands of Ørsted and Linnaeus, and Norway, the young country of the old heroes. Iceland is a stop on the homeward journey. The geyser no longer spouts, and the volcano has died, but the rocky island still stands in the foaming sea, the memorial stone of the sagas.

'There's a lot to see in Europe,' say the young Americans. 'You need a whole week, as so-and-so has shown in his guidebook, *See Europe in Seven Days*.'

FIVE PEAS FROM THE SAME POD

HERE WERE ONCE five peas in a pod; they were green, and the pod was green, so they thought that the whole world was green, and that was quite right. The pod grew and the peas grew; they all made space for each other, five in a row. The sun shone and kept the pod warm, and the rain fell and kept it clean. It was a snug little home, light in the day and dark at night, just as it should be. As the peas grew, they began to think for themselves; after all, they had to do something to pass the time.

'Shall I be stuck here forever?' each said in turn. 'I'm afraid I'll get hard from sitting here so long. I wonder if there's something outside; I have a feeling there is.'

Weeks passed. The peas turned yellow and the pod turned yellow. 'The whole world is turning yellow,' they said, and they had a perfect right to say it.

Then they felt the pod being pulled; they were in a man's hand, being shoved into a pocket alongside some other pods. 'Soon we shall be opened,' they said. That's what they were waiting for.

'I wonder which of us will go furthest,' said the smallest pea. 'We'll soon see.'

'What will be, will be,' said the biggest.

Pop! The pod split, and all five peas rolled out into the bright sun. They were in a little boy's hand. He said they were just the peas for his peashooter.

He fired off the first.

'Now I'm flying out into the wide world! Catch me if you can!' And it was gone.

'I shall fly right up to the sun,' said the second. 'That's the pod for me!' And off it went.

'We don't care, so long as we keep rolling!' said the next two, for they were rolling on the floor. But they went into the peashooter anyway. 'We'll go furthest!' they cried.

'What will be, will be,' said the last pea, as it was shot into the air. It lodged in a crack in the attic windowsill; the rotten wood was already stuffed with moss and earth, and the pea stuck there. It lay hidden, though not hidden from God.

'What will be, will be,' it said.

In the little attic room lived a poor woman who did heavy work, such as cleaning stoves and chopping wood. But though she was strong and willing, however hard she worked she was still as poor as ever. Living with her was her daughter, who had been lying in bed for a whole year. The little girl was terribly thin and delicate; it seemed she could neither live nor die.

'She'll go to her little sister,' said the woman. 'I had two children, but it was so hard to look after them both, so God went shares with me and took one for himself. I'd like to keep the other, but God doesn't want them to be parted, so she'll go to her sister.'

But the sick girl stayed on. She lay patient and quiet in bed all day, while her mother went out to earn their keep.

It was spring, and one sunny morning, just as the mother was getting ready to go out to work, the girl noticed something through the lowest windowpane. 'Whatever is that green thing, peeping in at the window? It's swaying in the breeze.'

The mother opened the window a crack. 'Well, I never!' she said. 'It's a little pea plant; you can tell by the green leaves. However did that get there? It will be a little garden for you to look at.'

So the sickbed was moved nearer to the window, so the girl could keep an eye on the pea as it sprouted, while the mother was at work.

'I feel I'm getting better, Mother,' said the young girl that evening. 'The sun has been shining in on me so warmly today. The little pea is getting stronger, and so am I. Soon I will be out in the sunshine, too!'

'I hope so,' said the mother, but she did not believe it. Still, because the little plant had cheered her daughter up, she found a stick and tied it up, so that the wind wouldn't break it. And she ran a string up the window, to give the pea something to climb up, which it did. You could see it grow from one day to the next.

'I do believe it's going to flower,' said the mother one morning, and now she too began to hope that her sick daughter might get well. She thought how lately the girl's talk had been livelier, and how each morning she sat herself up in bed and looked with sparkling eyes at her little garden of one pea plant.

Next week, the girl got up for the first time and sat happily in the sunshine for a whole hour. The window was open, and the pea's pink flower was in bloom. The girl leaned out and kissed the delicate petals. That was a red letter day.

'God himself planted that pea and made it thrive to bring hope to you and joy to me, my darling,' said the happy mother, and she smiled at the flower as though it were an angel from heaven.

But what happened to the other peas? The one who flew out into the wide world shouting, 'Catch me if you can!' was swallowed by a pigeon. He lay in its stomach like Jonah in the whale. The two who didn't care fared no better, for they were eaten by pigeons, too—so at least they made themselves useful. But the other one—the one who wanted to fly up into the sun—that one fell down into the gutter and lay there for weeks in the dirty water. It began to bloat.

'Bigger is better,' it said. 'Soon I shall be so fat I shall burst, and that's as much as any other pea can do, or ever has ever done. I'm the most remarkable of the five peas in our pod.'

And the gutter agreed.

The little girl stood at the attic window with shining eyes and glowing cheeks. She folded her delicate hands over the pea flower and gave thanks to God for it.

'I still think my pea's the best,' said the gutter.

THE BEETLE

HE EMPEROR'S HORSE was given gold shoes— a gold shoe for each hoof.

Why was he given gold shoes?

He was a handsome beast—good legs, wise eyes and a mane that fell over his neck like a silken veil. He had borne his master through bullets and smoke on the battlefield—he had used his teeth and hoofs to clear a way through the enemy and had jumped right over a fallen horse to carry the emperor to safety. He had saved the emperor's golden crown, and his life as well—and that was even more precious than gold. So that was why he was given gold shoes—a gold shoe for each hoof.

Then the dung beetle came out of the manure heap.

'First the big, then the little,' he said, holding out a foot to the blacksmith. 'Not that size is important.'

'What do you want?' asked the smith.

'Gold shoes,' replied the beetle.

'Are you mad?' said the smith. 'Why should you get gold shoes?'

'Why not?' said the beetle. 'Aren't I as good as that clumsy brute, who needs to be waited on hand and foot—groomed, fed and watered? Don't I live in the same stable?'

'But why has the horse been given its gold shoes? You don't understand!'

'Understand! I understand when I'm not wanted!' said the beetle. 'Insults and ridicule! I've had enough. I'm going out into the world to make my fortune.'

'Good riddance to bad rubbish,' said the smith.

'Oaf!' said the beetle.

Then the beetle flew outside, to a flower garden filled with the scent of roses and lavender.

'Isn't it lovely here?' asked a ladybird, showing off the smart black spots on her red wings. 'Isn't it fragrant?'

'It's not a patch on what I'm used to,' said the beetle. 'Call this beautiful? Why, there isn't even a manure heap.'

The beetle flew over to the shade of a gillyflower, on which a furry caterpillar was crawling. 'What a wonderful world this is!' said the caterpillar. 'The sun is so warm, everything is perfect. And when I fall asleep—what some people call dying—I shall wake up as a butterfly.'

'Wherever did you get such a notion?' said the beetle. 'Don't give yourself airs! I come from the emperor's stable, and no one there—not even the emperor's horse—has ideas like that. Go on, grow some wings and fly away! I'm going to.' And the beetle flew off.

'I try not to get annoyed,' he muttered, 'but I am annoyed, all the same.' So he dropped onto the lawn and went to sleep.

Then the heavens opened—it poured with rain. The beetle was woken up by the rain, and he tried to burrow into the earth, but he couldn't. The water overturned him—now he was swimming on his front, now his back. Flying was out of the question. It looked like this would be the end for him. There was nothing to do but lie there—so there he lay.

When the rain stopped for a moment and the beetle blinked the water out of his eyes, he caught sight of something white. It was a piece of linen left out on the grass to dry. It was soaking wet. The beetle crept into a fold. It wasn't as good as the manure heap, but beggars can't be choosers. So he stayed there for a day and a night, and the rain stayed too. The beetle didn't poke his head out of the fold until morning; he was that vexed.

Two frogs came and plopped down on the linen. Their eyes were shining with pleasure. 'What glorious weather!' one said.

'It's so refreshing, and this linen really soaks it up! You could swim in it!'

The other said, 'I'd like to know if the swallow, who can't stay in one place for five minutes, has ever come across a better climate than ours. Such drizzle and damp! It's as good as living in a ditch. A frog who is tired of such weather is tired of life.'

'I don't suppose you've ever been in the emperor's stables,' said the beetle, 'but there, the wetness is spicy and warm. That's my kind of damp—but you can't take it with you when you travel. Can you tell me, is there a greenhouse in this garden, where a refined type like me would feel at home?'

The frogs couldn't understand him—or rather they wouldn't.

'I only ask once,' said the beetle, after he had asked three times and never got an answer.

He went on and came to a bit of broken flowerpot. It shouldn't have been left lying there; but as it had been, several families of earwigs had taken shelter under it. Earwigs don't need a lot of room; but they do like company. The mothers all love their children and think that they are the cleverest and most beautiful of all.

'My boy is engaged already,' said one. 'The little innocent! So full of boyish pranks! His ambition is to climb into a priest's ear. Bless him!'

'My boy,' said another, 'is a likely lad—he came sizzling out of the egg, and he's sowing his wild oats already. And that warms a mother's heart. Don't you agree, Mr Beetle?' For she had recognised him by his shape.

'You are both right,' said the beetle, so they invited him to come in and make himself at home.

'You must meet my little one,' said a third mother.

'They're such sweethearts, and so full of fun,' said a fourth. 'They're never naughty unless they have a tummy ache—though they do get rather a lot of those.'

All the mothers chattered on about their children, and the children themselves pulled at the beetle's beard with the little pincers they have in their tail.

'The little rascals!' said the mothers. 'Always up to something!' And they positively dribbled with motherly love. But the beetle was bored and asked directions to the greenhouse.

'It's far, far away, on the other side of the ditch,' said one of the earwig mothers. 'If one of my children were to travel so far from home, it would be the death of me.'

'All the same that's where I'm going,' said the beetle, and he left without saying goodbye, as important people do.

In the ditch he came across some relatives—all dung beetles.

'We live here,' they said. 'We're as snug as bugs. It's the land of plenty! Come in; you must have had a tiring journey.'

'Yes, I have,' said the beetle. 'I've been lying on linen in the rain, and there's only so much cleanliness a beetle can bear. And now I've got aches and pains in my wings from standing under a draughty piece of flowerpot. What a relief to be back among my own kind!'

'Do you come from the greenhouse?' asked the oldest of them.

'Higher up,' said the beetle. 'I was born with gold shoes on my feet; I come from the emperor's stable. Now I've been sent on a secret mission. But it's no use pumping me about it—I won't say a word.'

With that the beetle eased itself down into the mud.

There were three girl beetles there, fluttering their feelers.

'They're none of them engaged,' said their mother, and the girls giggled shyly.

'Even in the royal stables, I've never seen more beautiful girls,' said the adventurous beetle.

'Don't take advantage of my little girls! Don't pay court to them unless you mean it. But I see you are a gentleman, so I give you my blessing.'

'Hurrah!' cried all the others, and so the beetle became engaged. First engaged; then married; there was no reason for delay.

The first day was good enough; the second jogged along; but by the third day it was all too much—he couldn't be doing with wives and maybe even children.

'They took me by surprise,' thought the beetle. 'So now I'll surprise them.'

And he did. He ran away. His wives waited all day and all night, and then they knew they had been abandoned. The other beetles said, 'He was a good-for-nothing playboy,' because now they would have to take care of his deserted wives.

'So now you are innocent young girls again,' said their mother. 'But shame on that no-good beetle for leaving you like that!'

In the meantime the beetle was sailing across the ditch on a cabbage leaf. Two men taking a morning stroll happened to see him and picked him up. They turned him this way and that and looked at him from every angle, for they were experts.

The younger one said, '"Allah sees the black beetle in the black stone in the black mountain." Isn't that what it says in the Koran?' And then he translated the beetle's name into Latin and gave an account of its species and their habits. But the older one said, 'There's no need to take this one home; we have better specimens already.'

The beetle's feelings were hurt by this, so he flew out of the scholar's hand and up into the sky. His wings had dried off, so he made it all the way to the greenhouse. A window was open, so he flew straight in and make himself at home in some fresh manure.

'This is the life!' he said.

Soon he fell asleep and dreamed that the emperor's horse was dead and that he, Mr Beetle, had been given its gold shoes and promised two more. It was a sweet dream.

When the beetle woke up, he climbed out of the manure and took a look about him. How magnificent the greenhouse was! The

sun was shining down through the palm leaves onto flowers as red as fire, as yellow as amber, and as white as new-fallen snow.

'Such greenery!' exclaimed the beetle. 'It will be delicious once it goes bad. What a fine larder! Now I must see if I can find any of my relations here. I can't mix with just anybody; I have my pride and I'm proud of it.' And then he allowed himself to daydream about the emperor's horse dying, and being given its gold shoes.

Suddenly a hand grabbed the beetle, pinching him and turning him over.

It was the gardener's son and one his friends; they had seen the beetle and wanted to have some fun with him. They wrapped him in a vine leaf and put him in a warm trouser pocket, where he wriggled about until he got another pinch from the gardener's son.

The boys ran down to the lake at the bottom of the garden. They made a boat out of an old wooden clog. A stick was the mast, and the beetle—who was tied to the stick with a thread of wool— was the captain. Then the boat was launched.

The lake was so big the beetle thought it was the ocean. He flipped over on his back from fright and lay there lashed to the mast, with all his legs kicking in the air.

The wooden clog sailed across the water. When it got too far out, one of the boys would roll up his trousers and fetch it back. But then, the boys were wanted. They were called so sharply they ran home and forgot all about the boat. It drifted on and on. The beetle was terrified, but he couldn't fly away as he was tied to the mast.

A fly buzzed up to him.

'Lovely weather we're having,' said the fly. 'And what a delightful spot this is. Just the place for a snooze in the sun.'

'Stuff and nonsense!' said the beetle. 'Can't you see I'm tied up?'

'I'm not tied up,' said the fly, and flew away.

'Now I know the world,' said the beetle. 'It's a mean world, and I'm the only decent one in it. First I'm refused my gold shoes; then I'm made to lie on damp linen and stand in a draft; then I'm tricked into marriage. When I boldly set out into the world to try my luck, up comes some human puppy who ties me up and sets me adrift on the raging waves. And all this while the emperor's horse is prancing around in his gold shoes! That's what really riles me. And do I get any sympathy?

'What a life I've had—but what's the use if no one knows my story? The world doesn't deserve to hear it. Not after refusing me gold shoes when the emperor's horse just had to stretch out its legs for them. No, they had their chance. I would have been a credit to the stable. But it's their loss, the world's loss. It's all over.'

But all was not over, for two girls were rowing on the pond.

'Look! There's a wooden clog!' said one.

'It's got a beetle tied up in it!' said the other. And she lifted the boat out of the water and carefully cut the thread with a small pair of scissors, without harming the beetle. When they reached the shore, she set him down safely on the grass. 'Off you go!' she said. 'Crawl small or fly high—go on, try!'

The beetle flew straight in through the open window of a large building—and collapsed into the long silken mane of the emperor's horse, who was standing in the stable where they both belonged. He clung tight to the mane while he tried to gather his thoughts.

'Here I am, sitting on the emperor's horse, riding high ... What was that? Yes, now it's coming clear. Now I understand. Why was the horse given gold shoes? That's what the smith asked me. And now I know. It was for me. That's why the horse was given gold shoes.'

The beetle was happy now. 'Travel broadens the mind,' he said, 'and puts everything into perspective.'

The sun shone bright through the window. 'It's not such a bad world after all,' said the beetle, 'if you learn to roll with the punches.' All was right with the world now, for the emperor's horse had been given gold shoes so that the dung beetle could ride him.

'Now I'll dismount,' thought the beetle, 'and go and tell the other beetles what has been done for me. I'll tell them all my adventures in the wide world. But I won't go on my travels again. I'll stay at home, until the horse wears out his gold shoes.'

THE TOAD

HE WELL WAS DEEP, so the bucket was on a long rope, and water was hard to fetch. Although the water was clear, the sun never reached down far enough to touch it, but as far as it did shine, green moss grew between the stones.

A family of toads lived there. They were newcomers; they had followed their mother when she fell head over heels down the well. The green frogs, who had lived there swimming in the water for ages, called them 'cousins', and pretended the toads were only on a visit. But the toads had no intention of leaving. They liked it in the 'dry part' of the well, as they called the damp stones.

Mother Frog had once been on a journey—all the way to the top in the water bucket. But the light hurt her eyes. Luckily she managed to scramble out of the bucket and fall back *splosh!* into the well—where she lay for three whole days with a bad back. She hadn't much to tell about the world above—only that the well was not the whole world. Mother Toad could have told them more than that, but she never answered when she was spoken to, and so they never asked her.

'She's fat, ugly and slimy,' said the children, 'and her brats are slimier still.'

'That's as may be,' said Mother Toad, 'but one of them has a precious jewel in their head—or is that me?'

The young frogs didn't like the sound of that; they pulled faces at her and dived back into the water. But the young toads stretched their hind legs in sheer pride, and held their heads perfectly still.

Then they pestered their mother. 'What is it we're being proud of?' they asked. 'What is a jewel?'

'It is something so valuable and fine,' said Mother Toad, 'that I can't begin to describe it. You wear it for your own pleasure, and to upset other people. And that's enough of your questions; I've said my say.'

'Well I'm sure I don't have the jewel,' said the littlest toad. 'It sounds too precious for the likes of me. And if it would upset other people, it wouldn't give me pleasure. All I wish is that I could go to the top of the well, just once, and look out. That must be wonderful.'

'Best stay put,' said Mother Toad. 'You know where you are here, and here's where you belong. Stay out of the way of that bucket, or it might squash you; and if you do get caught in it, jump out. Though there's no guarantee you'll land as well as I did, with legs and eggs intact.'

Croak! said the littlest toad, as if she were swallowing her words.

But she still longed to go to the top of the well and glimpse the green world above; so next morning when the water bucket was lowered, the little toad, quivering with excitement, jumped off its ledge into the full bucket and was hauled to the top.

'*Ugh!* What an ugly brute!' said the man who had pulled it up—and he poured the water away and aimed a kick at the toad. She only just escaped being badly hurt by hopping into some nettles.

In among the nettles, the toad looked up and saw the sun shining through the leaves, which seemed transparent, it was the same as when we go into a tall wood and look up to see the sun filtering through the high branches.

'It's much nicer here than in the well,' said the little toad. 'I could stay here forever.' She stayed for one hour, she stayed for two. But then she began to wonder what lay beyond the nettle patch. 'As I've come this far, I might as well go on.'

She hopped out onto a road. The sun was hot on her back, and she was soon coated with dust from the highway. 'This really is dry land,' she said. 'It's almost too much of a good thing; it's making me itch.'

She came to the ditch, where forget-me-nots and meadowsweet grew; in the hedge were elder and hawthorn, twined round with flowering bindweed. What a picture it was! And there was a butterfly fluttering about, which the toad decided must be a flower that had left home to see the world—and that was quite a shrewd guess.

'If only I could go so fast,' said the toad. *Croak! Croak!* 'It's so nice here.'

She stayed in the ditch for eight days and nights, and never went short of food. But on the ninth day she thought, 'I must be getting along.' Though it was hard to imagine that anywhere could be more delightful than the ditch, yet it was lonely; and the wind last night had carried the sounds of other toads or frogs.

'It's wonderful to be alive,' she said, as she set off once more. 'It's wonderful to come up out of the well, to lie in a forest of nettles, to march across a dusty road and to rest in a wet ditch, but I must go on. I'll look for those other toads or frogs, for one can't do without society. Nature is not enough!'

She made her way through the hedge into a field and across it to a pond surrounded by reeds.

'Isn't this a bit wet for you?' said the frogs who lived there. 'But you're welcome all the same—a girl just as much as a boy.'

They invited the toad to join them for a singsong that evening. A lot of bellowing in squeaky voices—you know the kind of thing. There were no refreshments, just all the water you could drink.

'I must be getting on,' said the little toad. She felt a desire for something better.

She saw the stars twinkling in the sky, she saw the new moon, she saw the sun rising ever higher. 'I am still in a well,' she thought. 'But a bigger well. I must go higher yet. I'm so restless, I feel strange longings in me.'

Later, when the moon was full, the poor creature thought, 'I wonder if that is a bucket being lowered down for me to jump into. That would take me higher! Or maybe the sun is the great bucket—it shines so brightly, and I'm sure it's big enough to take us all. I must take my chance when it comes. Oh! how my head is filled with its light. I'm sure it gleams brighter than any jewel. So I don't regret not having one of those. I just want to go higher, higher to glory and joy. I have faith, and yet I'm fearful. The first step is so hard, but I must go on—onward and upward!'

And she put her best foot forward, and soon came back to the road. Then she came to a place where humans lived—there were both flower and vegetable gardens, and the toad rested under a cabbage leaf.

'How many different creatures there are!' she said. 'There's always something new in this big, lovely world! As long as you keep on the move!' She took a look around the vegetable garden. 'How green it is!'

'I should say it is,' said a caterpillar that was sitting on a cabbage leaf. 'And my leaf is the greenest of them all. It's so big it covers half the world, but that's the half I don't bother myself about.'

Cluck! Cluck! The hens were coming. The one at the front had the sharpest eyesight—she spied the caterpillar on the leaf and pecked at it. It fell to the ground and lay there wriggling. The hen peered at it first with one eye and then with the other, wondering what all that wriggling was for. 'It can't be doing it for fun,' she thought, and she lifted her head to strike.

The toad was horrified, and began to crawl at the hen.

'It's called up reinforcements,' thought the hen. 'A horrible crawling thing! It would only have tickled my throat, anyway.' So she left the caterpillar alone.

'I wriggled out of that one,' said the caterpillar. 'I kept my nerve. But the problem is, how do I get back onto my cabbage leaf? Where is it?'

The little toad offered her sympathy to the caterpillar and said she was glad her ugliness had frightened the hen away.

'What do you mean?' said the caterpillar. 'I saved myself by my own wriggling. Though it's true you are ugly. I don't owe you a thing. Now where's my leaf? I smell cabbage … Here it is! There's no place like home. But I must climb up higher.'

'Yes, higher!' thought the little toad. 'Ever higher! It feels just as I do. A fright like that would give anyone a funny turn. But we all want to go higher.'

The little toad looked up as high as it could. On the farmhouse roof was a stork's nest, and father stork and mother stork were chatting away with their long beaks. 'Imagine living so high up,' thought the toad. 'If only I could go up there!'

Inside the farmhouse lived two students. One was a poet, and the other was a naturalist. The first sang and wrote about the wonder of God's creation, and how it was mirrored in his heart. His poems were short and simple yet full of meaning. The second looked at the world itself, in all its individual parts. He considered the creation as a matter of science—add here, take away there, and eventually the sum works out. He wanted to know and understand it all. He had a searching mind; a fine mind. They both loved life.

'Look, there's a good specimen of a toad,' said the naturalist. 'I'll catch it and preserve it in alcohol.'

'You've already got two. Leave it in peace,' said the poet.

'But it's so wonderfully ugly,' said the naturalist.

'If only we could find the precious jewel in its head, it might be worth dissecting it,' said the poet.

'Precious jewel!' said the other. 'What kind of natural history is that?'

'It's folklore, not natural history. I like the thought that the toad, the ugliest of creatures, has a precious jewel hidden inside its head. It's the same way with human beings—think of the precious jewels that Aesop and Socrates had inside their ugly mugs.'

THE TOAD

The two friends walked away, and the toad escaped being preserved in alcohol. So she didn't hear any more and didn't understand half of what she had heard. But she knew they had been talking about the precious jewel. 'It's just as well I don't have it, or I might have been in trouble,' she thought.

Father Stork was still chattering away on the roof. He was giving his family a lecture, and keeping an eye on the young men in the garden at the same time. 'Human beings are the most conceited of all animals,' he said. 'Listen to them jabbering away in their silly lingo. They're so proud of being able to speak, yet if they travel as far as we storks go in a single day, they find they can't understand a word! Whereas we storks speak the same tongue all over the world—the same in Egypt as in Denmark.

'And humans can't fly at all! They have to get in a machine that does it for them, and then they break their silly necks in it! It gives me shivers up and down my beak to think of it. The world can do without them. We don't need them; all we need are frogs and worms.'

'What a magnificent speech,' thought the little toad. 'The stork must be a very important creature, it lives so high up. I've never seen anything like it.' Just then the stork launched itself into the air. 'And it can swim too!' thought the toad.

Meanwhile Mother Stork was telling her children all about Egypt and the waters of the river Nile, and all the glorious mud to be found in foreign parts. It all sounded wonderful to the toad.

'I must go to Egypt,' she said. 'If only Father Stork will take me with him—or perhaps one of the youngsters would. I'd pay him back somehow. Yes, I'll go to Egypt, I'm sure of it. I'm so lucky. I'm sure my dreams are better than any precious jewel.'

But she *did* have the most precious jewel—her endless longing to go upward, ever upward. That was the jewel, and it gleamed with joy and yearning.

At that moment the stork came. He had seen the toad in the grass. He snatched her up in his beak, squeezing her in half. It hurt, but the little toad was sure she was going to Egypt. Her eyes shone with anticipation—it was as though a spark was flying out of them.

Croak!

Her heart gave up; the toad was dead.

But what of the spark that flew from her eyes? What of that?

The spark was caught up in a sunbeam and carried away. But where was it taken, that precious jewel from inside the toad's ugly head?

Don't ask the naturalist; ask the poet. He'll tell you the answer in a fairy tale. A caterpillar will be in the story; and a family of storks, too. The caterpillar transforms itself into a butterfly; the stork flies right across the ocean to Africa, then finds the shortest way home again to Denmark—back to the very same nest. It's almost too magical and mysterious—yet it's true. Go and ask the naturalist—he'll have to admit it. And you know it yourself, for you have seen it with your own eyes.

But what about the jewel in the toad's head?

Seek it in the sun! You might find it there!

But the light is too bright. We do not have eyes that can gaze on all the glory that God has created. But we shall get them one day. That will be the most wonderful fairy tale of all; for we shall be in it ourselves.

DANCE, DANCE, DOLLY MINE!

'THAT MUST BE A SONG for very little children,' declared Aunt Malle. 'I think it's silly, that "Dance, dance, dolly mine!"'

But little Amalie liked it—she was only three years old, and she was always playing with her dolls. She was bringing them up to be as clever as Aunt Malle.

There was a student who came to the house to help Amalie's brothers with their homework, and he often took the time to talk to Amalie and her dolls. He wasn't like anyone else—Amalie thought he was very funny. Aunt Malle said he had no idea how to speak to children—their little heads couldn't possibly take in his tomfoolery. But little Amalie's could—she even learned by heart all the words of his ditty, 'Dance, dance, dolly mine!' and sang it to her three dolls. Two of them were new—a girl and a boy—but the third was old. Her name was Lisa, and she liked listening to the song because she was mentioned in it.

> *Dance, dance, dolly mine!*
> *Oh, you look so very fine!*
> *And your boyfriend looks good too—*
> *His trousers white, his jacket blue,*
> *Shoes so tight they pinch his toe,*
> *And his hat and gloves just so.*
> *He is fine and she is fine,*
> *Dance, dance, dolly mine!*

Look, look, Lisa's here,
My dear dolly from last year!
She has brand-new flaxen hair
And a face that's clean and fair.
Now she looks quite young again—
Lisa is my oldest friend.
She must join the fun, and so,
All three of you—put on a show.

Dance, dance, my dollies bright,
Get the steps and rhythm right.
Keep your back straight, don't forget,
Point your toe and pirouette.
The dance is nearly over now—
Leap, twirl and take a bow.
You really are a sight to see—
Dance, dance, my dollies three.

The dolls understood the song, little Amalie understood it, and the student understood it too—but then, he had written it, and he said it was an excellent song. Only Aunt Malle did not understand it—she had long since climbed over the fence between childhood and adulthood, so she thought it was nonsense. But little Amalie didn't agree, and she kept on singing the song.

It is from her singing that we have it.

THE FLAX

HE FLAX WAS in full bloom. Its lovely blue flowers were as soft as the wings on a moth, and even more delicate. The sun shone on the flax and the rain watered it, and this was as good for the flax as it is for little children to be washed and then kissed by their mother. They're so much nicer afterwards, aren't they? And it was the same for the flax flowers.

'People say I am doing so well,' said the flax, 'and growing so tall, that they'll get a fine piece of linen from me. How lucky I am! Everything is as it should be, and I've got a future to look forward to. The sun is so warming, and the rain is so refreshing. Yes, I'm extremely lucky. I am the luckiest of all!'

'Ha! Ha! Ha!' groaned the wooden stakes in the hedge. 'You don't know the world! We do—we've got knots in us.' And they croaked gloomily,

> *Snap and bend!*
> *Snap and bend!*
> *Every song*
> *Must have an end!*

'That's not true!' said the flax. 'The sun will shine again tomorrow, and the refreshing rain will fall. Why, I can feel myself growing. I'm blooming! Yes, I'm the luckiest of all.'

But one day people came and grabbed hold of the flax and pulled it up by the roots—it did hurt! Then it was thrown into water as if to be drowned, and after that roasted on a fire, as if to be cooked. It was cruel.

'Life can't always be good,' said the flax. 'You have to suffer to understand that.'

But things got even worse. The flax was bruised and broken, hacked and thwacked, and then put on a spinning wheel, which whirred so loudly the flax couldn't hear itself think.

'I've been amazingly lucky,' thought the flax, through its pain. 'I must be thankful for the happy times I've had. Thankful, yes, thankful!' And it was still saying this when it was placed on the loom. And there it was turned into a fine big piece of linen—all the flax from the same field was turned into one piece.

'Oh, this is wonderful! I never expected this! I am so lucky! A lot they knew about it, those hedge stakes. The song's not ended at all! It's only just beginning. How wonderful life is! It's true I've suffered—but it's made me what I am today. I am the luckiest of all. I'm so strong, and yet so soft! So white and so long! This is much better than being a plant. Even when you're in bloom, no one waters you, you have to wait for the rain. Now I have a servant who turns me round every morning and bathes me each evening. Why, the parson's wife herself said I was the best piece of linen in the parish. Nothing could be better than that!'

Next the linen was taken into the house and cut up with scissors. It was clipped and cut and stuck through with needles! That was no fun! But at last the linen was made into twelve pairs of—well, we won't mention what they were, but everyone has to wear them, all the same.

'So this was my destiny! It's too wonderful for words! It's a pleasure to be useful, I'm sure. And though we've been turned into twelve garments, we're still together—we are a dozen! What incredible luck!'

The years passed—and at last they could hold together no longer.

'All things must pass,' they said. 'We should like to have lasted longer, but it's no good asking for the impossible.'

Then they were torn into rags. They thought they were done for. They were hacked and mashed and boiled and who knows what else—and at the end of it all, they had been turned into beautiful white paper.

'That's a surprise! A lovely surprise!' said the paper. 'Now I am finer than ever, and I shall be written on! I wonder what will be written on me? I really am so lucky.'

And wonderful fairy tales were written on it, stories that were read aloud, and which people listened to again and again. People got so much joy from the words written on that paper.

'This is better than I ever dreamed, when I was just a field of blue flowers,' said the paper. 'How could I know that one day I should bring such pleasure to people? I can hardly grasp it, even now. Yet it is so. And it's none of my doing, really—it has all just happened! I've gone from happiness to happiness. Each time I tell myself, "Every song must have an end," it is simply the beginning of something even better. I wonder what will happen now. Perhaps they will send me travelling around the world, so that all mankind can enjoy me. I expect so. Once I had blue flowers, now the flowers have been replaced by beautiful thoughts. I am the luckiest of all!'

But the paper did not go on its travels. Instead it was sent to the publisher, and everything that was written on it was set in type and printed in a book—hundreds and hundreds of books. Many more people could enjoy that stories that way. If the paper itself had been sent round the world it would have been worn out by the time it was half way.

'Yes, this is the wisest course,' thought the paper. 'It's better this way. I shall stay at home and be respected like an old grandfather. The words were written on me first, the ink flowed directly on to me from the pen. I shall be glad to stay at home, and let the printed books do all the running around. How lucky I am!'

So the paper was bundled up and laid on a shelf. 'Rest is sweet after hard work,' said the paper. 'It is good to have time to collect one's thoughts. It's given me a chance to really get to know

myself—and self-knowledge is the beginning of all knowledge, or
so they say. What will happen next, I wonder? Something new and
exciting, I'm sure.'

One day the paper was thrown on the fire to be burned—for it
mustn't be sold to the grocer to wrap his butter and sugar in. All
the children in the house clustered round the fire. They wanted to
see it flare up, and they wanted to count the red sparks that dart
to and fro among the ashes—blazing and dying so fast. 'Those are
the children, hurrying from school,' they said. 'And the last spark
of all is the schoolmaster!' When you think the fire's gone out, the
schoolmaster pops up, always a little after the rest.

All the paper lay in a bundle on the fire. *Oh!* How quickly it
caught fire! *Ah!* it sighed, and then it burst into flame. It blazed so
high—higher than the flax had ever been able to lift its blue
flowers. And it shone so bright—brighter than the linen ever had.
For an instant, all the letters written on it burned red, and then all
the writer's words and thoughts were consumed by the fire.

'Now I am going to join the sun!' said the flame. It was as
though a thousand voices cried it at once. The flame shot right up
the chimney.

And all around it hovered invisible tiny beings, just as many as
there were blossoms on the flax. They were even lighter than the
flames that bore them, and when the flame had died away, and
nothing remained of the paper but dark ash, they danced across it,
and wherever their feet touched it they left red sparks. The
children were hurrying out of school, and last of all was the
schoolmaster.

The children of the house enjoyed the show, and then
they sang,

> *Farewell old friend!*
> *Farewell old friend!*
> *Every song*
> *Must have an end!*

And the tiny invisible beings replied, 'The song will never end! That is the joy of it! We know it now, and therefore we are the luckiest of all!'

But the children could neither hear nor understand them—and that was as it should be, for children mustn't know everything.

THE GARDENER
AND HIS MASTER

FEW MILES FROM the capital stood an old manor house with thick walls, towers and stepped gables. It was the summer home of a rich nobleman and his wife; it was the best and handsomest of all the houses they owned. It was so well kept it looked as if it was new built, and inside it was comfortable and welcoming. The family arms were carved in stone over the entrance, surrounded by climbing roses.

The garden in front of the house was laid to lawn, with both pink and white may trees. There were even rare flowers of the kind you usually see in a greenhouse, for the nobleman employed a skilled gardener. The flower garden, the orchard, even the kitchen garden, were delightful. By the kitchen garden you could still make out some of the original garden design, with box hedges clipped into the shape of crowns and pyramids. Beyond that towered two ancient trees, almost bare of leaves, that looked as if the wind had been pelting them with great lumps of muck—but every lump was a bird's nest.

Here, for time out of mind, rooks and crows had built their nests. The two old trees were a regular settlement of screaming birds. They were the oldest family on the estate, and they regarded themselves as its true masters. They scorned the flightless creatures below, and didn't pay them much attention except when they started banging away with their guns, when the birds would flap into the air squawking *Caw! Caw!*

The gardener often suggested cutting the trees down, as they were an eyesore, and if they were gone, the screaming birds would go, too. But the master wouldn't hear of it, for the trees and the birds were part of the garden—something from the old days, that shouldn't just be thrown away.

'Those trees belong to the birds now. Leave them alone, my good Larsen,' he would say. The gardener's name was Larsen, though that's neither here nor there. 'Haven't you got enough to do already, Larsen, what with the flower garden, the orchard, the kitchen garden and the greenhouse?'

It was true, the gardener was responsible for all these, and he worked hard and well. The master and mistress knew this, but all the same they couldn't resist telling him every now and then how they had seen flowers or eaten fruit at other people's houses that were better than anything in their garden. The gardener was always cast down at this, for he did his best. He had a good heart, and he was good at his job.

One day the master sent for him and told him—in a friendly but patronising way—that the day before, while dining with some distinguished friends, they had been served apples and pears so juicy and mouthwatering that all the guests had been really impressed. The fruit was obviously not homegrown but, if they would stand the climate, trees should be imported. As the fruit was known to have been bought at the city's leading greengrocer's, the gardener should ride in and find out where the apples and pears were from, and order cuttings.

The gardener knew the greengrocer's well, for that was where, with his master's permission, he sold off the surplus fruit and vegetables from the garden. So he went to town and asked the greengrocer where he had got the apples and pears that had been so admired.

'Why, they were from your own garden!' said the greengrocer. He showed the gardener some of the fruit, and he recognised it at

once. The gardener was thrilled. He hurried home and told his master the good news that the fruit came from his own garden.

But the master and mistress wouldn't believe it. 'There must be some mistake, Larsen. Go and get the greengrocer to put it in writing.'

So Larsen got a written certificate from the greengrocer.

'How strange!' said the master.

From then on, the dining table at the manor always had a great bowl filled with apples and pears from the garden. The master had fruit crated up and sent as presents to friends in the city and elsewhere—some even overseas. What an excitement! Though they had to admit that it had been an unusually good year for fruit trees across the country.

Some time later the master and mistress were invited to dine with the king. The next day, they sent for the gardener. The king had served some exquisite melons from the royal greenhouse.

'You must go to the royal gardener, Larsen, and ask him for some melon seeds.'

'But the royal gardener got his seeds from us,' said Larsen, highly delighted.

'Then the man has improved the fruit in some way,' snapped the master. 'Every melon was perfect.'

'I'm very pleased to hear it,' said Larsen. 'I should explain that the royal gardener has had no luck with his melons this year. When he saw ours, he begged three of them for the king's table.'

'Do you mean to say that we were eating our own melons?'

'I'm sure you were.' And Larsen went to the royal gardener and got him to write a certificate confirming that the king's melons had come from the manor garden.

The master was quite taken aback. But soon he was showing the certificate around, and sending melon seeds far and wide, just as he had with the apples and pears.

The seeds were a great success, and they were named after the manor house—so now the house's name was known in England, Germany and France. Who would have thought it?

'I do hope the gardener won't let it go to his head,' said the master.

He didn't, but he did want to become one of the best gardeners in the land. Each year he tried to excel at something, and he often succeeded. But people often said that nothing was ever quite as good as his very first fruit, the apples and pears. The melons, of course, were good in their way; his strawberries were all very well, but no bigger or juicier than those to be found elsewhere.

The year the radishes failed, no one could talk of anything else, although other things had turned out well. It was almost as if the master felt quite relieved to be able to say, 'A poor year, Larsen.' It pleased him to say it: 'A poor year.'

Twice a week the gardener would take fresh flowers up to the house. He arranged them with great skill, so that nothing clashed, each bouquet was a delight.

'You're blessed with good taste, Larsen,' said the mistress. 'Though of course that's a gift from God, and nothing to be proud of.'

One day his arrangement was a crystal bowl with a water lily leaf floating on the surface. On top of this, with its stalk going down into the water, was a brilliant blue flower as big as a sunflower.

'An Indian lotus flower!' exclaimed the mistress. She had never seen anything like it.

The bowl was placed where the sun would catch it in the daytime, and it would reflect the candlelight at night. Everyone who saw it thought it was as lovely as it was unusual.

The young princess—who was good and kind—admired it so much that the master and mistress gave it to her to take back to the royal castle. Then they went into the garden to try to pick another for themselves; but they couldn't find one. So they called the gardener and asked him where he had got the Indian lotus flower from. 'We've looked everywhere,' they said. 'It's not in the greenhouse or in the flower garden.'

'No, it's not,' said the gardener. 'It is only a humble flower from the kitchen garden. But all the same, it's lovely isn't it? It's like a blue cactus—the flower of the artichoke.'

'You should have made that perfectly clear,' said the master, 'instead of letting us think it was a rare foreign flower. Now you've shown us up in front of the princess. She was so taken with the flower that we gave it to her. She knows a lot about botany, and she didn't know what it was, but then, botany doesn't have anything to do with vegetables. My good Larsen, how could you have sent such a thing into the house? You've made fools of us.'

So the beautiful blue flower from the kitchen garden was banished from the manor house, where it didn't belong. The master sent his apologies to the princess, explaining that the lotus flower was nothing but a common vegetable. It was the gardener's fault, and he had been given a good dressing down for his impudence.

'What a shame! It's not fair,' said the princess. 'He has opened our eyes to a beautiful flower that we had overlooked. I will order the royal gardener to bring me an artichoke flower every day, for as long as they are in bloom.'

And she did; so the master and mistress told Larsen that, after all, he might bring them another artichoke blossom. 'It really is a remarkable flower,' they said, and they complimented Larsen on it.

'Larsen loves praise,' they said. 'He's like a spoiled child.'

That autumn there was a violent storm. A number of trees on the estate were torn up by the roots. To the master's regret, the two ancient trees with the birds' nests were among those that were blown down. The birds beat on the manor windows with their wings, shrieking their anger.

'I suppose you're happy now, Larsen,' said the master. 'The storm has brought the trees down, and the birds have fled to the wood. Soon there'll be nothing left to remind us of the old days. It's very sad.'

The gardener said nothing. He had long ago thought what he would do with this sunny area once the trees were gone. He meant to make it the most beautiful part of the garden.

The big trees had destroyed the old topiary hedges in their fall. In their place, he planted shrubs and trees from the countryside—the kind of plants no other gardener would think worthy of a garden. Each was planted in shade or sunshine, depending where it would thrive, and all were tended with loving care.

Junipers from the heaths of Jutland raised themselves high like Italian cypresses. The wild green holly was a delight to the eye in summer and winter. Ferns of many kinds grew like miniature palm trees. The burdock—which is despised as a weed—blossomed with flowers worthy of any bouquet. In damper soil, the common dock spread out its sculptural leaves. Mulleins like giant candlesticks, woodruff, primroses, lilies-of-the-valley—each plant had its place. It was a joy to look at.

In front was a row of espaliered pear trees, specially imported from France, and tended so carefully that soon they were bearing as well as they would have done in their homeland.

Where the two old trees had stood was a flagpole flying the Danish flag, and a second pole twined with sweet-smelling hops. In the winter, a sheaf of oats was hung from this pole for the birds to eat at Christmastide; it was an old custom.

'The good Larsen is getting sentimental in his old age,' said the master. 'But he's a loyal old stick.'

In the New Year, one of the illustrated papers carried a picture of the manor house, with the flag staff and the sheaf of oats. It singled out the sheaf of oats, saying how refreshing it was to see the old traditions kept up in this way.

'Whatever Larsen does gets a fanfare,' said the master. 'He's a lucky man. We ought almost be proud to have him.'

But they weren't proud. They knew that they were the master and the mistress, and they could turn Larsen off with a month's notice if they chose to. They didn't, because they were decent people. There are many like them, which is just as well for the Larsens of this world.

That's the story of 'The Gardener and His Master'. Make of it what you will.

THE BOOK OF
FAIRY TALES

HERE WAS AN OLD manor house with a dashing young squire. He and his wife enjoyed their wealth and fortune, and liked to share it with others. They wanted everybody to be as happy as they were.

On Christmas Eve, a beautifully decorated Christmas tree stood in the great hall. A fire was burning in the hearth, and the frames of the family portraits were hung with branches of fir. Here the master and mistress and their guests would sing and dance the night away.

Earlier in the evening, Christmas was celebrated in the servants' hall. Here, too, stood a big Christmas tree glittering with red and white candles, and trimmed with little Danish flags, and swans and fishing nets cut out of paper and filled with candy. The poor children from the village had all been invited. Their mothers came too, but they weren't interested in the tree so much as the tables laden with Christmas presents: useful woollens and linen to make dresses and trousers. Only the little children stretched out their hands to the candles, the tinsel and the flags.

They had come early in the afternoon, and they all got some Christmas pudding, as well as roast goose and red cabbage. Then when they'd all admired the Christmas tree, and the presents had been handed out, they all had a little glass of punch and some apple cake.

When they got back to their own poor cottages, they all said,

'That's what I call the good life,' and sat back to digest their meal, and have a proper look at their presents.

Now, one couple were called Garden-Kirsten and Garden-Ole. They both worked in the manor house garden, weeding and digging, and that kept a roof over their heads and bread in their mouths. Every Christmas they got their share of presents. They had five children, and the squire's generosity clothed them all.

'They're kind-hearted folk, the master and mistress,' they would say. 'But, of course, they can afford it, and it makes them feel good.'

'Here are some good hard-wearing clothes for the four youngest,' said Ole, 'but isn't there anything for poor Hans? They don't usually forget him, even though he can't come to the party.'

Hans was their eldest son. When he was small he'd been the quickest and liveliest child, but then he suddenly went 'wobbly' in the legs, and couldn't stand or walk. For five years now he had been bedridden.

'Well, I did get something for him,' said his mother, 'but it's nothing really—just a book for him to read.'

'A fat lot of use that will be to him,' said his father.

But Hans was pleased with it. He was a very bright boy, who liked reading. Even though he had to lie in bed, he did what work he could, knitting socks and even bedspreads; the mistress of the manor had praised his work, and bought some.

It was a book of fairy tales that Hans had been given, with lots to read, and lots to think about.

'There's not much use for that sort of thing in this house,' said his parents. 'Still, let him read. It passes the time, and he can't always be knitting.'

Spring arrived. The flowers came up in the garden, and so did the weeds, which meant there was plenty of work for the gardener and his apprentices, and also for Garden-Kirsten and Garden-Ole.

'It's nothing but wasted effort,' they both said. 'As soon as we've raked the paths out, they get messed up again, what with the endless visitors they have at the manor. Just think of the cost! But the master and mistress are rich enough.'

'It's a funny old world,' said Ole. 'The parson says we are all God's children. Why is it so unfair?'

'It's because of the Fall,' said Kirsten.

They talked it over again that evening, while Hans lay in bed reading his book of fairy tales.

Drudgery had hardened their hands, and poverty had blunted their minds. They couldn't make it out; they weren't up to it. As they talked they got more and more hot and bothered.

'Some people are rich and happy, while others just scrape by. Why should we suffer just because Adam and Eve were disobedient and inquisitive? We would never have behaved like those two.'

'Yes you would!' exclaimed Hans. 'It's all written down in my book.'

'What does the book say?' asked his parents.

So Hans read them the old tale of 'The Woodcutter and His Wife'. They had had the same argument: Adam and Eve were the cause of all their misery, and they would never have been so inquisitive.

Just then, the king passed by. 'Come home with me,' he said. 'You shall live as well as I do, with seven courses for dinner. Only don't open the tureen that's on the table; if you touch it, that will be the end of your fine living.'

'I wonder what's in the tureen,' said the wife.

'It's no business of ours,' said the husband.

'It's not that I'm nosy,' said the wife, 'I'd just like to know why we may not lift the lid. It must be some delicacy.'

'As long as it's not some machine,' said the husband, 'that will go off like a pistol and wake the whole house.'

'Oh!' said the wife, and she left the tureen alone. But that night

she dreamed that the lid lifted itself, and she smelled the finest punch, the kind that you get at weddings and funerals. And there was a silver coin, with the inscription, 'Drink this punch, and you will become the richest people in the world, and all the rest will be beggars.' When she woke up, she told her husband about it.

'Try to put it out of your mind,' he said.

But she said, 'We could just lift the lid a little. As gently as can be.'

'Very gently,' said the husband.

So the wife raised the lid a fraction, and out sprang two lively little mice, and disappeared down a mousehole.

'Good night!' said the king. 'Now you can go home and stew in your own juice. Don't be so critical of Adam and Eve—you've been just as inquisitive and ungrateful yourselves.'

'I wonder where the book got that story from,' said Ole. 'It might have been us! That's given us something to think about.'

The next day they went back to work. They were scorched by the sun and soaked by the rain, and they got cross and grumpy.

That evening, they brooded over their thoughts. It was still light when they had eaten their milk porridge, so Ole said, 'Read us the story of the woodcutter and his wife again.'

'There are lots of stories in the book,' said Hans. 'Stories you don't know.'

'I don't care about them. I want to hear the one I know.'

So Ole and Kirsten listened to the story again. Many an evening they came back to that same story.

'It still doesn't explain everything,' said Ole one night. 'People are like milk. Some of it separates into rich curds, and some of it into watery whey. Some people have all the luck. They live like lords and never know sorrow or want.'

Hans was listening. Though he was weak in the legs, he was wise in the head. So he read them another tale from his book—the one about 'The Man Who Didn't Know Sorrow or Want'.

The king lay sick and could not be cured, except by wearing the shirt off the back of a man who had never known sorrow or want.

Messengers were sent far and wide to all the kings and noblemen, who should have been happy. But all of them had known sorrow and want at one time or another.

'Well, I haven't,' said the swineherd, who sat laughing and singing in the ditch. 'I'm the happiest man alive.'

'Then give us your shirt,' said the messengers. 'You shall have half the kingdom for it.'

But the swineherd, though he said he was the happiest man in the world, did not possess a shirt.

'That was a smart chap!' shouted Ole, and he and his wife had their best laugh in years.

The schoolmaster was passing by, and he said, 'What's up? Have you won the lottery?' For the sound of laughter was not often heard from that cottage.

'Nothing like that,' answered Ole. 'Hans has been reading us the story of the man who didn't know sorrow or want. That man didn't even have a shirt to his back! It makes you laugh till you cry to hear something like that, especially all written down in a book. Well, we all have our troubles to bear, and knowing you're not the only one always cheers you up.'

'Where did you get the book from?' asked the schoolmaster.

'Hans was given it the Christmas before last, as a present from the manor, because he's bedridden and likes reading. At the time we would rather have had a couple of new shirts, but the book is a real eye-opener. It seems to answer your thoughts.'

The schoolmaster picked up the book and opened it.

'Let's have the same story again,' said Ole. 'I haven't taken it all in yet. And then we can have the one about the woodcutter.'

These two stories were enough for Ole. They were like two sunbeams shining into that dark cottage, and into his stunted mind, that could be so sullen and grouchy.

Hans had read the whole book time and again, for the tales took him out into the world, where his legs couldn't carry him.

The schoolmaster sat on his bed and talked with him about it, and they both enjoyed themselves.

From then on, the schoolmaster often came to see Hans in the afternoon, while his parents were out. These visits were great fun for the boy, for the old man told him about the size of the earth, and its many lands, and how the sun was almost half a million times bigger than the earth and so far away that it would take a cannon ball twenty-five years to reach it, though the sun's rays reach the earth in just eight minutes. Every schoolboy knew these things, but they were new to Hans, and even more wonderful than the stories in his book of fairy tales.

The schoolmaster sometimes dined at the manor, and on one visit he told the master and mistress how much the book had meant to that humble home. Two stories alone were an inspiration and a blessing. By reading them, the clever young invalid had brought laughter and food for thought into the house.

As the schoolmaster was leaving, the mistress gave him some money to give to Hans.

'That should go to my parents,' said Hans, when the school-master gave him the money.

And Ole and Kirsten said, 'Bless him! Hans is some use after all.'

A few days after that, the mistress stopped her carriage outside the cottage. She was so delighted that her Christmas present had given so much pleasure to the boy and his parents that she had brought some more. There was fine bread, fruit and a flask of sweet syrup, but best of all was a blackbird in a gilded cage. She put the cage on a chest of drawers not far from the boy's bed, so that he could see the bird and listen to its lovely song. In fact, even passers-by could hear the bird singing.

Ole and Kirsten didn't get home until long after the mistress had gone. Though they could see how happy Hans was, they felt the present was just another burden. 'It's just another thing for us to look after,' they said, 'for Hans can't do it. These rich folk, they never think things through. In the end the cat will get it.'

A week passed, and then another. The cat often came into the room, but it did not harm the bird, or even frighten it. Then one afternoon, while the parents and the other children were out at work, it happened. Hans was reading his book of fairy tales. He'd got to the story about the fisherman's wife, who had all her wishes granted. She wished to be a king, and she was. She wished to be an emperor, and she was. Then she wished to be God—and ended up back in the ditch where she started.

The story didn't have any bearing on the bird and the cat. It was just the one Hans was reading at the time, and he remembered it ever after.

The cage stood on the chest of drawers; the cat sat on the floor, fixing the bird with its greeny-yellow eyes. It seemed to say, 'You look good enough to eat!'

Hans could read it in the cat's face.

'Shoo, cat!' he shouted. 'Get out!' But it tensed itself for the pounce.

Hans couldn't reach it, and he had nothing to throw but his treasure, the book of fairy tales. So he threw that; but the binding had come loose, and it flew one way and pages flew the other. The cat turned round and glared at the boy, as if to say, 'Don't meddle in my affairs, little Hans. I can run and jump, and you can't do either.'

Hans kept his eye on the cat. He was getting worried, and so was the bird. There was no one he could call. It was as if the cat knew it. Again it got ready to leap. Hans flapped his bedcover at it, and finally hurled it across the room, but the cat took no notice. It just jumped up onto a chair, and then the windowsill, so that it was right next to the bird.

Hans could feel his blood pounding, but he wasn't thinking of

himself, he was only thinking of the cat and the bird. He couldn't get out of bed; his legs wouldn't carry him. It felt as if his heart turned over inside him, when he saw the cat spring from the windowsill to the chest of drawers and knock the cage over. The bird was fluttering against the bars.

Hans shrieked and, without a thought of what he was doing, jumped out of bed, snatched up the cage and shooed the cat away. With the cage in his hand he ran out of the door and into the road. Tears were streaming down his face, and he shouted at the top of his voice, 'I can walk! I can walk!'

He had regained the use of his legs. Such things can happen, and it happened to him.

The schoolmaster lived nearby. The boy ran to him in his bare feet and nightshirt, carrying the bird in its cage. 'I can walk!' he shouted. 'Thanks be to God!' and he burst once more into tears of joy.

And there was joy at home with Ole and Kirsten. 'We shall never see a happier day,' they said.

Hans was called up to the manor, though he hadn't been that way for years. The trees and bushes seemed to nod to him, saying, 'Hello, Hans! It's good to see you.' The sun shone on his face and in his heart.

The master and mistress were as happy as if Hans was their own son; especially the mistress, because she had given him both the book of fairy tales and the caged bird.

It is true that the bird had died—died of fright—but it had been the cause of his recovery; and the book had been an inspiration to the boy and his parents. He meant to keep it and read it always, however old he grew. And now he would be able to learn a trade— perhaps become a bookbinder. 'Then I would get all the new books to read!' he said.

Later that day the mistress sent for Kirsten and Ole. She wanted to talk with them about Hans, who was so bright and eager, and quick to learn. For 'Heaven helps those who help themselves.'

That night Ole and Kirsten were very happy, especially Kirsten; but a week later she was crying, for dear Hans was leaving them. He was all dressed in new clothes, and he was going over the salt sea, to school. It would be years before they saw him again.

He left the book of fairy tales behind, for his parents wanted it to remember him by. Ole often read it, though only the two stories that he already knew.

Hans wrote to them of course, and each letter was happier than the last. The family he was boarding with were good to him, and school was wonderful. There was so much to learn, he wished he could live to be a hundred, and be a schoolmaster.

'If only we could live to see the day!' said his parents, and they pressed each other's hands, as solemn as if they were in church.

'What a turnabout for Hans!' said Ole. 'It shows, God doesn't forget the poor man's child. Why, it's just like something Hans might have read us from his book of fairy tales!'

Fairy Tales of Hans Christian Andersen was published by The Reader's Digest Association Limited, London, using material supplied by The Albion Press Limited.

First edition copyright © 2004
The Reader's Digest Association Limited, 11 Westferry Circus,
Canary Wharf, London E14 4HE
www.readersdigest.co.uk

Text copyright © 2004 Neil Philip
Illustrations copyright © 2004 Isabelle Brent

We are committed to both the quality of our products and the service we provide to our customers. We value your comments, so please feel free to contact us on **08705 113366** or via our web site at **www.readersdigest.co.uk**

If you have any comments or suggestions about the content of our books, you can contact us at: gbeditorial@readersdigest.co.uk

PICTURE ACKNOWLEDGMENTS
7 © Odense City Museums/The Hans Christian Andersen Museum 9 Topham Picture Library/Polfoto 10 © Odense City Museums/The Hans Christian Andersen Museum 13 © Odense City Museums/The Hans Christian Andersen Museum 14 © Odense City Museums/The Hans Christian Andersen Museum

READER'S DIGEST PROJECT TEAM
EDITOR John Andrews
DESIGNER Kate Harris
PROOFREADER Barry Gage
PICTURE RESEARCH Rosie Taylor

READER'S DIGEST GENERAL BOOKS
EDITORIAL DIRECTOR Cortina Butler
ART DIRECTOR Nick Clark
EXECUTIVE EDITOR Julian Browne
MANAGING EDITOR Alastair Holmes
PICTURE RESOURCE MANAGER Martin Smith
PRE-PRESS ACCOUNT MANAGER Penelope Grose

PRINTING R.R. Donnelley & Sons Company, China

CONCEPT CODE UK1633/G/OP
BOOK CODE 400-143-01
ISBN 0 276 42830 7
ORACLE CODE 250008889H.00.24